AN OUTLINE HISTORY OF
ENGLISH LITERATURE

Other books by the author:

An Introduction to the Study of Literature

AN OUTLINE HISTORY OF ENGLISH LITERATURE

WILLIAM HENRY HUDSON

RUPA

Published by
Rupa Publications India Pvt. Ltd 2015
7/16, Ansari Road, Daryaganj
New Delhi 110002

Sales centres:
Bengaluru Chennai
Hyderabad Jaipur Kathmandu
Kolkata Mumbai Prayagraj

Edition copyright © Rupa Publications India Pvt. Ltd 2015

All rights reserved.
No part of this publication may be reproduced, transmitted, or stored in a retrieval system, in any form or by any means, electronic, mechanical, photocopying, recording or otherwise, without the prior permission of the publisher.

P-ISBN: 978-81-291-3539-1
E-ISBN: 978-81-291-3631-2

Twenty-fourth impression 2024

25 24

Printed in India

This book is sold subject to the condition that it shall not, by way of trade or otherwise, be lent, resold, hired out, or otherwise circulated, without the publisher's prior consent, in any form of binding or cover other than that in which it is published.

Contents

Preface		*vii*
1.	Introductory	1
2.	English Literature Before Chaucer (500–1340)	9
3.	The Age of Chaucer (1340–1400)	17
4.	From Chaucer to *Tottel's Miscellany* (1400–1557)	30
5.	Development of Drama to 1561	39
6.	The Age of Shakespeare (1558–1625): Non-Dramatic Verse	45
7.	The Age of Shakespeare: Drama	54
8.	The Age of Shakespeare: Prose	69
9.	The Age of Milton (1625–1660): Milton	78
10.	The Age of Milton: Other Poets and Prose Writers	88
11.	The Age of Dryden (1660–1700): Verse	93
12.	The Age of Dryden: Prose and Drama	101
13.	The Age of Pope (1700–1745): Verse	111
14.	The Age of Pope: Prose and Drama	122
15.	The Age of Johnson (1745–1798): General Prose	134
16.	The Age of Johnson: The Novel	146

17. The Age of Johnson: Verse   160
18. The Age of Wordsworth (1798–1832): The Older Poets   183
19. The Age of Wordsworth: The Younger Poets   197
20. The Age of Wordsworth: General Prose   206
21. The Age of Wordsworth: The Novel   214
22. The Age of Tennyson (1832–1887): Verse   222
23. The Age of Tennyson: General Prose   238
24. The Age of Tennyson: The Novel   250
25. The Age of Hardy (1887–1928)   261
26. The Present Age (1930–1955)   287

Preface

The purpose and plan of this little book may easily be gathered from the introductory chapter. Only a few words of preface, therefore, are needed.

As I conceive it, a history of English literature, however brief, should still be a history of English literature in fact as well as in name; and for a history something more is required than a list of authors and their books, and even than a chronologically arranged collection of biographical sketches and critical appreciations. It is true that a nation's literature is made up of the works of individual writers, and that for the ordinary purposes of study these writers may be detached from their surroundings and treated separately. But we cannot get a history of such literature unless and until each one has been put into his place in the sequence of things and considered with reference to that great body of literary production of which his work must now be regarded as a part. A history of English literature, then, must be interested primarily in English literature as a whole. Its chief aim should be to give a clear and systematic account, not of the achievements of successive great writers merely, as such, but of national changes and development.

This does not imply neglect of the personal factor. On the contrary, it brings the personal factor into relief; for if each writer is to be considered with reference to literature as a whole, one main subject of enquiry must be the nature and value of his particular contribution to that whole. But it does mean that, together with the personal factor, the great general movement of literature from age to age has to be investigated, and that every writer has to be interpreted in his connection with this general movement. To exhibit the interplay of the personal and the impersonal in the making of history is, indeed, one of the fundamentals of the historian's task; and since history, properly understood, is as much concerned with the explanation of facts as with the facts themselves, it follows that a history of English literature must also include some record of the forces which, period by period, have combined in the transformation of literary standards and tastes.

I have put these ideas, into different, and perhaps rather simpler language in my introductory chapter. Here, therefore, I have only to say that this Outline History represents a modest attempt towards a real history of English literature in the sense which I attach to the term. One special feature of the book may be noted. It appears to be an accepted principle with many critics that literature is produced, as it were, in a vacuum, and by men who stand outside all conditions of time and place, and that therefore it may best be studied as a thing in itself. I, on the other hand, believe that the literature of any age is necessarily shaped and coloured by all the elements which entered into the civilisation of that age. So far as the limits of my space would allow, therefore, I have tried always to suggest the vital relationship between English literature and English life.

William Henry Hudson

1

Introductory

1. What Is a History of English Literature? Perhaps it seems hardly worthwhile to put this question, because the answer to it is so very obvious. A history of English literature, we reply without a moment's hesitation, is simply a chronological account of the books which have been written in the English language, and—since we cannot think of a book without thinking also of its author—of the men who wrote them.

In a rough way, this answer is all right so far as it goes. But it is too vague, and it does not go far enough. It will be well for us, therefore, to pause at the outset of our own work to consider a little closely what it is that a history of English literature, however brief, really involves.

Stress may first of all be laid upon the personal element in it which our answer already recognises. We cannot, we say, think of a book without thinking also of its author. Every book, in other words, takes us back immediately to the man behind it, of whose genius it is a product, and whose thoughts and feelings it embodies. In a history of English literature, therefore, we must fix attention upon the personalities of the men by whom this literature has been made. In a short sketch we cannot, of course, examine in detail their lives, experiences, and characters. This must be left for a more extended study. But we must try nonetheless to understand the distinctive quality in the genius of each man who comes before us. The reason of this is clear. Genius means many things, but at bottom it means strength of personality and, as a consequence, what we call originality. Every great writer, it has been well said, brings one absolutely new thing into the world—himself, and it is just because he puts this one new thing into what he writes that his work bears its own special hallmark, and has something about it which makes it unlike the work done by anyone else. In the detailed study of any great writer this essential element of individuality is the chief feature to be considered, and in an historical survey, no matter how slight, it must be carefully noted too, for otherwise we cannot learn why such a writer counts as he does in the literature of his nation. A history of English literature, then, is concerned to indicate the nature and value of the particular contribution which each writer personally has made to that literature.

This, however, is only a small part of its task. A mere list of authors, taken separately, and of their books, does not constitute a history of literature, for literature as a whole grows and changes from generation to generation, and in tracing this growth, history must show the place which each writer occupies in it, and his relations with those who went before, and with those who came after him. A writer of exceptionally powerful personality is certain to stamp his impress upon his age, and amongst those who follow him many will always be found who, whether they are conscious of it or not, reveal his influence in their thought and style. Moreover, the popularity obtained by any writer with a particular kind of work will naturally breed imitations, and what has once been done successfully will for a time be done again and again. In this way 'schools' are formed and 'movements' initiated, which last for a while, and then, when tastes presently change, and other 'schools' and 'movements' arise, disappear. Thus we speak of the 'school' of Pope, meaning the whole succession of poets who wrote in the particular style which he had brought to perfection and made current; of the 'classic' movement in verse which, following his lead, these writers carried on; of the 'romantic' movement in prose fiction which owed its principal impulse to Scott's historical novels; and so on. Such schools and movements always play a large part in the development of literature, and are often as important to the student as the individual writers themselves. It must be remembered, too, that even the most original men—the men who are most completely themselves—have their intellectual ancestry, and are often deeply indebted to others for inspiration and example. I have just spoken of Pope's particular style; but this was not his own independent creation; and while it assumed perfection in his hands, it was really the final result of a long 'movement' in verse which had already found one great representative in his immediate predecessor, Dryden. Scott was educated in a 'romantic' school before he became in his turn a supreme master in that school. We frequently think of Shakespeare, as if he stood altogether apart in the literature of his day, but in fact, he took the drama up at the point which it had reached when he began to write for the stage, and followed the lines which his forerunners had laid down. The history of literature, then, must take account of all these things. It must bring out the relationships between writer and writer and group and group; it must trace the rise, growth, and decline of 'schools' and 'movements'; and whenever any given writer had been specially prominent in their evolution, it must consider the influence he exerted in making literature either by keeping it in the old channels or in directing it into new.

We have, however, to go much farther even than this. I have said that literature as a whole grows and changes from generation to generation. This means that, as each age has its own particular lines of interest and its own particular way of thinking and feeling about things, so the literature which it produces is governed by certain prevailing tastes; that these tastes last for a time only; and that the tastes of one age are sure to differ, and are often found to differ enormously, from those of every other. Near as we are to the great Victorian era—which was simply the era of our fathers—there is much in its literature which now seems as foreign to us as its fashions in dress. We all know that authors did not write and that there was no public to enjoy the same kind of poetry in Pope's day as in

Spenser's, or in Scott's day as in Pope's. In Spenser's day there was boundless enthusiasm for *The Faery Queene*; in Pope's, for the *Essay on Man*; in Scott's, for *The Lady of the Lake*. Now the great central purpose of a history of literature—the purpose to which everything else in it is secondary and subordinate—is to give a clear account of the whole transformation of literature from period to period, and so far as possible to mark out the causes which have combined to produce it. Among these causes, as I have already suggested, we have to reckon the influence of individual men; for a great writer will often create a new taste, and make a fresh departure in the literature of his time. Yet, while full weight must be given to personal initiative and example, we must be careful not to emphasise their importance to the exclusion of all other considerations. Even the greatest genius is necessarily moulded by the culture, ideals, and mental and moral tendencies of the world into which he is born, and the character of what he produces is therefore to a large extent determined by these. If a man of powerful personality stamps his impress upon his age, as I have said, he also takes the impress of his age, and the success of his work, entirely original as it may seem to be, is often due to the way in which it meets or anticipates the general taste of the public to which he appeals. In this sense we have to regard every writer as a 'product' of his time, and so regarding him, we have to inquire into the nature of the influences which shaped his thought, directed his taste, and helped to give a distinctive character to his work. Such inquiry, it is evident, will often lead us rather far afield. Sometimes the influences in question are purely 'literary'; that is, they belong to the sphere of books and scholarship. Thus, for example, one of the principal forces behind the English literature of the Elizabethan era was the immense enthusiasm for the Greek and Latin classics which had come with what we call the Renaissance; our writers and readers alike were under the powerful spell of Italian literature during the same period, under that of French literature at the end of the seventeenth century, under that of German literature a hundred years later; while, to give one more illustration, the re-awakening, from about 1750 onward, of popular interest in the long-neglected art and literature of the middle ages inspired that 'medieval revival' which presently culminated in Coleridge and Scott. In such cases we see how literary influences introduce new currents of taste, which carry even the most independent writers along with them. But often the influences which most profoundly affect literature are not 'literary'; they are influences which belong, not to books and scholarship, but to general life, politics, society. Whatever brings fresh interests and ideas into the life of an age, whatever tends to modify its ways of thought and feeling and to change its attitude towards men and things, must of necessity enter as a vital factor into the making of its literature. We must never think of a book as though it were written outside the conditions of time and space. We must think of it as the work of a man who, living in a certain age, was affected, according to the nature of his own personality, by the atmosphere and the movements of that age. The Reformation, Puritanism, the French Revolution, the enormous progress of science during the nineteenth century—it is enough to mention these to show the intimate connection between the history of literature and general history.

We are now, I hope, in a position to realise what it is that a history of English literature should undertake to do. Its principal object is to trace the progress of English literature through all its transformations from age to age, and, in following the varying course of its development, to explain the successive changes which have taken place in its matter, form, and spirit. It has therefore to consider the influences by which these changes have been wrought, and thus it becomes a record both of individual men and their special contributions to literature and of the forces, personal and impersonal, which went to the shaping of their work.

2. English Literature and English History. This suggests one point which is so important that I trust that the reader of these pages will think about it carefully for himself. Every man belongs to his race and age, and no matter how marked his personality, the spirit of his race and age finds expression through him. A history of English literature has therefore a national as well as a personal character and interest. It is not only an account of the work done by a number of separate English writers; it is also an account of a great body of literature which in its totality is to be regarded as the production of the genius of the English people. Everything that for good or evil has entered into the making of our nation's life has also entered into the texture of its literature. Ordinary English history is our nation's biography; its literature is its autobiography; in the one we read the story of its actions and practical achievements; in the other the story of its intellectual and moral development. As we follow the history of our literature through all its transformations, therefore, we are brought into direct and living contact with the motive forces of the inner life of each successive generation, and learn at first hand how it looked at life and what it thought about it, what were the things in which it was most interested and by which it was most willing to be amused, by what passions it was most deeply stirred, by what standards of conduct and of taste it was governed, and what types of character it deemed most worthy of its admiration. In studying English literature according to the chronological method of history, let us always try to think of it as the progressive revelation of the mind and spirit of the English people.

3. The Periods of English Literature. We ought now to have no difficulty in understanding why the history of English literature is always divided into periods. This division is made, it is true, primarily as a matter of convenience, since for purposes of study it is necessary to break a large subject up into parts; but there is also a real justification for it. A period in the sense which we properly attach to the term, is a certain length of time during which a particular kind of taste prevails, and the literature of which is therefore marked by various common characteristics of subject-matter, thought, tone, and style. While the individual writers of such a period will of course differ immensely, one from another, in all the specific qualities of personality, these common characteristics will nonetheless be pronounced features in the work of all of them. Then with a decisive change of taste, the period in question may be said to come to a close while another period opens.

We must be on our guard against treating these periods as if they were rigorously fixed and self-contained, with actual boundary-walls between each one and the next. History recognises only a continuous flow, and knows nothing of absolute endings and beginnings. Hence, in fact, age overlaps age, and in strict chronology a man's work may begin in one and end in another. We can see at once that all proposed divisions have something arbitrary about them when we remember that Dryden was a man of forty-three when Milton died, and outlived him only twenty-six years, and that we yet always consider them not as contemporaries, but as representatives of different epochs. Still, on the whole, the periods of literature are fairly well defined, and in practice they are of the utmost value because they help us to concentrate attention upon the things which are most important in each successive stage of that great gradual transformation which, as we have learned, it is the main business of a history of literature to record.

In tabulating these periods various methods may be adopted. It is very usual to label them with epithets derived from history, and to speak, for example, of the Elizabethan Age, the Age of the Restoration, the Victorian Age, and so on. But perhaps it is better to take our descriptive terms from literature itself, and to designate each period by the name of its most characteristic and representative writer. This is the course I purpose to adopt here. Leaving out of consideration for the moment literature before Chaucer and for a hundred and fifty years or so after his death, we shall thus have the Age of Chaucer, the Age of Shakespeare, the Age of Milton, the Age of Dryden, the Age of Pope, the Age of Johnson, the Age of Wordsworth, and the Age of Tennyson, as the large divisions of our study. The appended table will show the rough limits of these periods, and their relations with the periods of general history.

It must be borne in mind that as this is to be a little book on a big subject, the various questions with which, as I have shown, the history of English literature has to deal, must be very briefly treated. In view of the limitations of our space, we shall also have to confine our attention almost entirely to what is commonly known as general literature. The literature of special subjects—of science, theology, philosophy, and so forth—save in exceptional cases in which there is some particular reason for mentioning it—will therefore be omitted from our survey.

PERIODS OF ENGLISH LITERATURE

Literary Periods	Approximate Dates	Historic Periods
Pre-Chaucerian Period	500–1340	Anglo-Saxon and Anglo-Norman periods
The Age of Chaucer (Chaucer, 1340–1400)	1340–1400	Middle Plantagenet (or Angevin) period
From Chaucer to *Tottel's Miscellany*	1400–1557	Later Plantagenet (Angevin) period Early Tudor period
The Age of Shakespeare (Shakespeare, 1564–1616)	1557–1625	The Elizabethan Age The Jacobean Age (Age of Renaissance)
The Age of Milton (Milton, 1608–74)	1625–60	The Caroline Age
The Age of Dryden (Dryden, 1631–1700)	1660–1700	The Age of Restoration
The Age of Pope (The Augustan Age) (Pope, 1688–1744)	1700–45	The Queen Anne Age Early Georgian Age
The Age of Johnson (Johnson, 1709–84)	1745–98	Middle Georgian Age
The Age of Wordsworth (Wordsworth, 1770–1850)	1798–1832	Later Georgian Age or the Age of the Revolution
The Age of Tennyson (Tennyson, 1809–92)	1832–87	The Victorian Age
The Age of Hardy (Hardy, 1840–1928)	1887–1928	
The Present Age	1930–55	

2
English Literature Before Chaucer (500–1340)

4. The Place of Old English Literature in our Study. Among historians of our language it was formerly the practice to draw a sharp dividing line between what they called 'Anglo-Saxon' and that new speech, which they distinguished as 'English', which after the Conquest gradually arose from the union of this Anglo-Saxon with the Norman French brought over by the Conqueror. This dividing line is not recognised by modern writers, who insist that in its foundations English is essentially a Teutonic language, that the English of the fourteenth century grew out of the Anglo-Saxon of the fifth by a regular course of evolution, and that nothing occurred at any stage to break its continuity. For this reason, the term Anglo-Saxon is now commonly dropped and 'Old English' used instead.

A corresponding change has naturally taken place in the interpretation of the history of literature. Here, again, the idea of unbroken continuity is emphasised, and as what was once called Anglo-Saxon is regarded as an early form of English speech, so what was once called Anglo-Saxon literature is regarded as an early form of English literature. According to this conception, English literature did not begin, as used to be said, with Chaucer. It began far back with the beginnings of the history of the English people on the continent of Europe, before bands of them had settled in the little island which was presently to become the home of their race.

I am not now going to question the modern scientific view; yet we may still recognise the practical convenience, if not the scientific accuracy, of the older view which it has displaced.

It is true that we can trace the gradual growth of Chaucer's language by a process of slow unbroken development out of that which Caedmon had used some seven centuries earlier. But there is still one fundamental difference between Chaucer's English and Caedmon's. We have to learn Caedmon's Old English as we learn a foreign language, while though Chaucer's Middle English is full of words and idioms which puzzle us, we rightly feel that it is only an archaic form of the same tongue that we use today. So with literary style: that of Caedmon is based on principles radically different from ours; that of Chaucer, on principles which are substantially those of our own poetry.

Continuous, then, though the history of English literature is from the fifth century to the twentieth, we may still hold that literature before Chaucer constitutes a special field of study, and that it is only with Chaucer that modern English literature definitely begins. Adopting this view, here, we will merely sketch with the utmost brevity the growth of our literature prior to the middle of the fourteenth century, and take this period as the real starting-point of our narrative.

5. English Literature before the Conquest. A considerable body of Anglo-Saxon poetry has been preserved, including one piece of immense interest, the epic *Beowulf*. Of the authorship of this nothing is known, and its history is still a matter of controversy. But it is probable that it grew up in the form of ballads among the ancestors of the English in Denmark and South Sweden, that in this form it was brought by invaders to this country, and that it was here fashioned into an epic, perhaps by some Northumbrian poet, about the eighth century. Manifestly heathen in origin, it is as it stands the work of a Christian writer. It tells with rude vigour of the mighty feats of the hero whose name it bears; how, first, he fought and killed the monster Grendel, who for twelve years had wasted the land of the King of the Danes; how, next, he slew Grendel's mother; and how at last, a very old man, he went out to destroy a fiery dragon, receiving as well as giving a mortal wound. Vivid pictures of life in war and peace among our remote forefathers add greatly to the value of a fine old poem.

Apart from *Beowulf*, the most important surviving examples of our oldest English poetry are to be found in the works of Caedmon and Cynewulf, both of whom belong to the north, and to the period immediately following the conversion of the Anglo-Saxons to Christianity, which began at the end of the sixth century.

Caedmon, who died about 680, was a servant attached to the monastery of Whitby in Yorkshire. According to a pretty tale told by the Venerable Bede, the power of verse came to him suddenly as a divine gift. He had never been able to sing to the harp as others did in festive gatherings in the monastery hall, and when, his turn came round, he had always been used to retire in humiliation. But one night, having gone to the stables to look after the horses of which he had charge, he fell asleep, and an angel appeared to him in a vision, and told him to sing. Then when he asked, 'what shall I sing?' the heavenly visitor replied, 'Sing the beginning of created things;' and waking, he found himself, to his astonishment, endowed with the faculty of poetry. Three free paraphrases of scripture which have come down to us in a manuscript of the tenth century, have been attributed to him; one dealing with the creation and the fall; the second, with the exodus from Egypt; the third with the history of Daniel; but it is now believed that a considerable portion of these poems, if not the whole of them, is the work not of Caedmon himself but of his imitators. They were first printed about 1650 by an acquaintance of Milton, and it has been thought, though there is no proof of this, that the great poet may have taken hints from the *Genesis* in writing *Paradise Lost*.

A miraculous element also enters into the story of Cynewulf's career. Born, it is conjectured, between 720 and 730, he was in earlier life, as he himself tells us in his *Dream of the Rood*, a wandering gleeman and a lover of pleasure, but converted by a vision of the cross, he dedicated himself henceforth to religious themes. His works include a poem called *Christ*, treating of the Incarnation, the Descent into Hell, the Ascension, and the Last Judgment; *Elene*, an account of the finding of the true cross, according to the legend, by Helena, the mother of Constantine; and *Juliana*, a tale of Christian martyrdom.

While generally sacred in subject, and profoundly earnest in feeling, Anglo-Saxon poetry is full of a love of adventure and fighting, and sometimes its martial spirit bursts out into regular war poetry, as in *The Battle of Brunanburh* (937), of which Tennyson made a spirited translation. A fondness for the sea, ingrained in our English character, is also another striking feature of it. In form, it rests upon principles of composition radically different, as I have said, from those which govern modern English versification. In place of our rhyme (or 'end rhyme' as it is more strictly called) it employs 'beginning rhyme', or alliteration, that is, the regular and emphatic repetition of the same letter; while the lines are quite irregular in regard to the number of unaccented syllables introduced. To state the broad rule: each line of an Anglo-Saxon poem consisted of two divisions; the first of these contained two accented syllables, the second at least one; and the accented syllables in each case began with the same letter. This gives us the normal type of Anglo-Saxon verse, as in this line from *Beowulf*:

> Grendel gongan, Godes yrre baer
> (Grendel going God's anger bore).

Another illustration will be given later from a fourteenth century poem, in which the old alliterative system was preserved (see §13).

Anglo-Saxon poetry flourished most in the north; prose developed later in the south. In general, while interesting from the linguistic and antiquarian points of view, the prose writings which have come down to us possess but little value as literature. Though hardly more than a translator, King Alfred (849–901) holds an honourable place as the first to put the vernacular to systematic use. Among the works rendered by him into 'the language which we all understand' (to adopt his own significant phrase) was the Latin *Ecclesiastical History* of the Venerable Bede, or Baeda (673–735), who wrote at Jarrow in the kingdom of Northumbria. But the greatest monument of Old English prose is the *Anglo-Saxon Chronicle*, which, though it already existed before Alfred, was under his guidance transformed into a national history, and which was so continued till 1154, when it closed with the record of the death of King Stephen.

6. From the Conquest to Chaucer. From the Norman Conquest to the beginning of the thirteenth century English had a severe struggle to maintain itself as a written language, and as a consequence, English literature, which for nearly two hundred years before William's landing had shown little sign of life, now for another period of a hundred and fifty years almost ceased to exist. Its revival began in the reign of John, by which time the long-standing hostility between the native population and the invaders had been to a large extent outgrown, and, as the famous incident of Magna Charta shows, the two elements had been welded into a single people. The loss of the French possessions of the English crown tended still further to confirm the growing unity of the nation. In these circumstances English began to assert itself beside the rival tongue, which was already losing ground, and with this English literature assumes a certain historical interest. It now becomes clear how much has been gained in the meantime by the accumulation of fresh materials from various sources. We see this in the case of the first noteworthy production of the revival, *Brut*, completed about 1205 by Layamon, a parish priest of Worcestershire. This enormous poem of some 30,000 lines contains the legendary history of ancient Britain, beginning with Æneas, whose descendant Brutus was the supposed ancestor of the British people, ending with Cadwallader, the last of the native kings, and including by the way, among innumerable episodes, the stories of Lear and King Arthur; but the point of special importance in connection with it is, that it is a paraphrase with additions of a versified chronicle, *Brut d'Engleterre*, of the Anglo-Norman poet Wace, which in its turn had been based upon the so-called *History of Britain* (1132) by the romancing Welsh annalist, Geoffrey of Monmouth. In Layamon's poem, then, three streams of influence—Celtic, French, and English—run together; while, though in versification it follows the Anglo-Saxon principle of alliteration, French taste is reflected in the occasional appearance of rhyme. A little later came *Ormulum* (about 1215), a series of metrical homilies, in short lines without either rhyme or alliteration, by a Lincolnshire priest named Orm; and a prose treatise, the *Ancren Riwle* (about 1225), or *Rule of Anchoresses*, prepared by some unknown writer for the guidance of three ladies entering the religious life. A charming dialogue poem, *The Owl and the Nightingale* (about 1220), in which the two birds discuss their respective merits, is historically interesting, because it discards alliteration and adopts French end-rhyme. This is the only other piece of native thirteenth century literature which calls for mention. The principal productions of the early fourteenth century—Robert Mannyng's *Handlyng Synne* (*Manual of Sins*, 1303); the prose *Ayenbite of Inwyt* (*Remorse of Conscience*, 1340)—both translated from the French; and the *Cursor Mundi* (about 1320), a versified account of scripture history together with many legends of the saints—belong to religious rather than to general literature.

7. The Making of the English Language. The period between the Conquest and Chaucer is, however, much more important from the point of view of our language than from that of our literature. During these three hundred years, while little was being produced in prose or verse of any intrinsic value, modern English was gradually evolving out of the conflict of opposing tongues, and assuming national rank as the speech of the whole people. To trace the stages of this evolution does not, of course, fall within the scope of a primer of literary history. It is enough for us to note that the final product of it was a mixed or compound language, the grammatical structure and vocabulary of which alike were the result of Norman

French influences acting upon the old Anglo-Saxon material. It was this new tongue which ultimately displaced that of the Conquerors. Norman French long continued, indeed, to be the only recognised official language and to some extent, the language of fashion. But by the beginning of the fourteenth century it had entirely lost its hold upon English life at large, and the complete triumph of English was signalised by a statute of 1362, which proclaimed that henceforth all proceedings in the law courts should be in that language instead of French. For more than a hundred years before this numerous English translations of French romances had shown the growth of a literary public among those who, as the phrase then ran, 'had no French.'

We must, however, remember that while French was thus disappearing, there was as yet no standard form of the new tongue to take its place. English was broken up into dialects. There was a Northern English, a Midland English, and a Southern English, which differed fundamentally from one another, and which were yet subdivided within themselves into numerous minor varieties. In this confusion, little by little, East Midland English tended to gain ascendancy, because it was the speech of the capital and of the two centres of learning, Oxford and Cambridge. Then when Chaucer began to write, he chose this as his vehicle, and it was largely on account of his influence that what had hitherto been only one of several provincial dialects attained the dignity of the national language.

We thus come round to Chaucer, the first of our really national English poets.

TABLE OF ENGLISH LITERATURE BEFORE CHAUCER

Settlement of the Jutes, Saxons and Angles in Britain, 449-547

Christianity introduced into Kent by St. Augustine, 597; into Northumbria, 627-35

    Caedmon's *Paraphrases*, 670-80
    Cynewulf, b. between 720 and 730
    Fashioning of *Beowulf* into an epic, ? 8th century.

Alfred, King of Wessex, 871-901   Alfred's translations, 9th century
Norman Conquest, 1066
John, 1199-1216

    English Revival
    Layamon's Brut, about 1205
    Orm's *Ormulum*, about 1215
    The *Ancren Riwle*, about 1225
    The *Owl and the Nightingale*, about 1220

    Mannyng's *Handlyng Synne*, 1303
    Cursor Mundi, 1320-25

Edward III, 1337-77   *Ayenbite of Inwyt*, 1340
    Chaucer, b. 1340?

3

The Age of Chaucer
(1340–1400)

8. The Age of Chaucer. Geoffrey Chaucer was born in the reign of Edward III, lived through that of Richard II, and died the year after Henry IV ascended the throne. His life thus covers a period of glaring social contrasts and rapid political change. Edward's reign marks the highest development of medieval civilisation in England. It was also the midsummer of English chivalry. The spirit of his court was that of the romantic idealism which fills Chaucer's own *Knight's Tale*, and the story of his successive wars with France, and of the famous victories of Crécy and Poictiers, as written in the *Chronicles* of Froissart, reads more like a brilliant novel than a piece of sober history. Strong in its newly established unity, England went forth on its career of foreign conquest in a mood of buoyant courage, and every fresh triumph served to give further stimulus to national ambition and pride. But there was another side to this picture. The king and his nobility led a very gay and debonair life. Trade expanded, and among the commercial classes wealth increased. But the masses of the people were meanwhile sunk in a condition of deplorable misery. Pestilence after pestilence ravaged the land, and then in 1348–9 came the awful epidemic called the Black Death, which in a single year swept away more than a third of the entire population, and which reappeared in 1362, 1367, and 1370. Famine followed plague; vagrants and thieves multiplied; tyrannous laws passed to regulate labour only made bad matters worse. The French wars, which had given temporary glory to the arms of Edward, were fraught with disastrous consequences for his successor. Their enormous cost had to be met by heavy burdens of taxation, which were the immediate cause of a general rising of the common folk under Wat Tyler, Jack Straw, and the unfrocked priest, John Ball. Though soon quelled, this was a sign of widespread social unrest. Political troubles also grew apace under Richard's unwise and despotic rule, and the constitutional conflicts between the king and his subjects resulted in endless discord and confusion. The temper of the England of Chaucer's closing years was therefore very different from that of the England into which he had been born. Much of the glamour had gone from life, and men were more conscious of its stern realities.

Among the causes which greatly contributed to the increasing evils of Chaucer's age we must also reckon the corruption of the Church. Of spiritual zeal and energy very little was now left in the country. The greater prelates heaped up wealth, and lived in a godless and worldly way; the rank and file of the clergy were ignorant and careless; the mendicant friars were notorious for their greed and profligacy. Chaucer himself, as we shall presently have to note, took little serious interest in social reform; yet the portraits which he draws for us of the fat, pleasure-loving monk, the merry and wanton friar, and that clever rogue, the pardoner, who wanders about hawking indulgences and relics, show that he was alive to the shocking state of things which existed in the religious world of his time. It is at this point that we recognise the importance of the work of John Wyclif (about 1320–84), 'the morning star of the Reformation.' That earnest and intrepid man gave the best of his life to the great task of reviving spiritual Christianity in England, and in the carrying out of his mission, he wrote religious pamphlets, sent his 'poor priests' or itinerant preachers far and wide with the message of the Gospel, and with the help of his disciples produced a complete English version of the Bible—the first translation of the scriptures into any modern vernacular tongue.

Social unrest and the beginnings of a new religious movement were thus two of the chief active forces in the England of the later fourteenth century. A third influence which did much to change the current of intellectual interests, and thus affected literature very directly, came from the new learning. Thus far, scholarship had been largely the concern of the Church, and men's thoughts and feelings about themselves and the world had been governed almost entirely by theology. Ecclesiastical ideas and the medieval habit of mind were still the controlling elements in Chaucer's period, but their sway was now to some extent broken by the influx of a fresh and very different spirit. That spirit had arisen in Italy, chiefly from a renewed study of the literature of classical antiquity, and from the consequent awakening of enthusiasm not only for the art, but also for the moral ideas of Greece and Rome. An enormous impetus was thus given to intellectual expansion and to men's efforts to liberate themselves from theological trammels. The leaders of this great revival were the two celebrated Italian writers, Petrarch (1304–74) and Boccaccio (1313–75), and it was through their work in the main that the influence of humanism (as the new culture came to be called) passed into England, where its effect was soon shown in the quickened sense of beauty, the delight in life, and the free secular spirit which began to appear in our literature. It is here that we mark the rise of the vast and complex movement, which was presently to culminate in the Renaissance, and of which we shall have much more to say later. We shall indeed learn that in England adverse conditions long held this movement in check, and that as in the field of religious activity, so in that of intellectual activity, this country had to wait till the sixteenth century before the promises of the fourteenth were fulfilled. But, though of little power as yet, humanism has to be included among the formative influences of the literature of Chaucer's age.

9. Chaucer's Life. Geoffrey Chaucer, who is so much the

greatest figure in the English literature of the fourteenth century that he has thrown all his contemporaries completely into the shade, was born about 1340 in London, where his father did a flourishing business as a merchant vintner. We know practically nothing about his childhood, but it is evident from the wide and varied scholarship which characterises his writings that he must have enjoyed the advantages of a liberal education. At seventeen he received a court appointment as page to the wife of the Duke of Clarence, Edward III's third son. In 1359 he was with the English army in France, where he was taken prisoner; but he was soon ransomed, and returned to England. Sometime after this he married, and became valet of the king's chamber. From that time onward he was for many years closely connected with the court. He was often entrusted with diplomatic missions on the continent, two of them being to Italy. He was thus brought into direct touch with Italian culture in the days of the early Renaissance, and may even have met Petrarch and Boccaccio, to the former of whom he makes pointed reference in the Prologue to the *Clerk's Tale*. During these years he received many marks of royal favour, and for a time sat in Parliament as Knight of the shire of Kent. But after the overthrow of the Lancastrian party and the banishment of his special patron, John of Gaunt, he fell on evil days, and with approaching age felt the actual pinch of poverty. Fortunately, on the accession of John of Gaunt's son, Henry IV, things mended with him, and the grant of a royal pension at once placed him beyond want and anxiety. At Christmas, 1399, he took a long lease of a house at Westminster, which suggests that he still looked forward to many years of life. But he died before the next year was out, and was buried in that part of Westminster Abbey which afterwards came to be known as the Poets' Corner.

  In studying Chaucer's work it is important to remember that his education as a poet was two-fold. Part of it came from literature; but part of it came from life. He was a thorough student, and in one of his autobiographical passages (in *The House of Fame*) he tells us how after a long day over his accounts, he would go home at night and there pore over his beloved volumes till he was completely dazed. But he was not a mere bookman, nor was he in the least a visionary. Like Shakespeare and Milton, he was, on the contrary, a man of the world and of affairs. He had travelled much; he had seen life; his business at home and abroad brought him into intimate relations with people of all sorts; and with his quick insight into character and his keen eye for everything dramatic and picturesque and humorous, he was precisely the kind of poet to profit by such varied experiences. There is much that is purely bookish in his writings; but in the best of them we are always aware that he is not merely drawing upon what he has read, but that his genius is being fed by his wide and deep knowledge of life itself.

10. Chaucer's Work in General. It is usual and convenient to divide Chaucer's literary career into three periods, which are called his French, his Italian, and his English period, respectively. His genius was nourished, to begin with, on the French poetry and romance which formed the favourite reading of the court and cultivated society during the time of his youth. Naturally he followed the fashion, and his early work was done on French models. Thus, besides translating portions at least of the then popular *Roman de la Rose*, he wrote, among other quite imitative things, an allegory on the death of Blanche, John of Gaunt's wife, which he called *The Boke of the Duchesse* (1369), and which is wholly in the manner of the reigning French school. Then, almost certainly as a direct result of his visits to Italy, French influences disappear, and Italian influences take their place. In this second period (1370–84), Chaucer is the disciple of the great Italian masters, for *The House of Fame* clearly owes much to Dante, while *Troylus and Cryseyde*, by far his longest single poem, is based upon, and in part translated from, Boccaccio's *Filostrato*. To the close of this period the unfinished *Legende of Good Women* may also be referred. Finally, he ceases to be Italian as he had ceased to be French, and becomes English. This does not mean that he no longer draws freely upon French and Italian material. He continues to do this to the end. It simply means that, instead of being merely imitative, he becomes independent, relying upon himself entirely even for the use to which he puts his borrowed themes. To this last period belong, together with sundry minor poems, the *Canterbury Tales*, in which we have Chaucer's most famous and most characteristic work.

11. The Canterbury Tales. These are a collection of stories fitted into a general framework which serves to hold them together. Some of them were certainly written earlier, and before the framework had been thought of; but we put the *Tales* as a whole into Chaucer's third period, because it was then that most of them were composed, and that the complete design shaped itself in the poet's mind. That design explains the title. A number of pilgrims on the eve of their departure meet at the Tabard Inn in Southwark, where, as it chances, Chaucer himself is also staying; and, as he too is bent on the same errand, he is easily persuaded to join the party. Pilgrimages were very popular in the fourteenth century; they were often undertaken, as here, in companies, partly for the sake of society by the way, and partly because of the dangers of the roads; and, it must be admitted, their prevailing spirit was anything but severely devotional. Sometimes the pilgrims went, as Chaucer's Wife of Bath had already done, as far afield as Rome and Jerusalem; but one of the favourite expeditions nearer home was to the shrine of the murdered St. Thomas a Becket at Canterbury; and there these particular pilgrims are bound. The jolly host of the Tabard, Harry Bailly, gives them hearty welcome and a supper of his best—good victual and strong drink to match; and, after they are satisfied, he makes this proposal: that to beguile the tedium of the journey each member of the party shall tell two tales on the way to Canterbury, and two on the way back; that he himself shall be the judge; and that the one who tells the best tale shall be treated by all the rest to a supper on their return to the Tabard Inn. The suggestion is applauded, and these *Canterbury Tales* are the result.

All this is explained in the *Prologue*, after which Chaucer proceeds to introduce his fellow-pilgrims. Though limited to what we may broadly call the middle classes, the company is still very comprehensive. The military profession is represented by a knight, a squire, and a yeoman; the ecclesiastical, by a prioress, a nun (her secretary), a monk, a friar, a sumnour (summoner of those charged under the jurisdiction of the ecclesiastical courts), a pardoner (or seller of pardons), a poor parson, and a Clerk of Oxford, who is a student of divinity. Then we have a lawyer and a physician, and, running down the social scale, a number of miscellaneous characters whom one cannot well classify—a franklin (freeholder of land), a merchant, a shipman (sailor), a miller, a cook, a manciple (caterer for colleges), a reeve (land steward), a haberdasher, a carpenter, a weaver, a dyer, a tapycer (tapestry maker), a ploughman (the poor parson's brother), and a well-to-do west-country cloth-maker named Alison, who, however, is better known as the Wife of Bath. In his descriptions of the most prominent of these people Chaucer's powers are shown at their very highest, and this *Prologue* is a masterpiece of insight, sureness of touch, fine discrimination, and subtle humour. All the characters are individualised, yet their thoroughly typical quality gives unique value to Chaucer's picture of men and manners in the England of his time.

As according to programme each of the pilgrims was to have told four stories, the poet's plan was a very large one. He lived to complete a small portion only, for the work, as we have it, is merely a fragment of twenty-four tales. Yet even as it stands its interest is wonderfully varied, for Chaucer is guided by a sense of dramatic propriety, and so the tales differ in character as widely as do those by whom they are told. Thus, to take extreme examples, we have the chivalrous epic of the Knight and the Clerk's beautiful account of the patient Griselda's wifely devotion balanced in strange contrast by the coarse farcical stories of the Miller and the Reeve. It should be noted that in no case are the tales original in theme. Chaucer takes his raw material from many different sources, and the range of his reading and his quick eye for anything and everything which would serve his purpose wherever he found it, are shown by the fact that he lays all sorts of literature, learned and popular, Latin,

French, and Italian, under contribution. But whatever he borrows he makes entirely his own, and he remains one of the most delightful of our story-tellers in verse.

His finest work as a narrative poet is the *Knight's Tale*, which in accordance with the law of dramatic propriety is heroic in subject, chivalrous in sentiment, and romantic in tone. Based on the *Teseide* of Boccaccio, it tells of two young cousins of royal blood, named Palamon and Arcite, who, when Duke Theseus makes war against their city of Thebes, are taken captive by him, and imprisoned in a tower of his palace. From their window one May morning they chance to see Emily, the beautiful sister of the Duke's wife, walking in the garden beneath; whereupon their life-long friendship is shattered in an instant and they become rivals in love. Arcite is presently ransomed, but unable to endure banishment from Emily, returns to Athens in disguise, and finds a menial place in the Duke's service. Then, after several years, Palamon makes his escape. The cousins meet in duel, but are surprised and interrupted by the Duke and his train as they ride out to hunt. Theseus dooms them both to death on the spot, but relenting on the petition of the ladies, spares their lives on condition that each shall collect a hundred knights, and that the case shall be decided in a great tournament, the hand o Emily being the victor's prize. In this tournament Arcite falls, and the story ends with the nuptials of Palamon and Emily. Brilliant in itself this fine tale is also intensely interesting as the embodiment of that romantic spirit which, as we have seen, prevailed in the court circles of Chaucer's youth. Nominally it is a tale of the heroic age of Greece, but as yet no notion existed of what we call historic truth, and everything in it—characters, sentiments, setting—is medievalised. It is in fact an idealised picture of the fastvanishing middle ages, and is steeped in the atmosphere of chivalry. Its account of the tournament, its presentation of the principles of knightly ethics, and the vividness with which it portrays the chivalrous conception of love, are among the features of it which we should specially note in studying it from the historical point of view.

12. General Characteristics of Chaucer's Poetry. Chaucer was not in any sense a poet of the people. He was a court poet, who wrote for cultured readers and a refined society. The great vital issues of the day never inspired his verse. He made his appeal to an audience composed of the favoured few, who wanted to be amused by comedy, or touched by pathos, or moved by romantic sentiment, but who did not wish to be disturbed by painful reminders of plagues, famines, and popular discontent. Thus, though he holds the mirror up to the life of his time, the dark underside of it is nowhere reflected by him. It is significant that his only mention of the Peasants' Revolt is in the form of a humorous reference in the *Nonnes Priestes Tale* of the Cock and the Fox. It is true that, as we have seen, he felt the religious corruptions of the world about him, and not only his satiric portraits of unworthy churchmen, to which I have referred, but also his beautiful companion study of the poor parson, who was indeed no hireling, but a real shepherd, show his sympathy in a general way with some of Wyclif's ideas. But on the whole he left burning questions alone. His was an easy-going, genial, tolerant nature, and nothing of the reformer went to its composition. The serious note is indeed sometimes heard in his poetry; as when, for example, he writes:

> That[1] thee is sent receyve in buxomnesse[2]
> The wrastling of this world asketh a fal;
> Here is no hoom,[3] here is but wildernesse.
> Forth, pilgrim, forth! forth, best[4] out of thy stal!
> Look upon hye, and thonke God of al.

But this is not its characteristic tone; its characteristic tone is that of frank pleasure in the good things of life. Chaucer's temperament thus explains his relations with his age. Little touched by its religious or social

---

[1]That which.
[2]Cheerfulness.
[3]Home.
[4]Beast.

movements, he responded readily to the influence of Italian humanism, and it is through him that its free secular spirit first expresses itself in our poetry. If Wyclif was 'the morning star of the Reformation', Chaucer may be called 'the morning star of the Renaissance'.

A specially charming feature of his poetry is its fresh out-of-doors atmosphere. His descriptions of the country are often indeed in the conventional manner of his time, and his garden landscape and May flowers are to some extent things of tradition only. But he has a real love of nature and particularly of the spring, and when he writes of these, as in the *Prologue* and the *Knight's Tale*, the personal accent is unmistakable.

We have already spoken of Chaucer's importance in the history of our language. His fourteenth century (or 'Middle') English looks very difficult at first, but only a little time and perseverance are needed to master it, and these will be amply repaid by the pleasure we are sure to find in the felicity of his diction and the melody of his verse. It will be observed that he abandons altogether the Old English irregular lines and alliteration—'rim, ram, roff' as he jestingly calls it—and adopts the French method of regular metre and end-rhymes. Under his influence rhyme gradually displaced alliteration in English poetry.

13. Other Poets of Chaucer's Age. Chaucer's chief rival in poetry was John Gower (1332?–1408). The two poets were long friends, and Chaucer's dedication of his *Troylus and Cryseyde* to the 'moral Gower', as he calls him, and Gower's warm reference to Chaucer towards the end of his *Confessio Amantis*, show their reciprocal esteem; but later on, jealousy and misunderstandings arose between them. Gower was a most industrious and well-meaning writer, and his work is extremely voluminous, learned, and careful; but he had nothing of Chaucer's vivacity and charm, and for the most part he is hopelessly dull. Unlike Chaucer, who from the first realised the possibilities of the English tongue, he found it hard to make up his mind concerning the best medium for his poetry, and of his three long poems, one—*Speculum Meditantis*—is in French; another—*Vox*

Clamantis—in Latin; the third—*Confessio Amantis*—in English. It is in this last named that he most distinctly challenges comparison with Chaucer, for the body of it consists of tales introduced to illustrate the evils wrought by the seven deadly sins. In temper and attitude towards life, again, the two poets differed radically. Gower took a very gloomy view of the social conditions of the time. His *Vox Clamantis* is largely concerned with Wat Tyler's rebellion, and his criticism of the clergy is frequent and severe. Yet his standpoint was that of a strong conservative, and he had no more sympathy than Chaucer with the teachings of Wyclif and his followers, the Lollards.

In striking contrast with both Chaucer and Gower, who, deep as were their individual differences, were alike poets of the court, stands a third writer of this age, William Langland (1330?–1400), who was essentially a poet of the people. Of the man himself we know very little. He seems to have been the son of a franklin; to have been born in the neighbourhood of Malvern; and to have lived a life of poverty and struggle. Of his character, however, we have a clear revelation in his work, *The Vision of William Concerning Piers the Plowman*, an enormous allegorical poem which in its final shape runs to upwards of 15,000 lines. Rambling, confused, and almost formless, the *Vision* has small claim to be regarded as a piece of literary art; but its defects on this side are redeemed by its vigour and moral earnestness. Under the conventional device of a dream, or more exactly a series of dreams, the poet boldly attacks the social and ecclesiastical abuses of the day, the greed and hypocrisy of the clergy, and the avarice and tyranny of those who sit in high places. It is to this *Vision* that we have to turn if we would complete Chaucer's picture of fourteenth century England by putting in the dark shadows. Langland's spirit is strikingly puritan and democratic. He was not indeed a Wyclifite, nor politically was he a revolutionist. But he was profoundly moved by the misery of the masses; he was an ardent champion of their cause; and he sought to bring English religion back to the simplicity and purity of gospel truth. It is an interesting commentary upon the character of the poem that, written expressly for the people instead of the court, its language and style are far more rustic and old-fashioned than those of Chaucer's work. Its dialect is a mixture of Southern and Midland English, and—the last important poem to be written in this way—it adheres to the Anglo-Saxon principle of alliteration; as in the opening lines:

> In a sorrier seson whan soft was the same
> I *sh*ope me in *sh*roudes as I a *sh*epe were.[5]

One other fourteenth century poet deserves passing mention—the Scottish John Barbour (1316?–95), who for a time was Archdeacon of Aberdeen. As the real father of Scottish poetry, he holds a certain place in literature. His fame rests on his long poem *The Brus*, in which the great deeds of Robert Bruce are recorded in spirited narrative.

14. Prose of Chaucer's Age. Under this head there is little to record. Chaucer's own few prose writings—such as his translation of Boëthius and his *Treatise on the Astrolabe*—are not important. Wyclif's Bible is an interesting example of vigorous artless English, and his controversial pamphlets helped to show the capabilities of the vernacular at a time when Latin was deemed the only fitting vehicle for theological discussion. But the great prose work of this period is the singular volume which goes by the title of *The Travels of Sir John Maundeville*. According to the specific statement of the preface, this Maundeville was born at St. Albans, and set out on his journey in 1322; and his book purports to give a circumstantial account of what he had seen and heard during many years of wanderings in the Holy Land and the far east. It is now established, however, that no such person as the alleged author ever existed; that the work is a translation from the French of a certain Jean de Bourgogne; and that, instead of being a genuine record of travel, it is simply a compilation of fabulous stories out of Pliny, Friar Odoric, Marco Polo, and other retailers of the marvellous. The fact that the supposed Maundeville describes a bird which could carry an elephant away in its claws, a phoenix, and a weeping crocodile, a valley in which

---

[5] I arrayed myself in garments as if I were a shepherd.

devils were jumping about like grasshoppers, and rocks of adamant which drew the nails out of passing ships, will show that his book is at least amusing; while, even though it is only a translation, it keeps its place as the first English prose classic.

TABLE OF THE AGE OF CHAUCER

Edward III, 1327–77

John Barbour, b. 1316?
William Langland, b. 1332?

Beginning of the Hundred Years' War with France, 1338

Chaucer, b. 1340?

Battle of Crécy, 1346
The Black Death, 1348–49
Battle of Poictiers, 1356

The Romaunt of the Rose, 1360-65?
Boke of the Duchesse, 1369
Langland's *Vision*, 1362–90
Barbour's *Brus*, 1375

Richard II, 1377–99

Speculum Meditantis, 1378?
Wyclif's Bible, 1380

Wat Tyler's Rebellion, 1381

Official condemnation of Wyclif's opinions, 1382

Troylus and Cryseyde, 1380–83

Vox Clamantis, 1382?

House of Fame, 1383–84
Legende of Good Women, 1384–85
Canterbury Tales, 1385 onward
Confessio Amantis, 1393?

Henry IV ascends throne, 1399

Chaucer, d. 1400
Langland, d. 1400
Maundeville's *Travels*, 1400
Gower, d. 1408

4

From Chaucer to *Tottel's Miscellany* (1400–1557)

15. The Fifteenth Century. With Chaucer English literature made a brilliant beginning, but it was only a beginning, and after his death we enter upon a long barren period in its history. In trying to explain the unproductiveness of the fifteenth century we have, of course, to remember that there can never in any circumstances be great books unless men are born who are capable of writing them, and that the dearth of great books for a hundred years and more after Chaucer may therefore simply be the result of a dearth of literary talent. It is perhaps noteworthy that the fifteenth century was not in England an age of great men in any field of activity. But we must also recognise that even when talent exists it depends upon favourable conditions for its expression, and in the fifteenth century conditions were the reverse of favourable. Little affected by the labours of Wyclif, religion continued to degenerate, and persecution was employed to stamp out all efforts towards reform. The free movement of thought was thus checked. The country was distracted by political conflicts, which culminated in the thirty years' struggle for power (1455–86) between the Houses of York and Lancaster. In these Wars of the Roses many of the great nobles were killed, and the old order of feudalism severely shaken at its foundations. The low state of education has also to be emphasised. Such mental activity as still was to be found in the universities was wasted in endless and profitless controversies over the dry abstractions of medieval philosophy; while outside these centres of learning, and especially among the fast rising middle classes, a mercenary and sordid spirit prevailed, which was hostile to intellectual interests of any kind. In fifteenth century England, therefore, there was little enough to inspire, and much to repress literary genius. We shall indeed see presently that signs of new life became increasingly apparent as the century ran its course. But we may conveniently postpone the consideration of these till we come to deal with the revival of the early sixteenth century.

16. Poetry of the Fifteenth Century. The poor quality and general lifelessness of fifteenth century verse is at once suggested by the fact that the greater part of it is imitative. Nearly all the poets tried to walk in Chaucer's footsteps and, with little of his genius, laboured to reproduce his matter and style. Here and there real sympathy of mind and a touch of genuine power gave birth to work having a distinct merit of its own, as in the beautiful *The Flower and the Leaf*, a poem long ascribed to Chaucer himself, but now referred to some anonymous writer of his school. But on the whole, like all merely imitative things in art, such productions are of slight permanent value. Of these Chaucerians, who were numerous, the best known are Thomas Occleve, or Hoccleve (1370?–1450?), and John Lydgate (1370?–1451), both of whom were very voluminous. Hoccleve wrote a long poem called *The Governail of Princes*, in Chaucer's seven-line stanza (rhyming *ababbcc*) and in the prologue, in which he tells us much about himself, describes his grief on Chaucer's death and sings his master's praises. Among his minor poems is one entitled *Moder of God*, which was formerly printed with Chaucer's own works. Lydgate, a learned Benedictine monk of Bury St. Edmunds, poured out an enormous quantity of verse, his longer productions being the *Storie of Thebes* (designed as a new *Canterbury Tale*), the *Troy Boke*, and the *Falles of Princes*—the last based on a French paraphrase of a Latin work by Boccaccio.

The best poetry of the fifteenth century, however, was written in Scotland, where, though the influence of Chaucer was very marked, the spirit of originality was far stronger than in the south. There is not much originality, indeed, about *The King's Quair* (quire, that is, book), a long poem in which James I of Scotland (1394–1437) tells of his love for the Lady Jane Beaufort (the Duke of Somerset's daughter), who afterwards became his wife; but the genuineness of its personal feeling gives life to its verse. It is written in the Chaucerian seven-line stanza just referred to, which from this use of it is often called the 'rhyme royal'. In William Dunbar (1465?–1530?), the greatest British poet between Chaucer and Spenser, the individual quality is much more apparent. His graceful allegorical poem, *The Thistle and the Rose*, composed to commemorate the marriage of James IV of Scotland and Margaret, daughter of Henry VII of England, is quite in the manner of Chaucer's early poetry. But in much of his later verse, as in his satirical ballads and in his remarkable *Dance of the Seven Deadly Sins*, there is a combination of vigour, broad humour, and homely pathos, which belongs wholly to the character of the poet and to his native soil. The true Scottish quality is also in the ascendant in Robert Henryson (1430?–1506?), who followed the Chaucerian model in his *Testament of Cresseid*, but also produced in *Robin and Makyne* a story which anticipates Burns' *Duncan Gray*; and in Gawain or Gavin Douglas (1474–1522), Bishop of Dunkeld, whose *Palice of Honour* is full of Chaucer, while his original prologues to the successive books of his translation of the *Æneid* bear the stamp of the writer's own mind and style. The treatment of nature by these Scottish poets in general is specially interesting. Chaucer's May morning and garden landscape had become a convention which his English disciples were content to reproduce. In Scottish poetry, too, the convention reappears, but on the other hand we often find real Scotch scenery painted manifestly by men who, instead of adopting a mere literary fashion, had studied and were trying to depict the nature about them for themselves. Thus three of Douglas's prologues, just mentioned, deal with the country in spring, in autumn, and in winter, and though there are many stereotyped details, the pictures are evidently painted directly from reality, and with wonderful care and accuracy. This faithful rendering of landscape is a characteristic which should be remembered, for, as we shall learn in due course, Scottish poets did much to bring the love of nature into later English literature.

It will be seen that in speaking of these Scottish poets we have followed the Chaucerian tradition into the sixteenth century. But though they thus wrote on into a time when new ideas of poetry were beginning to arise, the general quality of their work leads us to class them with the fifteenth century men.

I must add that though poetically poor in other respects, this fifteenth century seems to have been rich in a particular kind of minor verse. We cannot indeed be sure when such poems as *The Battle of Otterburn*, the *Nut Brown Maid*, and the numerous ballads of the Robin Hood cycle, first took shape; but there is good reason to believe that ballad literature in general became increasingly popular in the century after Chaucer's death. Often rude in style, but often wonderfully direct and vigorous and full of real feeling, these ballads did much to foster a love of poetry among the English people.

17. Prose of the Fifteenth Century. Meanwhile, more promising work was being done in prose than in verse, for Englishmen were beginning to shape the rough materials of their native tongue into something like literary form for the various purposes of instruction and entertainment. Reginald Pecock (1395?–1460), Bishop of St. Asaph's and afterwards of Chichester, who took an active part in the religious controversies of his day, without, however, satisfying either the Lollards, for whom he was too conservative, or the orthodox churchmen, for whom he was too radical, made a bold break with a tradition which Wyclif had failed to shake, when he set out his arguments in English instead of Latin, and his *Repressor of Overmuch Blaming of the Clergy* and his *Boke of Faith*, must be mentioned as landmarks in the history of our prose. Some importance also attaches to the political treatise of Sir John Fortescue (1394?–1476?), *The Difference between an Absolute and a Limited Monarchy*, and to the miscellaneous writings of William Caxton, whose name will come up again directly. But the great prose production of the fifteenth century, which is indeed the one really great book of the age, is the *Morte d'arthur* of Sir Thomas Malory. Of the author we know nothing for certain except that he was a knight, and that, according to Caxton's statement, he completed his work in the ninth year of King Edward IV, that is, in 1470. This work is a compilation made from a number of French romances dealing with different portions of the vast cycle of legends which had grown up about King Arthur and his knights of the Round Table, Malory's object being to digest the scattered stories into a connected summary. To this end he treated his materials with a very free hand, selecting, rejecting, abridging, adapting, and rearranging, to suit his purpose. His narrative has little unity or proportion, yet when the immense difficulties of his task are considered, we must give him full credit for the measure of success which he certainly achieved. In an age when the medieval spirit was fast dying and the old feudal order rapidly becoming a thing of the past, Malory, a man of retrospective mind, looked back with sentimental regret, and his book is full (in Caxton's words) of 'the noble acts, feats of arms of chivalry, prowess, hardiness, humanity, love, courtesy, and very gentleness', which formed at least the ideal of the ancient system of knighthood. There is a good deal in his pages, nonetheless, which shows how very different in many matters his moral standards were from our own; but his general tone is sound. The *Morte d'arthur* holds a high place in literary history not only on account of its intrinsic interest, but also because it has been a well-spring of inspiration to many modern poets, such as Matthew Arnold, Swinburne, William Morris, and pre-eminently Tennyson, whose *Idylls of the King* are largely based upon it. In style, it is artless, for Malory pays little attention to grammar, and his sentence structure is often faulty. But he is wonderfully racy and picturesque, and on occasion he becomes really impressive.

18. The Revival of Learning. We have said that notwithstanding its literary barrenness, signs of new life became more and more apparent as the fifteenth century ran its course. To understand the place that it occupies in our literature as a period not of production but of preparation, we have to consider the growth of influences which were to contribute to the great intellectual awakening of the century following.

The origin of these influences is to be sought in the Italian revival of learning. That revival began, as we have learned, with Petrarch and Boccaccio in the fourteenth century, but it is with the fifteenth that we enter the great age of Italian humanism, when wealthy men, like the Florentine banker, Cosimo de' Medici, and his grandson, Lorenzo the Magnificent, became munificent patrons of scholarship and the arts, when monastic libraries were ransacked and innumerable long-forgotten treasures of Greek and Latin literature brought to light, and when a boundless enthusiasm for classic studies swept through the whole educated community. In the development of literature this revival of learning worked in two ways: it did much to emancipate thought from the bondage of medieval theology by restoring the generous spirit and ideals of pagan antiquity; and it presented writers with literary masterpieces which they might take as models for their own efforts. For these two reasons the Renaissance is rightly regarded as a chief force in the making of modern European literatures. Hence the importance of the fact that England now began to share in these new liberalising movements. English scholars crossed the Alps to study at Padua, Bologna, and Florence, bringing back with them the inspiration which they had received in these great centres of culture; and thus before the century was out, the new learning was firmly established at Oxford and Cambridge. Young Englishmen of rank considered a visit to Italy a necessary part of their education in the arts of life, and in this way another channel was opened up through which Italian humanism flowed into English soil. Nor must we forget how much the progress of the new learning and the diffusion of all the various influences which it bred, were helped by the introduction of printing, which by multiplying books, popularising knowledge, and disseminating ideas, did more than any other agency to break down the old intellectual boundaries and to change the spirit of the world. William Caxton, who, setting up his press at Westminster in 1476, became our first English printer, thus deserves recognition as one of the great forerunners of the intellectual revival of the sixteenth century.

19. Literature of the Early Renaissance in England. The results of this revival are first shown in the literature of the early Tudor period, which historically is of great significance as the prelude to that splendid outburst of creative energy which was to give glory to the age of Elizabeth.

In prose we find little as yet that can be classed as general literature, though a good deal that is important in connection with the special subjects which were beginning to occupy and agitate men's minds. William Tyndale's English New Testament (1525), the complete English Bible of Miles Coverdale (1535), and Cromwell's 'Great' Bible (1539), reflect the steady growth of popular interest in the scriptures during the years immediately preceding the Reformation, while they exerted great influence in the development of a standard English prose. The *Utopia* of Sir Thomas More (1478–1535) is one of the most thoroughly typical works of this time, for its description of an ideal state of society owes much, on the one hand, to Plato's *Republic*, and, on the other, to the general speculations about life, government, and religion, which the intellectual awakening had naturally brought in its train; but though written in Latin in 1516, it did not enter English literature till 1551, when it was translated by Ralph Robinson.[6] In Roger Ascham (1515–68) we have one of the earliest masters of original English prose. His *Toxophilus, or Schole of Shooting* (1545) was, in the author's own words, written 'in the English tongue for English men'; his much more famous educational treatise, *The Scholemaster*, was published by his widow two years after his death.

---

[6]The name *Utopia* is formed of two Greek words which mean Nowhere, and in the adjective Utopian has passed into our common speech.

In the revival of English poetry, which was meanwhile the principal feature in the literature of the period, the most pronounced direct influence was that of Italy. A few poets indeed either carried on the Chaucerian tradition or struck out on independent lines for themselves; among them, Stephen Hawes (d. 1523?), whose *Pastime of Pleasure* followed the old allegorical mode; and John Skelton (1460?–1528?), who began by imitating Chaucer, but later evolved a coarse, vigorous style of his own for his satiric attacks on Cardinal Wolsey. But the new movement in poetry really began at the thoroughly Italianised court of Henry VIII. In this new movement two names stand out conspicuously—those of Sir Thomas Wyatt (1503–42) and Henry Howard, Earl of Surrey (1516?–47). Both these men were filled with the spirit of the new culture, and had drunk deep of Italian poetry, and it was under these influences that, as the early critic Puttenham phrased it, 'they greatly pollished our rude and homely maner of vulgar [that is, vernacular] poesie, from that it had bene before.' Together they brought from Italy the love-poetry (or 'amourist' poetry, as it was called) which Petrarch and his followers had made popular, and with it the form called the Sonnet; while Surrey, in imitation of Italian models, was the first English poet to use (in his translation of two books of the *Æneid*) the unrhymed, ten-syllabled verse, to which the name blank verse is popularly applied.

Wyatt and Surrey are the chief poets represented in a collection of 'Songs and Sonnets' by various authors, which is commonly known, from the name of its publisher, as *Tottel's Miscellany*. Published in 1557—the year before Elizabeth came to the throne—this work deserves special mention in any history of English literature, for it distinctly marks the dawn of the new age.

It will be noted that thus far we have taken no account of the development of the drama during the periods which we have passed under review. We will deal with this important subject in our next chapter.

TABLE OF ENGLISH LITERATURE FROM CHAUCER TO TOTTEL'S MISCELLANY (1400–1557)

Henry IV, d. 1413	Hoccleve's *Governail of Princes*, 1412
	James I's *The King's Quair*, 1422
	Lydgate's *Falles of Princes*, 1430
	Pecock's *Repressor*, 1449
	Fortescue's *Difference between Absolute and Limited Monarchy*, 1450?
Wars of the Roses, 1455–86	Malory's *Morte Darihur*, 1470; pub. 1485
Progress of classical studies at Oxford and Cambridge, 1475 onward	
Caxton's printing press set up, 1476	Hawes's *Pastime of Pleasure*, 1506?
Battle of Bosworth, 1485	Dunbar's *Dance of the Seven Deadly Sins*, 1507
Henry VII, 1485–1509	
Henry VIII, 1509–47	Douglas' *Æneid*, 1513
	More's *Utopia*; Latin, 1516; English, 1551
	Sir Thomas Wyatt, 1503–42
	Henry Howard, Earl of Surrey, 1516–47
	Tyndale's New Testament and other portions of the Bible, 1525–36
	Coverdale's Bible, 1535
Edward VI, 1547–53	
Mary, 1553–58	*Tottel's Miscellany*, 1557

5

Development of Drama to 1561

20. The Beginnings of the English Drama—Miracle Plays. The history of the English drama takes us back to the century succeeding the coming of the Normans, the earliest mention of any dramatic representation in this country referring to a performance of a Latin play in honour of St. Katherine, at Dunstable about 1110. By the time of the Norman Conquest a form of religious drama, which in the first instance had evolved out of the rich symbolic liturgy of the Church, had already established itself in France, and as a matter of course it soon found its way into England. Its purpose was directly didactic; that is, it was the work of ecclesiastical authors, who used it as a means for instructing the unlettered masses in the truths of their religion. To begin with, the Church had this drama under complete control; performances were given in the sacred buildings themselves; the priests were the actors; and the language employed was the Latin of the service. But as the mystery or miracle play,[7] as it was called, increased in popularity, and on great occasions larger and larger crowds thronged about the church, it became necessary

---

[7] Attempts have been made to distinguish between 'mysteries' and 'miracle plays' on the ground that, strictly speaking, the former dealt with subjects taken from the Bible, the latter with the lives of the saints. This distinction is accepted on the Continent, but has never been established in England, where the current name for the religious drama in general has been miracle play.

to remove the stage from the interior of the building to the porch. Later, it was taken from the porch into the churchyard, and finally from the precincts of the church altogether to the village green or the city street. Laymen at the same time began to take part in the performances, and presently they superseded the clerical actors entirely, while the vernacular tongue—first French, then English—was substituted for the original Latin. But the religious drama in England did not reach its height till the fourteenth century, from which time onward at the festival of Corpus Christi, in early summer, miracle plays were represented in nearly all our large towns in great connected sequences or cycles. Arranged to exhibit the whole history of the Fall of man and his redemption, these Corpus Christi plays, or 'collective mysteries', as they are sometimes called, were apportioned among the Trading Guilds of the different towns, each one of which took charge of its own particular play, and their performance occupied several days. Four of these cycles have come down to us complete: the Chester cycle of 25 plays; the Coventry, of 42; the Wakefield, of 31; and the York, of 48. Each of these begins with the creation of the world and the Fall of man, and, after dealing with such prophetic themes as the Flood, the Sacrifice of Isaac, and the Exodus from Egypt, goes on to elaborate the last scenes in the life of Christ, the Crucifixion, Resurrection, and Ascension, and closes with the Last Judgment. In literary quality they are of course crude, but here and there they touch the note of pathos, as in the story of Abraham and Isaac, and the note of tragedy, as in the scene of the Crucifixion; while the occasional introduction of a comic element, as notably in the Shepherd plays of the Wakefield series, which are, in fact, rough country farces, only slightly connected with their context, shows even more clearly the growth of the dramatic sense. These religious performances lasted well on into the sixteenth century, and there is good reason to think that Shakespeare must have witnessed once at least those which, during his boyhood, were still being given annually at Coventry. Hamlet's advice to the players not to 'out-herod Herod' recalls the ranting braggart Herod of the old miracle plays.

21. Morality Plays and Interludes. A later stage in the evolution of the drama is marked by the morality play. This, like the miracle play, was didactic; but its characters, instead of being taken from sacred narrative, or the legends of the saints, were personified abstractions. The rise of this form of drama was very natural at a time when allegorical poetry was immensely popular. All sorts of mental and moral qualities thus appeared embodied in types—Science, Perseverance, Mundus, Free Will, the Five Senses, the Seven Deadly Sins (separately or together), Good and Bad Angels, Now-a-Days, Young England, Lusty Juventus, Humanum Genus, Everyman. Among such personifications (of which the foregoing are, of course, only examples), there was generally a place for the Devil, who had held a prominent position in the miracle plays. A later introduction of much importance was the so-called Vice, who was some humorous incarnation of evil taken on the comic side, and as such was the recognised fun-maker of the piece. He sometimes scored a tremendous popular success by jumping on the Devil's back, sticking thorns into him, belabouring him with a dagger of lath, and making him roar with pain. He is specially interesting as the direct forerunner of the clown of the Elizabethan stage. As the morality play was not, like the miracle play, obliged to follow the prescribed lines of any given story, it had greater freedom in the handling both of plot and of characters. During the excitement of the Reformation period it was much used for purposes of exposition, and even of controversy by both religious parties; one of the finest extant examples, the play *Everyman*, for instance, being written expressly to inculcate the sacramental doctrines of the Catholic Church. Little by little, as the personified abstractions came more and more to resemble individual persons, the morality passed insensibly into comedy.

What is known as the interlude was also a late product of the dramatic development of the morality play. There is indeed some confusion regarding the exact scope and proper use of this word, for many so-called interludes are only modified forms of the morality; but in its more specific sense it seems to mean any short dramatic piece of a satiric rather than of a directly religious or ethical character, and in tone and purpose far less serious than the morality proper. This form grew up early in the sixteenth century, and is rather closely associated with the name of John Heywood (1497?–1580?), who for a time was court musician and general provider of entertainments to Henry VIII. His *Four Ps*, a dialogue in which a Palmer, a Pardoner, a Pothecary, and a Pedlar exchange racy stories, and finally enter into competition as to which of them can tell the biggest lie, is the most amusing specimen of its class. Interludes were also used for scholastic purposes, as in the *Interlude of the Four Elements*; while in such a production as *Thersytes*, the addition of action turns the form into a sort of elementary comedy.

22. The Beginnings of Regular Comedy and Tragedy. These early experiments in play-writing are of great importance historically, because they provided a kind of 'Dame School' for English dramatic genius, and did much to prepare the way for the regular drama. It was, however, under the direct influence of the revival of learning that English comedy and tragedy alike passed out of these preliminary phases of their development into the forms of art. Filled with enthusiasm for everything belonging to pagan antiquity, men now went back to the classics for inspiration and example in the drama as in all other fields of literary enterprise, though it was the works of the Latin, not of the Greek playwrights, that they took as their models. At first, the comedies of Plautus and Terence, and the tragedies of Seneca were themselves acted at the universities, and on special occasions elsewhere, before audiences of scholars. Then came Latin imitations, and in due course these were followed by attempts to fashion English plays more or less precisely upon the patterns of the originals. In such attempts English writers learned many valuable lessons in the principles of dramatic construction and technique. Our first real comedy, *Roister Doister*, was written about 1550 by Nicholas Udall, head master of Eton, for performance by his schoolboys in place of the regular Latin play. It is composed in riming couplets, divided into acts and scenes in the Latin style, and deals in an entertaining way with the wooing of Dame Custance by the vainglorious hero, his various mis-adventures, and the pranks of Matthew Merrygreek the jester. Though greatly indebted to Plautus and Terence, it is everywhere reminiscent of the older humours of the miracle plays and the moralities. Our first real tragedy, on the other hand, is an almost pedantic effort to reproduce the forms and spirit of Senecan tragedy. It is entitled *Gorboduc* (or later, *Ferrex and Porrex*); is based upon an episode in Geoffrey of Monmouth's history (see §6); and was written by Thomas Sackville, Lord Buckhurst (1536–1608) and Thomas Norton (1532–84) for representation before the members of the Inner Temple at their Christmas festivities of 1561. It is an interesting point that this first English tragedy was also the first of our plays to use blank verse, which, it will be remembered, had been introduced into English poetry only a few years before (see §19).

TABLE OF THE DEVELOPMENT OF THE DRAMA TO 1566

Henry I, 1110–35	First recorded dramatic performance in England, *Ludus de S. Katherina*, about 1110
Henry III, 1216–72	Institution of the Festival of Corpus Christi, by which a great impulse was given to the performance of miracle plays, 1264
Edward III, 1327–77	York cycle, about 1340 Chester cycle, middle of 14th century Wakefield cycle, middle of 15th century
Henry VI, 1422–71 Richard III, 1483–85 Henry VII, 1485–1509	Coventry cycle, 15th century Earliest extant morality play, *The Castell of Perseverance*, middle of 15th century
Henry VIII, 1509–47	Interludes, early 16th century The *Four Ps*, about 1520

Edward VI, 1547–53   *Roister Doister*, about 1550
Many translations of Seneca's tragedies, second half of 16th century

Elizabeth, 1558–1603   *Gorboduc*, 1561
Gammer Gurton's Needle (by John Still, second English comedy), 1566

6
The Age of Shakespeare (1558–1625):
Non-Dramatic Verse

23. The Age of Shakespeare. We now enter what we broadly call the Shakespearean Age, by which we here mean the whole period extending from the accession of Elizabeth in 1558 to the death of James I in 1625. These 67 years fall naturally into three divisions—the first 21 years of the Queen's reign; the 24 years between the publication of Spenser's *Shepheardes Calender* and her death; and the 22 years of the reign of James I. We may call the first division, the time of preparation, or the springtide of Elizabethan literature; the second, its time of full fruition, or summer; the third, its time of decline, or autumn. Strictly speaking, it is of course to the first two divisions only that the term Elizabethan should be applied, while the proper designation for the third is Jacobean. But from the point of view of literary development there are good reasons why Elizabethan and Jacobean should alike be included in the general phrase which we use here—the Age of Shakespeare.

By virtue of its wonderful fertility and of the variety and splendour of its production, this period as a whole ranks as one of the greatest in the annals of the world's literature, and its greatness was the result of many co-operating causes. As we follow the course of history, we observe that sometimes the average mood of a nation is sluggish and dull, and sometimes it is exceptionally vigorous and alert. Men who, like Spenser, Bacon and Shakespeare grew from boyhood into youth in the early years of Elizabeth's reign, and reached maturity during the closing decades of the sixteenth century, were fortunate enough to find themselves in a world in which the tides of life were at their highest. Influences were everywhere at work which tended to expand thought, stir the feelings, dilate the imagination, and by nourishing as well as stimulating genius, to give breadth and energy to the literature produced. England now felt the full effect of the revival of learning, which was no longer limited to the scholarly few at the universities and about the court, since innumerable translations carried the treasures of the classics far and wide through that large miscellaneous public to which the originals would have been sealed books. In this way, as has been well said, 'every breeze was dusty with the pollen of Greece, Rome, and of Italy,' and even the general atmosphere was charged with the spirit of the new learning. An appetite for literature was thus fostered, and an immense impetus given to the sense of beauty and the growing love of everything that made for the enrichment of life. While the Renaissance aroused the intellect and the aesthetic faculties, the Reformation awakened the spiritual nature; the same printing press which diffused the knowledge of the classics put the English Bible into the hands of the people; and the spread of an interest in religion was inevitably accompanied by a deepening of moral earnestness. The recent discovery of new worlds beyond the seas, and the thrilling tales brought home by daring explorers, like Hawkins, Drake, Frobisher, and Raleigh, quickened popular curiosity and the zest of adventure, kindled fresh ideas about many things, and did much to enlarge the boundaries of men's minds. The general prosperity of the country was also increasing, and for the first time for many years it enjoyed the blessing of internal peace. England had thrown off the yoke of foreign power in the great rupture with Rome; the fierce feuds of Catholic and Protestant, by which it had long been rent, were now over; its discordant elements had been welded together into a united nation; and in the crisis in which, for the moment, its very existence was imperiled—the collision with Spain—Englishmen found themselves sinking minor differences to stand shoulder to shoulder in defence of their common country against their common foe. An intense patriotism thus became one of the outstanding features of the age, and showed itself in many ways—in a keen interest in England's past, pride in England's greatness, hatred of England's enemies, and extravagant loyalty to England's Queen.

Such were some of the conditions which combined to create the spirit of Shakespeare's age—an age in which 'men lived intensely, thought intensely, and wrote intensely.' At such a time, when passions were strong, and speculation was rife, and a great public existed eager to respond to the appeal of genius, everything conspired to bring out of each man the best that was in him, and whatever might be the individual quality of his work, the fulness and manysidedness of the life about him were certain to be reflected in it.

24. Elizabethan Poetry before Spenser. We may take the publication of Spenser's *Shepheardes Calender* in 1579 as marking the opening of the 'golden age' of Elizabethan literature. In the first half of the Queen's reign, while there was a good deal of poetic activity, little verse of any distinct value was produced. By far the best poetry of the period is to be found in the contributions of Thomas Sackville, Lord Buckhurst (see §22) to an extensive undertaking entitled *A Myrroure for Magistrates*. This originated in a publisher's scheme for a continuation of Lydgate's *Falles of Princes* (see §16), and was designed to include a long series of 'tragical histories' of famous Englishmen. A number of writers took part in it, but Sackville's two poems (which first appeared in the edition of 1563)—the *Induction* (or general introduction to the whole) and the *Complaint of Buckingham*—are immeasurably superior to the rest of the work. The noble, but sombre *Induction* in particular is worthy of attention as the finest single poem written in England between Chaucer and Spenser. The *Steele Glas* (1576) of George Gascoigne (1525?–77) possesses some interest as the first regular verse satire in the English language.

25. Spenser and his Poetry. Edmund Spenser, the greatest non-dramatic poet of an age which found its most natural literary expression in the drama, was born in London in 1552 and educated at the Merchant-Taylors' School and at Cambridge, where he read the classics and Italian literature, and came under the influence of the strong Protestant spirit which then pervaded the university. After a couple of years spent with relatives in Lancashire, he found a place in the household of the Earl of Leicester, with whose nephew, Sir Philip Sidney, he formed an intimate friendship. In 1580 he went to Ireland as secretary to the new Lord Deputy, Lord Grey de Wilton. The remainder of his life, save for brief visits to London, was passed in Ireland, in miserable exile among a lawless people whom he loathed. Again and again disappointed in every effort to secure a position at the court, and, with this, the means of returning to England, he found his only relief in the writing of his *Faery Queene*. In October 1598, rebellion broke out in Tyrone, where he was then living; his castle was fired and plundered by an infuriated mob; he and his family barely escaped with their lives. In failing health, and crushed in spirits, he reached London at the end of the year, and on 16th January, 1599, died in an inn at Westminster.

While Spenser's fame rests mainly on *The Faery Queene*, his minor poetry, which is voluminous, would itself have sufficed to assure him the place of pre-eminence among contemporary English poets. His *Shepheardes Calender* (1579) is a pastoral poem of the artificial kind, which the taste for everything classic which came in with the revival of learning had made popular in all European literatures, and in it Spenser follows the models set by the late Greek poet Theocritus, by Virgil in his *Bucolica*, and by French and Italian writers of the Renaissance who had imitated these. It is divided into twelve parts, one for each month of the year, and in it under the guise of conventional pastoral imagery—that is, of shepherds talking and singing—the poet writes of his unfortunate love for a certain mysterious Rosalind, deals with sundry moral questions, and discusses the religious issues of the day from the standpoint of strong Protestantism. Such conventional pastoral imagery was again used in *Astrophel* (1586), an elegy on the death of Sidney, to whom the *Calender* had been dedicated. His *Foure Hymnes* in honour of love and beauty show his wonderful power of melodious verse. His *Amoretti*, a series of 88 sonnets (such sonnet sequences in Petrarch's manner had gained great vogue in England under the influence of the widespread enthusiasm for Italian literature) describe the progress of his love for Elizabeth Boyle, whom he married in 1594. That event inspired his *Epithalamium*, the finest of all his minor poems and 'by common consent, the noblest wedding hymn in the language.'

26. The Faery Queene. Like the *Canterbury Tales*, *The Faery Queene* is a fragment, for of the twelve books which Spenser projected, six only were published during his lifetime, and portions of the seventh after his death. Even as it stands, however, it is one of the longest as well as one of the greatest of English poems. According to his own statement, his plan was that, while each of the twelve books should be independent and self-contained, they should nonetheless be connected as parts of a general comprehensive whole. His underlying scheme is explained at length in his prefatory letter to his friend, Sir Walter Raleigh. The Fairy Queen keeping her annual feast for twelve successive days, on each of these days a certain knight at her command undertook a particular adventure, each such adventure furnishing the subject of one book. Meanwhile, Prince Arthur, whom he chose as his central figure, because he was the hero of the greatest British legend-cycle of chivalry, having dreamed of the Fairy Queen, went forth in quest of her, falling in with the various knights who were engaged on their adventures, by the way. This appearance of Arthur at a critical juncture in each of the stories was specially devised as a link between one part and another of the gigantic design. Externally considered, *The Faery Queene*, like its principal models the Italian romantic epics, is compounded of the traditional materials of chivalry; giants, dragons, dwarfs, wizards, knights of superhuman prowess and courage, and distressed damsels of marvellous beauty provide its chief characters; enchantments, tournaments, love passages and endless fightings, are the staple of its plot. But Spenser's genius was fed by the Reformation as well as by the love of medieval romance and the culture of the Renaissance, and unlike his brilliant Italian master, Ariosto, who wrote only to amuse, his own great work is inspired by a high moral and religious aim. In other words, *The Faery Queene* is not simply a romance; it is a didactic romance, the poet throughout using his stories as vehicles of the lessons he wished to convey. He carries out his purpose by turning romance into allegory. His twelve knights-errant are types of the twelve cardinal virtues of Aristotle's philosophy, and the adventures of each knight are arranged to body forth symbolically the experiences, conflicts, and temptations of each such virtue in the turmoil of the world, and its ultimate triumph, with the aid of Arthur, the incarnation of Divine Power, over all its foes. Thus the first book contains 'the Legend of the Knight of the Red Cross, or of Holiness'; the second, that 'of Sir Guyon, or of Temperance'; the third, that 'of Britomartis, or of Chastity'; the fourth, that 'of Cambell and Triamond, or of Friendship'; the fifth, that 'of Artegall, or of Justice'; the sixth, that 'of Sir Calidore, or of Courtesy.' Involved with this ethical allegory, another kind of allegory enters into Spenser's plan which, as it is directly concerned with the political and religious problems of the age, we may call the historical; for the figures of his narrative are not merely personifications of moral and mental qualities, but often stand at the same time for individuals or institutions representing or embodying the qualities in question. Thus in the first book we have the story of the Red Cross Knight, who goes out to rescue the parents of the Lady Una from the power of a great dragon who for years has kept them confined in a brazen castle. As general allegory this represents the work of True Religion in rescuing Humanity from the power of the great dragon, Satan, while the friends and foes whom the knight meets are the forces which aid and the forces which oppose True Religion in the divine work of deliverance. But Spenser identifies True Religion with English Protestantism, and the foes of True Religion with the foes of England—the Papacy, and Rome's political allies, especially Spain and Mary of Scots; and so the two lines of allegory run together, and the poem becomes at once the medium of the poet's teaching and his reading of contemporary movements and events. As many of the immediate issues of Spenser's day are living issues no longer, much of his poem, if taken from this point of view, can have at best an historic value only. His allegory is sometimes confused, inconsistent, and obscure. Many readers will feel too that the constant intrusion of the symbolism sadly taxes the attention and detracts from the human interest of the poem. Yet as Spenser wrote this poem expressly for the purpose of embodying his ideas on many of the great questions of life, the allegory must never be altogether ignored.

The defects of *The Faery Queene* are very obvious. It suffers from its extreme artificiality. The old machinery of romance seems almost to collapse in places under stress of the new spiritual meanings with which it is loaded. Spenser is on the whole a rather languid story-teller; he has little dramatic power, and rarely rises to the full height of his opportunities. But, on the other hand, his merits are very many and very striking. He has a wonderful sense of beauty. He has splendid pictorial power. His work is filled with a noble moral spirit; while the quality of pure essential poetry—that quality which defies analysis, but can never be missed by any sympathetic reader—is to be felt on almost every page. It is this which enables us to understand why Spenser has been called 'the poet's poet', and why, as we shall learn later, he exercised such a stimulating influence on the literature of the eighteenth century romantic revival.

It should be noted that he was not only the greatest non-dramatic poet of his epoch; he was also the most completely representative. All the co-operating forces which made Elizabethan England what it was entered into the texture of his poem, which more than any other single work of the time represents the combination of the spirit of the Renaissance with the spirit of the Reformation. It is steeped in the humanism of the classics and Italian literature, and it everywhere testifies to the strenuous idealism and moral earnestness of Protestantism.

Two matters of detail must be touched on before we leave this epoch-making work. First, it must not be supposed that the language in which it is written was the actual English of Spenser's day. An ardent lover of Chaucer, he employed a dialect of his own which he purposely made archaic. Secondly, as his language was his own invention, so also was the stanza which he used, and which is now always known by his name. This is a nine-line stanza, rhyming *ababbcbcc*, the last line being what is called an Alexandrine, or line of six iambic feet instead of five. The genesis of this stanza is uncertain, but it is probable that Spenser evolved it by simply adding the Alexandrine to Chaucer's eight-line stave (*ababbcbc*) of *The Monkes Tale*.

27. Other Poets from 1579 to 1625. The minor poets of the Age of Shakespeare were very numerous, but it would serve no useful purpose to attempt a catalogue of them here. It is, however, necessary that we should learn something about the different kinds of poetry which were then written, and about a few of the men who helped to swell the chorus of Elizabethan song.

Following in the wake of *Tottel's Miscellany* came many collections of a similar character under curiously fanciful titles, such as *The Paradyse of Daynty Devises* (1576), *A Handefull of Pleasant Delites* (1584), *An Arbor of Amorous Devises* (1597), and—the most famous of all of them—*England's Helicon* (1600). These, like the regular song-books, which were also popular, have preserved for us many graceful pieces of verse by authors whose very names would otherwise have been forgotten. A special type of lyric which enjoyed great vogue was the sonnet, which on its introduction from Italy by Wyatt and Surrey, at once established itself among the recognised forms of English poetry. The Italian plan of writing sonnets in sequences was, as we have seen, also adopted by many poets. One such sequence—the *Amoretti* of Spenser—has already been mentioned, and to this we may now add, by way of further illustration, SIDNEY's *Astrophel and Stella*, DANIEL's *Delia*, DRAYTON's *Idea*, and the *Sonnets* of SHAKESPEARE. All these are love poems, which in the Italian manner trace the movements and fluctuations of passion, but while in some cases the experiences and sentiments are real, in others they are merely feigned.

Another class of poetry which historically is very significant, because it expresses the powerful patriotic feeling of the time, is that inspired by national themes. WILLIAM WARNER'S *Albion's England* (1586–1606), a poem of some 10,000 lines, sets forth the history of England from Noah's days to those of Elizabeth. SAMUEL DANIEL produced a versified chronicle in eight books on *The Civil Wars between the Two Houses of Lancaster and York* (1595–1609). MICHAEL DRAYTON, who is now best known by his spirited ballad *The Battle of Agincourt*, has a more substantial, if not a better, claim to recognition as the author of *England's Heroical Epistles* (1595), *The Barons' Wars* (1603), and *Polyolbion* (1612–22), an enormous poetical description of England in thirty books, which Drayton himself not unjustly refers to as his 'Herculean toil'. We must remember that such poems were the product of the same keen interest in, and love for, England which led scholars like Stow, Harrison, and Holinshed into laborious historical researches, and found dramatic expression in the chronicle plays of Shakespeare.

We have spoken of the Jacobean division of the Age of Shakespeare; as the period of decline. By this we mean that the Elizabethan inspiration was now waning, that its subject matter was getting exhausted, and that a tendency to imitation was setting in among the rising generation. Meanwhile, a new kind of poetry was beginning with JOHN DONNE (1573–1631), whose work belongs essentially to the time of James, though he was thirty years old when Elizabeth died. Donne, who was a celebrated divine and preacher, wrote songs, sonnets, marriage poems, elegies, and satires, all of which are characterised by much genuine poetic feeling, harsh metres, and those strained and whimsical images and turns of speech, which are called 'conceits'. His historical importance lies in the fact that he initiated the 'metaphysical' school of poetry, of which we shall have something more to say presently.

Note. For a Table of the Poetry of the Age of Shakespeare see pp. 76–8.

7

The Age of Shakespeare:
Drama

28. The Elizabethan Romantic Drama. The quarter-century or so which followed the production of *Gorboduc* was a period of great confusion in the English drama. On the one hand, there were scholars who cherished the ambition of naturalising the Senecan, or 'classic,' species of play, of which Sackville and Norton's tragedy had been an example, and their efforts were seconded by humanists like Sir Philip Sidney, who believed that the only sure way to a really artistic drama lay through the faithful imitation of ancient models. On the other hand, the writers and actors who catered for the amusement of the miscellaneous unscholarly public, knowing that their patrons cared little for the finer details of art, and much for exciting plots and vigorous action, rejected altogether the decorous Senecan conventions, and struck out into a variety of experiments, all of them very crude, in a type of play which rested upon entirely different ideas of construction. These experiments may be regarded as a natural elaboration of the dramatic elements of the older English stage, and as a groping in the dark after a larger and freer form of art than was possible under the cramping conditions of the Senecan style. There was thus a temporary conflict between the humanists, who stood for classical tradition, and sought to impose it upon the people, and the strong national taste of the English public, who demanded a quite different sort of thing. In the end, the national taste triumphed, and just before Shakespeare began his career as a playwright the 'romantic' form of drama was definitely established. The establishment of this romantic drama was the achievement of Shakespeare's immediate predecessors, a group of university men who had been trained in the school of the classics, and had learned much there about dramatic workmanship, but who, while profiting by their lessons, discarded their special principles of composition, and instead carried forward the free tradition of the popular stage.

Before we turn to their work, however, we must be sure that we understand, at least in a general way, the difference between the so-called 'classic' and 'romantic' types of play.

Confining our attention to the points which immediately concern us here, we may epitomise the principles of the classic drama under three heads: (1) it adhered rigorously to unity of subject and tone, and as a result, it kept the spheres of tragedy and comedy entirely separate. A tragedy had to be a tragedy from first to last; it had to maintain the proper tragic pitch and avoid all suggestion of familiarity, and no humorous episode was permitted in it; a comedy had to be a comedy from first to last, and no tragic element was allowed to enter into its composition; (2) there was little or no dramatic action, the incidents composing the plot taking place off the stage, and being reported to the audience in dialogue and set narrative; (3) in theory, at all events, the three unities of time, place and action controlled the construction, by which we mean, in the briefest possible statement (*a*) that the entire story of a play had to be confined to a single day, (*b*) and to a single scene, and (*c*) that it was to be one single story only, without subplots or minor episodes of any kind. These principles were derived, or more correctly speaking, were supposed to be derived, from the practice of the Attic writers of tragedy and the teachings of the great Greek critic Aristotle; but they came into the modern drama through the plays of the Latin poet Seneca, in which they were exhibited in their severest form. The particular type of drama which the humanists sought to introduce is now clear, and we are also in a position to understand the general characteristics of the opposed type, which Shakespeare's forerunners established in its place. For the romantic, or Shakespearean, drama (1) makes free use of variety in theme and tone, often blending tragic and comic incidents and characters in the same piece; (2) while it, of course, employs both action and narrative in carrying on a plot, it is essentially a drama of action, nearly everything that happens being represented on the stage; and (3) it repudiates the three unities (*a*) allowing the story, on occasion, to extend over months and even years; (*b*) changing the scene as often as is necessary, sometimes from one town or country to another; and (*c*) employing subplots and minor episodes in connection with its central subject.

29. Shakespeare's Predecessors. It will be seen that special importance attaches historically to the work of those playwrights who, coming just before Shakespeare, prepared the way for him by ensuring the triumph of that free and flexible form of drama which he was afterwards to make his own. In a loose sense, they constitute a group, and they are commonly known by the name of 'the university wits'. As this implies, they were all men of academic training, and had thus been brought into personal touch with the new learning, and had absorbed its spirit, at one or other of the two great institutions of scholarship. But, with one exception, they gave their talents to the public stage, and it is certain that the strongly pronounced taste of their audience had a good deal to do with the class of drama which they produced. Arranged roughly in order of time, they are: John Lyly (1554?–1606); Thomas Kyd (1557?–95?); George Peele (1558?–97); Thomas Lodge (1558?–1625); Robert Greene (1560?–92); Christopher Marlowe (1564–93); and Thomas Nash (1567–1601).

It would be of little use to give a mere catalogue of the dramatic works of these men, and a more detailed examination of their writings would be out of keeping with the design of this short sketch. We must think of them, therefore, mainly as a group, and must be satisfied with the general assertion that each contributed something to the evolution of the drama into the forms in which Shakespeare was to take it up. Concerning two of them only, a few further details must be added, because of their special significance in literary history and of the direct influence which they exerted upon Shakespeare himself. These are Lyly and Marlowe.

Lyly is most widely known as the author of a prose romance entitled *Euphues*, of which we shall speak in our next chapter. His dramatic work, with which alone we have now to do, consists of eight comedies, of which the best are *Campaspe*, *Endymion*, and *Gallathea*. These were all written for performance at the court, and the interest in them depends not on plot, situation, or even characterisation, but on language—that is, on the wit, point, ingenuity, and grace of the dialogue. At a time when the humours of the public stage ran often into coarseness and horse-play, Lyly helped to give comedy an intellectual tone. In this, as well as in his skill in clever repartee, and in his continual use of puns, conceits, and all sorts of verbal fireworks, he anticipated Shakespeare, whose early comedies, such as *Love's Labour's Lost* and *A Midsummer Night's Dream*, obviously owe much to his example. From Lyly Shakespeare also learned how to combine (as in the two plays just named) a courtly main plot with episodes of rustic blunders and clownish fooling. In these things Lyly set a fashion which others, including Shakespeare, followed, and in comedy he was undeniably Shakespeare's first master.

Marlowe's historical importance is even greater. A man of fiery imagination and immense though ill-regulated powers, who lived a wild Bohemian life, and while still young was killed in a drunken brawl, he was by nature far more of a lyric poet than a dramatist; yet his *Tamburlaine the Great*, *Dr. Faustus*, *The Jew of Malta*, and *Edward II*, despite the bombast and extravagance by which they are frequently marred, give him the place of pre-eminence among our pre-Shakespearean playwrights. In these plays he really fixed the type of tragedy and chronicle play for his immediate successors, and in them also he introduced blank verse (hitherto confined to classic plays and private representations) to the romantic drama and the public stage. That Shakespeare, who must have known him well, and who probably collaborated with him, was at first profoundly influenced by him, is evident. His early blank verse is fashioned on Marlowe's. His narrative poem, *Venus and Adonis*, is in part at least inspired by Marlowe's *Hero and Leander*. His *Richard III* and *Richard II* are clearly based on the model of chronicle play provided in *Edward II*. Even in *The Merchant of Venice* there are many details to show that Shakespeare wrote with *The Jew of Malta* in mind.

30. Shakespeare's Life. WILLIAM SHAKESPEARE was born on or about the 23rd April, 1564, at Stratford-on-Avon, Warwickshire. He was the son of a prosperous tradesman of the town, who a little later became its High Bailiff or Mayor. Though there is no actual record of the fact, it is practically certain that, like other Stratford boys of his class, he went to the local Grammar School, an excellent institution of its kind, where he was taught Latin and arithmetic. While he never became a learned man, his few years at school thus gave him a sound education as far as it went. Financial misfortunes presently overtook his father, and when he was about fourteen, he was taken from school that he might help the family by earning money on his own account. Of the nature of his employment, however, we know nothing. In his 19th year he married Anne Hathaway, a woman eight years his senior, the daughter of a well-to-do yeoman of the neighbouring village of Shottery. This marriage was hasty and ill-advised, and appears to have been unhappy. Three children were born to him: Susannah, and the twins, Judith and Hamnet. Tradition says that meanwhile he fell into bad company, and that a deer-stealing escapade in the woods of Charlecote Hall obliged him to fly from home. There may or may not be truth in this story—we cannot tell. It is certain that a few years after his marriage—roughly, about 1587—he left his native town to seek his fortunes in London. At this time the drama was gaining rapidly in popularity through the work of the University Wits. Shakespeare soon turned to the stage, and became first an actor, and then (though without ceasing to be an actor) a playwright. An ill-natured reference to him in a pamphlet written by Greene on his deathbed, shows that in 1592 he was well known as a successful author. He remained in London upwards of twenty years after this, working hard, producing on an average a couple of plays a year, and growing steadily in fame and wealth. He became a shareholder in two of the leading theatres of the time, the Globe and the Black-friars, and purchased property in Stratford and London. But the years which brought prosperity also brought domestic sorrows. His only son died in 1596: his father in 1601; his younger brother Edmund, also an actor, in 1607; his mother in 1608. Then between 1610 and 1612 he retired to Stratford, where he had bought a house—the largest in the town—known as New Place. His elder daughter had already (1607) married Dr. John Hall, who was later celebrated as a physician; on February 10, 1616, Judith became the wife of Thomas Quiney, whose father had been one of the poet's closest friends. By this time Shakespeare's health had broken down completely, and he died on the 23rd April of that year.

Shakespeare's biography proves conclusively that, like Chaucer, he was no dreamer, but a practical man of affairs. He reached London poor and friendless; he left it rich and respected; and his fortunes were the work of his own hand. Much light is thus thrown not only upon his personal character, but also upon his writings, in which great powers of creative imagination are combined with, and supported by a wonderful feeling for reality, sound commonsense, and a large and varied familiarity with the world. Of the learning which is shown in his plays, and about which so much has been written, it is enough here to say that it is not the learning of the trained and accurate scholar—of a Bacon or a Ben Jonson; but rather the wide miscellaneous knowledge of many things, which was naturally accumulated by an extraordinarily assimilative mind during years of contact with men and books at a time when all social intercourse and all literature were alike saturated with the classicism of the Renaissance. Translations gave him easy access to the treasures of ancient literature; the intellectual atmosphere of the environment in which he lived and worked was charged with new ideas, and was immensely stimulating; and Shakespeare was pre-eminently endowed with the happy faculty of turning everything that came to him to the best possible account.

31. Shakespeare's Works. A few miscellaneous and doubtful pieces omitted, Shakespeare's non-dramatic poetry consists of two narrative poems, *Venus and Adonis* and *Lucrece*, in both of which the classicism of the age is very marked, and a sequence of 154 sonnets, the first 126 addressed to a man, the remainder addressed or referring to a woman. These sonnets have given rise to endless discussion, and everything about them remains obscure. They purport to record a passionate history of disastrous love and broken friendship, but we cannot even be sure whether they deal with real or with imaginary things. The only certainty is that they contain in places the finest lyrical poetry of their time.

The commonly accepted canon of Shakespeare's dramatic work comprises 37 plays, though the authenticity of several of these is doubtful, and in some cases at least it is clear that his part in the dramas attributed to him was limited to the retouching of older material. His activity as a writer for the stage extended over some 24 years, beginning about 1588 and ending about 1612; and we may therefore say, in general terms, that 12 years of it belonged to the sixteenth and 12 to the seventeenth century. Shakespearean critics have agreed to subdivide these 24 years into four periods, and by arranging the plays within these periods as nearly as possible in their order of production, we are able to follow the evolution of his genius and art, and the remarkable changes which came over his thought and style. I will therefore give the names of his plays, approximately in their chronological sequence, indicating the specific characteristics of spirit and technique by which the work of each period is marked.

(i) 1588–93. Period of early and, to a large extent, experimental work. Shakespeare's apprenticeship begins with the revision of old plays, such as the three parts of *Henry VI* and *Titus Andronicus*. To this period belong his first comedies, in which the influence of Lyly is pronounced—*Love's Labour's Lost, The Two Gentlemen of Verona, The*

Comedy of Errors, and *A Midsummer Night's Dream*; his first effort in chronicle drama, distinctly reminiscent of Marlowe, *Richard III*; and a single very youthful tragedy, *Romeo and Juliet*. The work of this period as a whole is extremely slight in texture; the treatment of life in it is superficial; there is little depth of thought or characterisation; and the art is markedly immature. The prominence of rhyme in the dialogue, the stiffness of the blank verse, and the constant use of puns, conceits, and other affectations, are among its outstanding technical features.

(ii) 1594–1600. Period of the great comedies and chronicle plays. The works of this period are: *Richard II, King John, The Merchant of Venice, Henry IV*, Parts I and II, *Henry V, The Taming of the Shrew, The Merry Wives of Windsor, Much Ado about Nothing, As You Like It*, and *Twelfth Night*. Shakespeare now leaves behind him the influence of his early masters, his work becomes independent, and reveals immense development in power and technique. It is far more massive in quality, the knowledge of the world and of the motives and passions of men which it everywhere exhibits is infinitely more profound. The characterisation and the humour have become deep and penetrative, and there is a great growth in the weight of thought. Shakespeare has also outgrown, or is fast outgrowing, the immaturities of his former style. The youthful crudeness, extravagance, and strain are disappearing; rhyme is largely abandoned for prose and blank verse, and the blank verse itself has lost its stiffness, and is free and flexible.

(iii) 1601–08. Period of the great tragedies, and of the sombre or bitter comedies. In this period all Shakespeare's powers—his dramatic power, his intellectual power and his power of expression—are at their highest. This is the time of his supreme masterpieces. But what perhaps is most striking is the extraordinary change which has now occurred in the entire spirit of his work. His attention is pre-occupied, to the total exclusion of all other things, with the darker side of human experience, and his plays are made out of those destructive passions which shake the foundations of the moral order and bring ruin upon innocent and guilty alike. The sins and weaknesses of men form the staple of his plots, and even when he writes what are theoretically distinguished as comedies, the emphasis is still thrown on evil and the tone is either grave or fierce. The plays of this period are: *Julius Caesar, Hamlet, All's Well that Ends Well, Measure for Measure, Troilus and Cressida, Othello, King Lear, Macbeth, Antony and Cleopatra, Coriolanus,* and *Timon of Athens.*

(iv) 1608–12. Period of the later comedies or Dramatic Romances. Again we note a sudden and singular change in the temper of Shakespeare's work. It is as if the heavy clouds which had long hung over the fictitious world of his imagination now roll away, and the sky grows clear towards sunset. In these last plays the groundwork is still furnished by tragic passion, but the evil is no longer permitted to have its way, but is controlled and conquered by the good. A very tender and gracious tone prevails in them throughout. At the same time they show very fully the decline of Shakespeare's dramatic powers. They are often careless in construction and unsatisfactory in characterisation, while in style and versification they will not bear comparison with the work of the preceding ten years. Three plays entirely Shakespeare's belong to this period—*Cymbeline, The Tempest,* and *The Winter's Tale.* To these we have to add two which are only partly his—*Pericles* and *Henry VIII.* The latter was completed by his younger contemporary and friend, Fletcher (see §34).

To the much debated question how far Shakespeare's work is a revelation of his life and character it is impossible to give in brief a complete answer. We cannot, I feel sure, accept the judgment of those who maintain that he was so entirely the dramatist that no trace of his own thoughts and feelings is to be found in it. On the contrary, I am certain that it does tell us much about the man himself. But whether or not the changes which we mark in its successive stages were in any way the result of his own experiences—whether, for example, he wrote tragedies because his life was tragic and turned again to comedy when his spirit was once more restored to peace— we do not know. Read in their chronological order, his plays at least give us the record of his intellectual and artistic history.

32. Characteristics of Shakespeare's Works. Taken as a whole, Shakespeare's plays constitute the greatest single body of work which any writer has contributed to our literature. Perhaps their most salient feature is their astonishing variety. Other men have surpassed him at this point and that; but no one has ever rivalled him in the range and versatility of his powers. He was (though not equally) at home in tragedy and comedy, and his genius took in innumerable aspects of both; he was supreme, not only as a dramatist, but also as a poet to whom the worlds of high imagination and delicate fancy were alike open; and while not himself a very profound or very original thinker, he possessed in a superlative degree the faculty of digesting thought into phraseology so memorable and so final that, as we all know, he is the most often quoted of all our writers. He was almost entirely free from dogmatism of any kind, and his tolerance was as comprehensive as his outlook. In the vitality of his characterisation in particular he is unparalleled; no one else has created so many men and women whom we accept and treat not as figments of a poet's brain, but as absolutely and completely alive. His unique command over the resources of the language must also be noted; his vocabulary is computed to run to some 15,000 words, while that of Milton contains scarcely more than half that number.

The greatness of Shakespeare's work is apt to blind critics to his limitations and defects, but these must, of course, be recognized in any estimate of him, or otherwise we shall get him out of his proper focus. Broad as he was, he was essentially a man of his time, and while his plays are remarkable for their general truth to what is permanent in human nature, still his interpretation of human nature is that of 'an age in many respects very different from our own. He wrote hurriedly, and signs of hasty and ill-considered production are often apparent. Designing his plays expressly for the stage, and anxious to secure their success under the actual conditions of stage representation, he was willing at times to sacrifice consistency of character and the finer demands of art to the achievement of a telling theatrical effect. In his occasional coarseness he reflects the low taste of the 'groundlings' to whom he had to appeal. At places his psychology is hopelessly crude and unconvincing; his style vicious; his wit forced and poor; his tragic language bombastic. These and other faults will be conspicuous to any one who reads him in the least critically. But they are small things after all in comparison with those paramount qualities which have given him the first place among the world's dramatists.

33. Ben Jonson. Shakespeare's age was marked by tremendous dramatic activity, and the list of his contemporaries in the annals of the stage is a very long one. Among these, the most important is his friend Ben Jonson, not only because he was the greatest of them in the power and volume of his genius, but also because the aims and principles of his work were fundamentally different from Shakespeare's. He was born in London in 1573; was educated at the Westminster Grammar School, where he laid the foundation of his sound classical scholarship; became an actor about 1592; and in 1598 opened his career as a dramatist with the satiric comedy *Every Man in his Humour*. For many years he wrote plays both for the court and for the public stage. With the accession of Charles I, a decline in his fortunes set in; and henceforth he suffered from neglect, poverty, and ever-increasing ill-health. Long palsied and bed-ridden, he died in 1637, having outlived Shakespeare by twenty-one years. Jonson did a good deal of work outside the drama, including many translations and a large number of miscellaneous poems. His plays fall into three groups: his court masques; his historical tragedies, *Sejanus* and *Catiline*, which are very learned, very laborious, and very dull; and—by far the most significant part of his production—his numerous comedies, of which the best are *The Alchemist*, *Volpone or the Fox*, and *Epicoene or the Silent Woman*. In studying these comedies, we can realise at once the distinctive features of Jonson's genius and art, and can understand what is meant by the statement that he worked in a different field from Shakespeare, and on methods entirely his own. He was, to begin with, a realist; that is, the world of his comedy is not the world of romance, but of contemporary

London life, with its manners, types, foibles, and affectations. Of this world he gives a heightened picture. But his aim is not only to depict and, by depicting, to amuse; he takes his art seriously, and holding fast to the moral functions of the stage, he seeks also to correct and teach. A distinct ethical purpose is thus generally apparent, and is often expressly proclaimed in his work. His realism must therefore be further defined as didactic realism. In his principles of construction he repudiates the lawlessness of the romantic drama, and takes Latin comedy as his model. Finally, his characterisation is based on the idea that each man is possessed and governed by some one particular quality or 'master passion' which (for the purposes of the stage, at any rate) may be regarded as the backbone and central feature of his personality. Jonson accordingly seizes upon this master passion, or 'humour', as he calls it, and makes a whole character out of it, with the result that his men and women are not complex individuals, like Shakespeare's, but rather types; while, reverting to the old morality method, he often labels or tickets them with names which at once indicate their special 'humours'; as, for instance, Downright, Morose, Wellbred, Subtle, Pertinax Surly, Sir Epicure Mammon. In Jonson's comedies intellect predominates; they are products rather of learning, skill, and conscientious effort than of creative power; and, though astonishingly clever and rich in detailed pictures of the life of the time, they are heavy and wanting in spontaneity and charm. Historically, however, they are extremely important, for Jonson was the real founder of what is known as the Comedy of Manners, and his influence on succeeding dramatists was very great.

34. Other Dramatists of Shakespeare's Age. Of the crowd of lesser playwrights whose work extends from the time of Shakespeare's prime to the close of the period, I will name only a few who may be said to occupy the foremost positions in the second rank. John Webster (1580?–1625?) was a dramatist of sombre cast of genius and great power, though his morbid love of the violent and the horrible led him too often to sheer sensationalism. His *White Devil* and *Duchess of Malfi* contain scenes of tragic passion unrivalled outside Shakespeare.

In JOHN FORD (1586?–1639) a similar tendency towards repulsive subjects and unnatural emotions is apparent, but his pathos gives a distinction to his best work, like *The Broken Heart*. The names of FRANCIS BEAUMONT (1584–1616) and JOHN FLETCHER (1579–1625) are always associated, and they did much work in collaboration, though Fletcher continued to write with great fluency, for the nine years between his partner's death and his own. Their moral tone is often relaxing, their sentiment strained, and their characterisation poor; but they have many redeeming features, and such plays as *Philaster* and *The Maid's Tragedy* successfully challenge comparison with anything in the romantic drama outside Shakespeare. PHILIP MASSINGER (1583–1640), a ready writer in various styles, reached a high level in his comedy *A New Way to Pay Old Debts*. JAMES SHIRLEY (1596–1666) belongs to the reign of Charles I, but we may mention him here as, in Charles Lamb's phrase, 'the last of a great race'. In all these writers, and still more, in smaller men whom we need not pause to name, the decline of the drama is apparent. By the time we reach the end of the period we find that all the old creative power has gone, and that the stage has yielded completely to the fast-spreading immorality of the age; while even the formlessness of the blank verse employed gives one more sign of the general decay.

35. The Playhouses of Shakespeare's Time. It is desirable that the student of the drama should understand something of the theatrical conditions under which Shakespeare and his contemporaries did their work. In the early years of the regular drama plays had been performed in inn yards and other open spaces, where a scaffold could be erected and accommodation provided for the spectators. In 1576 two permanent playhouses were built—the Theatre and the Curtain—in what were then the open fields of Shoreditch. These were the only London playhouses when Shakespeare reached the metropolis; but by the end of Elizabeth's reign at least eleven were in existence. These were not in London, for the civic authorities would not permit their erection within their boundaries, but in the immediate outskirts, and chiefly on the banks, on the Surrey side, of the Thames. With two of these playhouses—the Globe in Southwark, and the Blackfriars, near the spot now occupied by the *Times* office—Shakespeare, as we have seen, was very closely connected. The theatrical profession had formerly been in very ill odour, and in order to avoid being treated as 'rogues and vagabonds', actors had been forced to obtain licenses from peers and other influential patrons, and to enrol themselves in companies as their 'servants'. Thus we read of Lord Leicester's Servants (afterwards the Lord Chamberlain's), to which company Shakespeare belonged, of the Lord Admiral's Servants, the Queen's Players, and so on. The playhouses were very small, were round or hexagonal, and were mainly of wood. There was nothing in the least luxurious about them, either in architecture or in appointments. The stage and the boxes, or 'rooms', as they were called, were roofed in with thatch, but the rest of the building was open to the sky. The boxes were frequented by the wealthier and more aristocratic play-goers, some of whom, however, assumed the privilege of sitting on the stage. No seats were provided for the 'groundlings' in the 'yard' or pit. Into this yard ran the stage, a simple platform, the limited dimensions of which seem to our minds to turn into absurdity those scenes of marching armies and pitched battles in which the Elizabethans delighted. The stage arrangements present some features of great interest. Of movable scenery there was practically none; though it was just beginning to come in towards the end of the Shakespearean period, it was not regularly used till the re-opening of the theatres after the Commonwealth. Stage 'properties', such as articles of furniture, were freely employed, and placards hung out bearing such legends as—This is Athens', and 'This is a wood'—to inform the audience where the scene was supposed to be laid.

Two prominent characteristics of the Shakespearean drama may be referred directly to this absence of painted scenery: the continual change in the locality of the action, and the frequency of descriptive passages, in which appeal was made to the imagination of the spectators. A small structure at the back of the stage, consisting of a balcony and an open space beneath, played an important part in the economy of the performance. The balcony itself stood for any elevated place, such as the walls of a city or the upper part of a house; the space beneath, which could be curtained off, was put to the most various uses when any sort of interior scene was required. Performances generally began about three in the afternoon, and lasted some two hours. There is every reason to believe that the art of acting was brought to a high pitch of perfection. But there were no actresses on the Shakespearean stage, women's parts being taken by boys and young men specially trained for the purpose. These 'boy actresses' must have been very clever, and when after the Restoration, women began to appear on the English boards, there were those, like the diarist Pepys, who regretted the change. But it is difficult for us to think that Shakespeare's heroines can ever have been quite adequately interpreted by such male performers.

Note. For a Table of the Drama of the Age of Shakespeare, see pp. 76–8.

8
The Age of Shakespeare:
Prose

36. Lyly and other Writers of Prose Fiction. While the Age of Shakespeare found its chief imaginative outlet in drama, it was also active in the field of prose fiction. It did not indeed produce what we specifically call the novel, by which we mean the long story of contemporary life and manners. This was not established in English literature till more than a century after Shakespeare's death. But in other lines of fictitious narrative considerable progress was made.

Some stimulus in this direction was given by the work of the translators, who familiarised the reading public with Spanish and Italian romance and with Italian *novelle*, or short stories. The last named have a great secondary interest as the sources upon which the Elizabethan dramatists, including Shakespeare, often drew for the materials of their plots. They were also adapted and imitated, and various collections of stories appeared, such as William Painter's *Palace of Pleasure*, which enjoyed much popularity.

The most important prose romance of the period is the work of John Lyly, whose comedies have already been mentioned—*Euphues, the Anatomy of Wit*, and its sequel, *Euphues and his England*. The former was published in 1579, and was therefore exactly contemporary with the *Shepheardes Calender*; the latter, the following year. The first part tells of a young Athenian named Euphues, wealthy, handsome, and clever, who sets out on his travels; reaches Naples, where he becomes an intimate friend of a certain Philautus, with whom he holds many long conversations on philosophical and ethical subjects; has several affairs of the heart, which come to nothing; and in the end returns to Athens leaving behind him a 'pamphlet', or letter, addressed to his friend and described as 'a cooling Carde for Philautus and all fond lovers', the purpose of which is to dissuade him from women's society and tender passion. It is a sort of love-story, but without action, and what little narrative there is, is merely an excuse for endless discourses and moralisings. In the second part Euphues visits England, and gives a long 'description of the countrey, the court, and the manners of the isle', which is so unqualified in its praise that, could we only take it as truthful, we should be convinced that in Lyly's time our land was a paradise, and its inhabitants absolute embodiments of all the virtues. The popularity of *Euphues* was extraordinary; in little more than half a century it went through ten editions—a great record at that time; everybody read it who read anything; and the ladies of the court used it as a moral handbook, a guide to polite behaviour, and a model of elegance in speech and writing. It owes its continued fame mainly to its style. Enthusiasm for the classics, the influence of Italian and Spanish literatures, and a widespread desire to lift and refine the vernacular tongue, led to all kinds of strange experiments in English prose. Lyly's style, or 'Euphuism', as it is called, is the most remarkable of these. It is characterised, in common with other contemporary efforts, by extreme elaboration and artifice, and, as distinguished from them, by a number of specific rhetorical devices which give it a quality of its own. It would take too much space to analyse these here, but it is necessary to indicate the most important of them. Perhaps the outstanding feature of Euphuism is the excessive use of balanced antithesis; as, for instance—'As you may suspect me of idleness in giving ear to your talk, so you may convince me of lightness in answering such toys'; in which, as will be seen, 'suspect me' and 'convince me', 'idleness' and 'lightness', 'giving ear' and 'answering', 'talk' and 'toys', are carefully arranged in contrasted pairs. This balanced antithesis is frequently combined with alliteration, as, for example—'Although I have *sh*rined thee in my heart as a *tr*usty *fr*iend, I will shun thee *h*ereafter as a *tr*othless *f*oe.' Lyly also indulges freely in similes, word-play, and punning; while another of his peculiar characteristics is a fondness for 'non-natural natural history', or the natural history, not of science, but of myth and fable. Thus we read to our astonishment of a bird named Attagen 'who never singeth any time after she is taken'; of a precious gem, Draconites, which is found in the dragon; of a herb, Dictannum, in which the wounded deer always finds an unfailing remedy; and so on. Shakespeare gives us an example of the same sort of fantastic pseudo-science when he writes of the toad as 'ugly and venomous', but as wearing none the less 'a precious jewel in his head'.

The second place in Elizabethan romance may be assigned to Sir Philip Sidney's *Arcadia*, completed about 1581, though not published till 1613. To some extent this work carries on the traditions of the older romances of chivalry, while it owes much of its form to the pastoral *Diana* of the Portuguese Montemayor and the *Arcadia* of the Italian Sannazaro. Unlike *Euphues*, in which there is practically no story, it is full of incident. Its principal interest is provided by the adventures of the two friends, Pyrocles and Musidorus, while seeking to win the two Arcadian princesses, Philoclea and Pamela; but a large number of other characters are introduced, each of whom becomes the centre of a separate story, and episodes arise within episodes to the great complication and confusion of the plot. Though Sidney does not overwork a few rhetorical devices, like Lyly, his prose is of an extremely ornate and poetical kind, and, while striking and beautiful in places, in the long run it becomes wearisome because of its total want of simplicity and restraint. Two of the pre-Shakespearean dramatists whom we have named—Lodge and Greene—have also a certain importance as writers of romance. In a general way they resemble Sidney in the use of the persons and machinery of conventional pastoralism, but their style is largely fashioned upon that of Lyly. Each produced amid much other work one book which is still of interest, not, however, on account of its intrinsic merits, but because of its connection with Shakespeare. Lodge's *Rosalynde, Euphues' Golden Legacy*, furnished the raw materials of *As You Like It*; Greene's *Pandosto, The Triumph of Time*, those of *The Winter's Tale*. A third of the 'University Wits', THOMAS NASH, has a place somewhat apart, for at a time when the tendency in fiction was almost entirely towards romance, he gave a distinct lead in the direction of realism of a coarse description. His *Unfortunate Traveller, or The Life of Jack Wilton*, a rambling record of adventure on the continent, is our earliest example of the picaresque novel,[8] or novel of rascality—a type of fiction which was already popular in Spain, and was later to be cultivated with great success by Defoe.

37. Bacon and his Essays. We must not suppose that the English literature of the Age of Shakespeare was entirely a literature of the imagination. England now felt the stimulus of the Renaissance on the intellectual as well as on the artistic side, and the result was the production of a great many prose works dealing with various subjects in which thoughtful people were then interested. Most of these belong to the special history of such subjects rather than to the general history of literature. But a few writers claim a place in our record, and among them is one of great importance—Bacon, the principal prose master of his time.

The second son of a famous lawyer and statesman, FRANCIS BACON was born on 22nd January, 1561. As a boy his wit and precocity attracted the attention of the queen, who used jestingly to call him her 'young lord keeper'—his father then being the Keeper of the Great Seal of England. He was educated at Trinity College, Cambridge, and in preparation for a career of statesmanship was sent to Paris in the suite of the English ambassador. His father's death in 1579 threw him upon his own resources; he chose the law as his profession; was called to the bar in 1582, and became Queen's Counsel in 1589. By this time he had also made his mark as an

---

[8] From the Spanish *picaro*, a rogue.

orator in the House of Commons. After the accession of James I, he rose rapidly in favour and fortune. He was knighted in 1603; became Attorney General in 1613; Privy Councillor in 1616; Lord Keeper in 1617; Lord Chancellor and Baron Verulam in 1618; Viscount St. Albans in 1621. Then came a sudden crash. He was impeached before the House of Lords on various charges of official malpractice, offered no defence, and was sentenced to a fine of £40,000, imprisonment during the king's pleasure, and perpetual banishment from parliament and court. This sentence, however, was never carried into effect, and ultimately he received a royal pardon. He spent the few remaining years of his life in scholarly pursuits, and died in 1626 from complications arising from a cold caught while he was making a scientific experiment. His character was compounded of contradictions and inconsistencies. He believed himself 'born for the service of mankind', and sincerely desired to devote his wonderful powers to the advancement of that knowledge which would lead to 'the glory of the Creator and the relief of man's estate'. Yet in practice he sacrificed much for the sake of wealth and power and the satisfaction of his inordinate ambitions; while his moral teaching too often resolves itself into the narrowest expediency and utilitarianism. He wrote voluminously on many subjects, and his greatest works—his *Advancement of Learning* and his *Novum Organum* (New Organ or instrument), in which he sets forth and illustrates the inductive or 'Baconian' method of studying nature—place him in the front rank of the world's epoch-makers. But these belong to the history, not of general literature, but of science and philosophy. His principal contribution to general literature is his little collection of *Essays, or Counsels Civil and Moral*, first published in 1597, and in much enlarged editions in 1612 and 1625. The writing of these *Essays* was doubtless suggested by the *Essais* of the great French thinker Montaigne, but both the matter and the manner of them are entirely Bacon's own. It should be noted that, like Montaigne, he uses the word 'essay' in its original etymological sense, now almost lost, and as equivalent to *assay*—a trial or attempt. The *Essays*, therefore, are intended merely as 'dispersed meditations', or informal thoughts on the subjects dealt with, not as exhaustive treatises. Thoroughly practical in character, they concern themselves for the most part with the conduct of life in private and public affairs, and thus with things which 'come home to men's business and bosoms'. Extraordinary insight and sagacity are their salient qualities; beyond perhaps any other book of the same size in any literature they are loaded with the ripest wisdom of experience; but we must never forget that the wisdom which they inculcate is on the whole of a distinctly worldly kind. Though according to his first biographer, Bacon in writing them 'did rather drive at a masculine and clear expression than at any fineness or affectation of phrases', his style nonetheless is marked by the general ornateness, the fondness for imagery, the love of analogy and metaphor, which were so much in the taste of the time. It is also very highly Latinised. But its most important characteristic is its marvellous terseness and epigrammatic force. Bacon had an almost unrivalled power of packing his thoughts into the smallest possible space, and, adapting a phrase in Marlowe's *Jew of Malta*, we may therefore describe these *Essays* as 'infinite riches in a little room'.

38. Other Prose of the Period. The varied interests of the time are well represented in its prose literature. History was cultivated by many writers; among them, RALEIGH in his vast and uncritical *History of the World* (1614); BACON in his judicial *History of the Reign of Henry VII* (1622); FOXE in his thoroughly untrustworthy *Acts and Monuments* or *Book of Martyrs* (1563); and RAPHAEL HOLINSHED in his *Chronicles of England, Scotland, and Ireland*—a work which Shakespeare often laid under contribution in his historical plays. At a time when the spirit of adventure was strong, the literature of travel naturally flourished, and of this one specially famous work, RICHARD HAKLUYT'S *Principal Navigations, Voyages, Traffiques, and Discoveries of the English Nation*, may be cited as an example. In the field of theology a great deal of important work was done, and while this does not properly concern us here, the masterly *Ecclesiastical Polity* (1594–97) of Richard Hooker may be mentioned in passing for the sake of its style, which, though still over-rhetorical and involved, is generally plainer and simpler than most contemporary prose. In this context we must recall the Authorised Version of the Bible (1611), which from the date of its appearance onward has never ceased to exercise a profound influence upon English writing. From the point of view of literary history there is also great significance in the development of the literature of criticism, for this shows that people were beginning to be interested in the forms and principles of literature as an art. The best known of these early treatises is Sidney's *Apologie for Poetrie* (about 1581). Other similar works of some importance are WILLIAM WEBBE'S *Discourse of English Poetrie* (1586) and GEORGE PUTTENHAM'S *Arte of English Poesie* (1589).

TABLES OF THE AGE OF SHAKESPEARE

1. Early Elizabethan Period 1558–79

Non-Dramatic Poetry	Drama	Prose
Sackville's *Induction to The Myrroure for Magistrates*, 1559		
	Sackville and Norton's *Gorboduc*, 1561	Foxe's *Acts and Monuments*, 1563
	Still's *Gammer Gurton's Needle*, 1566	
	Gascoigne's *Supposes* (trans. from Ariosto), the first English comedy in prose, 1566	
		Ascham's *Scholemaster*, 1570
	Tancred and Giomonda (Senecan tragedy), in rime, 1568; in blank verse, 1572	

Non-Dramatic Poetry	Drama	Prose
Paradyse of Daynty Devises, 1576	First London playhouses built, 1576	
Gascoigne's *Steele Glas*, 1576		Holinshed's *Chronicles*. 1577

II. Later Elizabethan Period 1579–1603

Non-Dramatic Poetry	Drama	Prose
The Shepheardes Calender, 1579	Lyly's first comedy, *Endymion*, 1579	Lyly's *Euphues*, 1579–80
		Sidney's *Arcadia* and *Apologie for Poetrie*, about 1581
Warner's *Albion's England*, 1586	Marlowe's first tragedy, *Tamburlaine the Great*, 1587	Webbe's *Discourse of English Poetrie*, 1586
	Shakespeare's first period, 1588–93	
		Greene's *Pandosto*, 1588
		Hakluyt's *Voyages*, 1589
		Puttenham's *Arte of English Poesie*, 1589
Faery Queene, Books I–III, 1590		Lodge's *Rosalynde*, 1590
Venus and Adonis, 1593 *Lucrece*, 1594	Death of Marlowe, 1593	
	Shakespeare's second period, 1594–1600	Hooker's *Ecclesiastical Polity*, 1594–97
		Nash's *Unfortunate Traveller*, 1594
Daniel's *Civil Wars*, 1595		
Faery Queene, Books IV–VI, 1596		

Non-Dramatic Poetry	Drama	Prose
Drayton's *Barons' Wars* and *Heroical Epistles*, 1596–98		Bacon's *Essays* (first edition, ten essays), 1597
	Jonson's first play, *Every Man in his Humour*, 1598	
Death of Spenser, 1599	Globe Theatre built, 1599	
	Shakespeare's third period, 1600–08	

III. Jacobean Period 1603–25

Non-Dramatic Poetry	Drama	Prose
	Death of Lyly, 1606	
	Beaumont and Fletcher's plays, 1607 onward	
	Shakespeare's fourth period, 1608–12	
	Webster's first play, *The White Devil*,? 1608–10	
Shakespeare's *Sonnets* published, 1609		Authorised Version of the Bible, 1611
Drayton's *Polyolbion*, 1613–22		
	Death of Shakespeare, 1616	Raleigh's *History of the World*, 1614
	Death of Beaumont, 1616	
	First Folio of Shakespeare's plays, 1623	
	Death of Fletcher, 1625	Bacon's *Essays* (third edition, 58 essays), 1625

9

The Age of Milton
(1625–1660):
Milton

39. The Age of Milton. The growth of Puritanism as a moral and social force, its establishment as the controlling power in the state, and the religious and political struggles by which these were accompanied, are for the student of the literature of Milton's age the principal features of its history.

At the time of the Reformation, though the counsels of the more moderate men prevailed, there were not wanting those of a more radical cast of mind who were dissatisfied with the religious settlement accomplished by Archbishop Parker and his colleagues, because they held that the Church of England as organised by them did not differ sufficiently from the Church of Rome. The true descendants of Wyclif and the Lollards, and now greatly influenced by the famous John Calvin of Geneva, these dissentients, while in many ways they failed to agree among themselves, were at one in their hostility to the episcopal form of ecclesiastical government and to the retention in the creeds and public worship of the national church of many ideas and ceremonies which they regarded as remnants of Popery. They also advocated very strict views concerning life and conduct, and thus came to be called Puritans—a name which appears to have originated about the year of Shakespeare's birth or shortly after and was at first used in derision, though it was soon accepted as a mere descriptive term. While the uncompromising spirit of this party spread steadily among the English middle classes during the reign of James I, it was not till the time of his successor that Puritanism emerged as a great national power. A combination of causes now led to its practical success. The fast-growing flippancy and profligacy of the upper classes, by drawing towards it the sympathies of serious men of various shades of opinion, greatly increased its moral and social influence. The high-handed policy of Laud, and his determination to enforce his will by persecution, meanwhile precipitated a fierce conflict within the religious world, and brought all the enemies of episcopacy into line. Then came the monstrous encroachments of Charles upon the rights of the Commons and the constitutional privileges of the English people. Their keen sense of the supremacy of God as the ruler of rulers, and of the prerogatives of the individual conscience, made the Puritans intolerant of earthly tyranny in any form. Thus Puritanism became a political as well as a moral and religious force and, at a very critical time, the great custodian and defender of our jeopardised liberties. After a stormy period of civil war, it triumphed with the triumph of Oliver Cromwell, and during the few years of the Commonwealth it was supreme.

Within its range, the influence of Puritanism upon the tone and temper of English life and thought was profound. The spirit which it introduced was fine and noble, but it was hard and stern. We admire the Puritan's integrity and uprightness; but we deplore his fanaticism, his moroseness, and the narrowness of his outlook and sympathies. He was an intense and God-fearing, but illiberal and unreasonable man. While in the light of the conditions of the time we can make the fullest allowance for his violent and extreme reaction against prevailing abuses, we are still bound to admit that his was a one-sided and unwholesome view of the world, for in his pre-occupation with moral and spiritual things he generally neglected, and often expressly denounced, the science and art, the knowledge and beauty, which give value to the secular life. To the extent of its power, Puritanism destroyed humane culture, and sought to confine literature within the circumscribed field of its own particular interests. While fatal to art it was thus almost fatal to literature. It was only here and there that a writer arose who was able to absorb all its strength while transcending its limitations. This was emphatically the case with Milton, the greatest product of Puritanism in our literature, in whose genius and work, however, the moral and religious influences of Puritanism are combined with the generous culture of the Renaissance.

40. Milton's Life. John Milton was born in Bread Street, Cheapside, London, on 9th December, 1608, or some four years before Shakespeare's retirement to Stratford. His father, though strongly Puritan in his sympathies, was nonetheless a lover of literature and art, and the child enjoyed all the advantages of a cultivated home. He was educated at St. Paul's School, and at Christ's College, Cambridge, where he remained seven years, taking his B.A. in 1629 and his M.A. in 1632. His systematic studies did not, however, close with the close of his college course. Realising that he could not conscientiously enter the church, for which he had been intended, and feeling no call to any other profession, he decided to give himself up entirely to self-culture and poetry. Fortunately his father was in a financial position to further his wishes, and on leaving Cambridge he accordingly took up his abode in the country house of the family at Horton, Buckinghamshire, some seventeen miles from London. While a boy at school, as he himself tells us, his books had kept him out of bed till midnight; at the university he had shown the same untiring devotion to learning; and now during six years of almost uninterrupted seclusion he was able to pursue his studious way undisturbed. Building steadily upon the firm foundations he had already laid, Milton thus became a very great scholar. This point must be carefully marked, not only because in the breadth and accuracy of his erudition he stands head and shoulders above all our other poets, but also because his learning everywhere nourishes and interpenetrates his poetic work. Having now reached his thirtieth year, he resolved to complete his studies by travel. He therefore left London in May, 1638, and went by way of Paris to Italy, whence, however, he was prematurely recalled by news of the critical state of things at home. 'While I was preparing to pass over into Sicily and Greece,' he writes, 'the melancholy intelligence which I received of the civil commotions in England made me alter my purpose; for I thought it base to be travelling for my amusement abroad while my fellow-citizens were fighting for liberty at home.' He was back in London in August, 1639, after an absence of fifteen months; and from 1640 onward was increasingly active as a supporter of the Puritan cause against the Royalists. As a pamphleteer he became indeed one of the great pillars of that cause, and on the establishment of the Commonwealth was appointed Latin Secretary to the Committee for Foreign Affairs. In 1643 he married Mary Powell, the young daughter of a Royalist, but the union proved a most unhappy one. Early in 1653 a terrible calamity overtook him; his sight, which had long been failing, was now ruined entirely by over-stress of work, and he became totally blind. Three years later he married again, but his wife; Catherine Woodcock, died within fifteen months. On the restoration of the monarchy, Milton was arrested and two of his books were publicly burnt by the hangman; but he was soon released and permitted to drop into political obscurity. He was now poor and lonely as well as blind; he felt bitterly the failure of the cause for which he had toiled so hard and sacrificed so much; and though his third wife, Elizabeth Minshull, brought comfort to his declining years, he was greatly distressed by the unfilial conduct of his daughters by his first marriage. It was in darkness and sorrow, therefore, that he now turned back upon the ambitious poetical designs which he had cherished many years before and had long set aside at the call of practical duty. His *Paradise Lost* was published in 1667; *Paradise Regained* and *Samson Agonistes* together in 1671. Three years later—on 8th November, 1674—Milton died.

41. Milton's Earlier Poetry. Milton's work falls naturally into four periods: (1) the college period, closing with the end of his Cambridge career in 1632; (2) the Horton period, closing with his departure for the Continent in 1638; (3) the period of his prose writings, from 1640 to 1660; and (4) the late poetic period, or period of his greatest achievement.

His college poems, Latin and English, are for the most part simply a young man's experimental work, and while interesting to the special student as the expression of his genius during its immaturity, they have little other importance. To this statement, however, one exception must be made in favour of the ode *On the Morning of Christ's Nativity*, which, though far from perfect and in places sadly marred by conceits and inequalities of style, is still a very remarkable production for a poet of twenty-one. To the Horton period, on the other hand, belong four minor poems of such beauty and power that, even if *Paradise Lost* had never been written, they would have sufficed to put their author high among the greater gods of English song: *L' Allegro* and *Il Penseroso* (1633), *Comus* (1634), and *Lycidas* (1637). Each of these may, of course, be enjoyed to the full for its own sake; but for the student the most significant thing about them is that, read in the order of their writing, they show that during these years of thoughtful leisure a profound change was taking place in the poet's mind. I have said that in Milton's work the moral and religious influences of Puritanism were blended with the generous culture of the Renaissance. It was this combination of elements which gave its distinctive quality to his greatest poetry; he could never have written as he did, had either of them been wanting. But from his earlier poetry we now learn that he began to write chiefly under the inspiration of the learning and art of the Renaissance; that the Puritan element was at first quite subordinate; and that it gradually gained in strength and depth till it became at last the dominant element. Thus in *L' Allegro* and *Il Penseroso*, with their charming contrasted pictures of man, nature, and art as seen through the medium of the mood, in the one case of gladness, and in the other of melancholy, there is little that is characteristically Puritan, and a good deal that is really un-puritan; for the poet dwells frankly upon the pleasures of romance and rustic sports, upon the delights of the playhouse and the Greek drama, and upon the beauty of church architecture and music—all of which things were to the religious fanatic objects of uncompromising hatred. Then with *Comus* we mark a distinct stage in the development of Milton's mind. Thus far latent only, the Puritan spirit now makes its influence felt, not alone in the poet's increased earnestness, but also in the specific quality of his moral teaching. On the literary side, this work too belongs to the Renaissance; for it is an example (and the finest example in our literature) of that type of drama which is called the Mask, which had been brought into this country from Italy, and which had ever since been extremely popular at court and among the nobility. That Milton should be willing to adopt it is proof that he was still far from sharing the intense hostility of the Puritan party to everything connected with the drama. But though he wrote in the forms of Renaissance art, he filled them with a strenuous moral spirit and meaning; for his simple story of the lady lost in the woods, lured away by Comus and his band of revellers, and rescued by her brothers with the help of an attendant spirit and the river nymph, is a patent allegory of virtue attacked by sensuality and conquering by divine aid. Here, then, we see the two streams of influence, by which Milton's genius was fed, running together, and note that while the drama is loaded with classical learning, the nobility of its tone and the superb faith in God which is expressed through it, testify to the growing power of religious inspiration over the poet's thought. Finally, in *Lycidas* we have a Puritanism which is political and ecclesiastical as well as spiritual and ethical. A monody on the death of Milton's college friend, Edward King, this, like Spenser's *Astrophel* (see §25) is in the conventional style of the classic pastoral elegy. In form, therefore, it belongs with *Comus* to the Renaissance. But the religious accent in it throughout is unmistakably Puritan, while its famous attack upon the corrupt church and the hireling clergy of the time openly proclaims Milton's adherence to the Puritan cause. Thus through these earlier poems we can trace the steady growth of the religious element in Milton's mind. The learning and the art of the Renaissance were not abandoned by him; but they were more and more used for the service of a Puritan philosophy of life.

42. Milton's Prose Writings. On his return to England from the Continent, Milton, then in his 31st year, threw himself into the fierce controversies of the hour, and thus in his own words embarked 'on a troubled sea of noises and hoarse disputes'. The ambition to write a great epic poem had already taken shape in his mind, but this he laid aside in order that he might give all his strength and industry to the performance of what he conceived to be a great public duty. Involved in political and religious controversies, he thus turned from poetry entirely, and for the next twenty years continued active as a writer of prose. When we remember that Milton was incomparably the greatest poet of his age, and that in the very prime of his manhood, and during a space of time almost equal to the whole period of Shakespeare's dramatic activity, he produced all told about a dozen sonnets, we can form some idea of what literature must have lost through his pre-occupation with temporary matters. His prose works are not today very interesting in themselves, nor indeed do they make very agreeable readings; for though they are often filled with noble earnestness and are redeemed by occasional bursts of splendid eloquence, they are too often marred by the coarseness of phrase and the intense bitterness of temper which were the prevailing characteristics of the polemical literature of their time. Moreover, their style is heavy and cumbrous. Milton himself said that they were the work of his 'left hand', and we can learn from almost every page that his left hand did not possess the cunning of his right. The long trailing sentences, the involved constructions, the parentheses, the Latin inversions, all in fact show that, when Milton wrote, modern English prose had not yet come into existence. One of these treatises, however, stands altogether apart—the great and noble *Areopagitica*. Directed against an order of Parliament which established a censorship of books, this is essentially a plea for freedom of thought and speech; and it should be read by every lover of literature and of intellectual liberty.

43. Milton's Later Poetry. It was not till the restoration of the monarchy drove him into private life and obscurity that Milton found leisure to accomplish the immense task which year by year he had kept in the background of his mind. Now in *Paradise Lost* he produced our greatest English poem. It is in the study of this stupendous masterpiece of intellectual energy and creative power that the full significance of that combination of qualities in his work of which we have spoken, becomes apparent. The inspiration and the subject-matter of the poem alike come from Milton's Puritanism; *Paradise Lost* is written as an exposition of his theology; upon the foundation of that theology it undertakes to 'assert Eternal Providence and justify the ways of God to men'. But if as a thinker and moralist he now belonged completely to Puritanism, as an artist he had not ceased to belong to the Renaissance; and in its form and style, its machinery and method, the poem everywhere takes us back to Milton's avowed models, the great epics of classical antiquity, while the vast and varied learning which is built into its fabric, shows how fondly in the blindness and loneliness of his old age, he recalled the wide secular studies of his happy earlier days. Even now, then, the Puritan in Milton had not killed the humanist. With the zeal for righteousness and the strenuous moral purpose which pertained to the one, there were still blended the love of learning and the passion for beauty which were the characteristics of the other. That Milton should have written the greatest regular epic poem in any modern literature, and should yet have written it, not on a classical but on a theological subject, and as the vehicle of Christian teaching, is thus one fact of capital importance in the consideration of his work.

In *Paradise Lost* he set forth the revolt of Satan against God, the war in heaven, the fall of the rebel angels, the creation of the world and man, the temptation of Eve and Adam, and their expulsion from Eden. Yet, while his central purpose was to show how 'man's first disobedience' brought sin and death in its train, it is characteristic of him that he does not close on the note of evil triumphant, but prophetically introduces the divine work of redemption. Though in this way he had apparently completed his original scheme, however, he was afterwards led to add a sequel in four books the substance of which was provided by the temptation of Christ in the wilderness; but, while not without its occasional passages of sublimity and of tenderness, *Paradise Regained* seems to most modern readers a very slight thing beside its gigantic predecessor. The 'dramatic poem' *Samson Agonistes* (Samson the Wrestler) crowns the labours of these closing years. In this as in *Paradise Lost*, Milton applies the forms of classic art to the treatment of a biblical subject, for the work is fashioned strictly upon the principles of Greek tragedy, while the matter is, of course, derived from the fate of Samson among the Philistines. This subject had been in Milton's thought many years before when he had been casting about for a theme for his epic, but it had then been discarded in favour of the fall of man. He returned to it now in all probability because he saw in the hero an image both of himself, blind, disappointed, and surrounded by enemies, and of the Puritan cause, overwhelmed by the might of its foes.

44. Characteristics of Milton's Poetry. After Shakespeare, Milton is the greatest English poet; which means that he is the greatest English poet outside the drama. Moreover, in the almost unanimous judgment of the critics, he is to be regarded as one of the three or four supreme poets of the world. In him we have a wonderful union of intellectual power and creative power, both at their highest. He is also a consummate literary artist, whose touch is as sure in delicate detail as in vast general effects. While many qualities thus go to the making of his work, however, the one which we most naturally think of, and which indeed we have come to denote by the epithet 'Miltonic', is his sublimity. He is the most sublime of English poets, and our one acknowledged master of what Matthew Arnold calls 'the grand style'. In sustained majesty of thought and diction he is unrivalled. His descriptive power, too, is astonishing, as we can learn for ourselves by turning, for example, to the scenes in Hell in the opening books of *Paradise Lost*; and, while he was entirely lacking in the true dramatic sense, the magnificent debate in the council of the fallen angels, and the whole conduct of the temptation of Eve, show an extraordinary insight into motive and character. Though in theory an epic poem is supposed to be quite impersonal, Milton's epic is throughout instinct with the spirit of the man himself. Narrow he often is; he is often hard and austere. But there is an intensity of individuality in everything he writes which is singularly impressive; and the loftiness of his temper and passionate moral earnestness make us feel as we read that we are indeed in the presence of one 'whose soul was like a star, and dwelt apart'.

In connection with the technical side of his poetry special note should be taken of the great and varied beauty of its style and versification. His blank verse in particular deserves the closest study. Though this form, as we now know, had long been used in the drama, it had not thus far been adopted for any important non-dramatic poem. Milton was therefore making an experiment when he took as the measure of *Paradise Lost* 'English heroic verse without rime.' Of this measure he remains our greatest master.

10

The Age of Milton:
Other Poets and Prose Writers

45. The Caroline Poets. As I have already pointed out (§3), the Age of Milton and the Age of Dryden, though in a broad way we are bound to distinguish between them, really overlap, and as a result it is extremely difficult, in grouping the writers of the period between 1625 and 1700 under one or the other head, to establish any quite satisfactory order among them. We will here, however, for the present confine our attention to those who, irrespective of dates, seem by the quality of their thought and style to belong to the older generation. Those who, while really contemporary with them, belong rather to the new generation, or for any reason may most conveniently be connected with it, will be dealt with in our next two chapters.

Under the term Caroline Poets[9] we include a number of verse writers whose work may in the bulk be roughly assigned to the reign of Charles I, though as a matter of fact many of them continued to produce through the years of the Commonwealth or even later. Some of them were secular, some religious poets. The most important of them, ROBERT HERRICK (1591–1674), wrote both secular and religious poetry with equal felicity, if not quite with equal success. In early life an associate of Ben Jonson, Herrick went into the church, found

---

[9]From *Carolus*, Latin for Charles.

himself in the banishment of his Devonshire parsonage as unhappy as Spenser had been in Ireland, was deprived of his living after the civil war, and reinstated at the Restoration. His religious poetry was published under the general title of *Noble Numbers*; his secular, in the same volume (1648), under that of *Hesperides*. It is in the latter that Herrick's powers are shown at their best. They are miscellaneous in character, comprising addresses to friends, fairy poems, occasional poems on all sorts of subjects, and many love poems; but they are all delightful in their naturalness and spontaneity, their exquisite fancy, and their lyrical charm and grace. Historically, perhaps their most singular feature is their complete detachment from the political interests of the hour. In that season of tumult and confusion, when the minds of men were stirred by the fiercest passions, Herrick held himself altogether aloof, preferring to sing of the joys of life, with a tender sense, all the same, of their brevity.

In the 'Cavalier' group of Caroline poets, whose inspiration was entirely or almost entirely secular, the principal names are those of THOMAS CAREW (1598?–1639), his friend SIR JOHN SUCKLING (1609–42), and RICHARD LOVELACE (1618–58). These are all poets in the lighter vein and made no pretence at treating their art seriously, but what they did they did extremely well. Carew's *He that loves a rosy cheek*, Suckling's *Why so pale and wan, fond lover?* and Lovelace's *To Althea from Prison*, may be cited as examples of the fine lyrical quality by which at its best their amatory verse is marked. With these we may here join ANDREW MARVELL (1621–78), because his earlier work exhibits many of the characteristics of the Cavalier school. But in politics and religion he was on the other side, and after the Restoration he changed his poetic note, and wrote fierce satire in rugged style on Charles II and his supporters.

Of the Caroline poets who found their main interest in religion, the most widely known, though not poetically the greatest, was GEORGE HERBERT (1593–1633), whose collection of lyrics entitled *The Temple* breathes the spirit of the purest piety. The sacred verse of RICHARD CRASHAW (1613?–49), though very unequal and at times quite ruined by conceits, has far greater fire and passion; that of HENRY VAUGHAN (1622–95), while directly and powerfully influenced by Herbert, is deeper in thought and much more mystical. The *Religious Emblems* of FRANCIS QUARLES (1592–1644), the text of which was illustrated by quaint engravings, must be placed on record because of their immense and long-enduring popularity.

46. Cowley and the 'Metaphysical' Poets. ABRAHAM COWLEY (1618–67) demands a little more attention, both because he was in his own day considered the greatest of English poets, and because he is usually regarded as the chief representative of that 'metaphysical' school which, as we have seen, took its rise in the work of Donne (see §27). The name 'metaphysical' was first applied to this school by Johnson, and though it is not a very good one, it has kept its place in our critical vocabulary. Johnson's explanation of his term is, however, excellent. The metaphysical poets, he writes, 'were men of learning, and to show their learning was their whole endeavour.... They neither copied nature nor life.... Their thoughts are often new, but seldom natural; they are not obvious, but neither are they just; and the reader, far from wondering that he missed them, wonders more frequently by what perverseness of industry they were ever found.' The salient features of this curious group of writers are here clearly indicated. Their work is packed with affectations and conceits; in their effort to surprise by the boldness and novelty of their images they indulge in strained metaphors, far-fetched similes, and the most extravagant hyperbole; they cultivate ingenuity at any cost; substitute philosophical subtleties and logical hair-splitting for the natural expression of feeling; and employ their vast out-of-the-way learning without the slightest regard to propriety. As a result they are in general violent, harsh, cold, and obscure. That from time to time they nonetheless give us passages or even whole poems of real power and beauty only proves that the promptings of genius were not altogether stifled by vicious theories. But when we find a poet of the quality of Crashaw ransacking earth and heaven for emblems of the eyes of the sorrowing Mary Magdalene, and describing them, for example, as

'Two walking baths, two weeping motions,
Portable and compendious oceans,'

we can realise into what frantic absurdities English poetry was for a time misled, as Johnson puts it, 'by voluntary deviation from nature in pursuit of something new and strange.' In Cowley's work we have the last important productions of this metaphysical school, but we must remember that its influences were very widely spread among the poets of the age in general. Thus the three chief religious poets who have been named above—Crashaw, Herbert, and Vaughan—were all more or less metaphysical. It should also be noted that in his later poetry Cowley discards much of his former extravagance, and approximates to the restrained and sober style which came in with the next generation.

A slightly younger writer—THOMAS TRAHERNE (?1634–1704)—might usually have been grouped with the three poets just named if most of his manuscripts had not been lost to sight for nearly two hundred years after his death. When they were found early in the present century, Traherne was at once recognized as one of the greatest religious and metaphysical poets of the seventeenth century through the volume of *Poems* first published in 1903. His *Centuries of Meditations* (1908) showed that he was a great prose writer also. Although Traherne's work presents much of the difficulty common to the metaphysicals it also has much beauty and eloquence as well as profundity of thought and spiritual feeling.

47. The Caroline Prose Writers. In the prose literature of Milton's age there are many names of importance, but it is only of the men whose interest is broad enough to justify their inclusion in a record of general literature that we have here to take account. Thus the *Holy Living* and *Holy Dying* of the eloquent divine, JEREMY TAYLOR (1613–67) and *The Saints' Everlasting Rest* of the Puritan RICHARD BAXTER (1615–91), though purely religious in matter and aim deserve reference as acknowledged classics of their kind. Another divine, the quaint, witty, and vivacious THOMAS FULLER (1608–61), though he also wrote much on religious subjects, is best remembered today for his delightful miscellaneous *Worthies of England*. SIR THOMAS BROWNE, a physician, was the author of a number of books full of varied and curious erudition, but his main title to fame is his personal confession of religious faith, *Religio Medici*. That a highly special subject may by sheer charm of treatment be endowed with the widest possible interest is strikingly shown in the case of *The Compleat Angler, or the Contemplative Man's Recreation*, by IZAAK WALTON (1593–1683), which, though ostensibly designed for the instruction of fishermen, has long been popular with countless readers who care nothing for the sport, on account of its pleasant gossipy style and genuine rustic flavour. Walton also wrote some admirable biographies. In history, in which much good work was now done, the first place is occupied by the *History of the Great Rebellion*, by EDWARD HYDE, EARL OF CLARENDON (1609–74), which, while untrustworthy by reason of its royalist bias, is justly admired for its stately diction and its skilful studies of character. The *Leviathan* of THOMAS HOBBES (1588–1679), advocating strong central government, apart from its theories, which do not now concern us, must be mentioned as the most important of the political treatises which were inspired by the unrest and speculations of the time.

Speaking of the work of all these men in general, and disregarding for the moment their individual qualities, we may say that we nowhere recognise in their style the characteristic tone and manner of our modern prose. What has been said about the prose of Milton is equally applicable to that of his contemporaries. Even in the greater colloquialism of Baxter there is still much to remind us that this is not the sort of prose we use today. We must therefore be careful to note the particular historical interest of the charming *Essays* of Cowley, the manner of which has a great deal in common with that simpler and clearer way of writing which the Age of Dryden, as we shall presently see, was to introduce.

Note. For a Table of the Literature of the Age of Milton, see pp. 109–111

11

The Age of Dryden
(1660–1700):
Verse

48. The Age of Dryden. The Stuart Restoration was followed by an immense change in the general temper of the English people. A sweeping reaction against Puritanism and everything that it had stood for set in; and this reaction went so far that together with the galling restraints which religious fanaticism had unwisely imposed, moderation and decency were too often cast aside. England now touched low-water mark in its social history. The court of Charles II was the most shameless this country has ever known; infidelity and profligacy became fashionable; the moral ideals of Puritanism were turned into jest, and those who still upheld the cause of domestic virtue laughed at as hypocrites or denounced as sour sectaries. Even outside the narrow circle of court and aristocracy, where things were at their worst, the spirit of corruption spread far and wide, and while piety and goodness were of course cherished among individuals, the general lowering of the moral tone was everywhere apparent. The effect of these conditions on literature will be anticipated by all who recall the great principle of interpretation, which preceding chapters have now made clear, that literature is a social product and inevitably reflects the life of the era out of which it springs. The literature of the age of Dryden was at times openly and defiantly corrupt; while even at its best, though it had many admirable qualities, it was generally wanting in moral strength and spiritual fervour. Real earnestness of purpose had passed away, and with this, strong passion, and with this again, great creative energy. The thoughts of men no longer scaled the heights; they moved along the plain. Literature ceased to soar and became pedestrian. Thus with the Restoration we enter upon a period in which literature is intellectual rather than imaginative or emotional, and though often brilliant, is on the whole a trifle hard and unsympathetic. This is true even of poetry, which became prosaic, was made to do the work of prose, and was judged by the standards of prose. The poet did not allow his thoughts to wander off with Spenser into fairyland, or to explore with Milton the mysteries of heaven and hell. He made his verse the vehicle of argument, controversy, personal and political satire. The era of the versified pamphlet thus began. This is a striking illustration of the changed mood of the times. Even more significant, perhaps, is the fact that the men of the Restoration were the real creators of our modern English prose.

In further illustration of the qualities of the literature of this period we must remember the direct and powerful influence exerted upon it by France. The European supremacy of Italy had now passed away, and France had become the world's great arbiter of taste. The political relations between the two countries naturally tended to give vogue in England to all things French, including French taste and French ideas of art. Now the contemporary literature of France was characterised particularly by lucidity, vivacity, and—by reason of the close attention given to form—correctness, elegance, and finish. It was essentially a literature of polite society, and had all the merits and all the limitations of such a literature. It was moreover a literature in which intellect was in the ascendant and the critical faculty always in control. It was to this congenial literature that English writers now learned to look for guidance, and thus a great impulse was given to the development alike in our prose and in our verse of the principles of regularity and order and the spirit of good sense. As in verse pre-eminently these were now cultivated at the expense of feeling and spontaneity, the growth of an artificial type of poetry was the inevitable result.

49. The Forerunners of Dryden. Of this epoch Dryden, 'the greatest man of a little age', as he has been called, was the one complete representative and exponent. But before we turn to his work, we must say a word about two writers, both some years his elders, whom he himself regarded as his masters, and who are still commonly considered the pioneers of the so-called 'classic' school of poetry—EDMUND WALLER (1605–87) and SIR JOHN DENHAM (1615–69). In general, these two writers were leaders in the reaction in taste against the excesses and obscurity of the metaphysical poets and in favour of good sense and of neatness and clearness of expression. In particular, they were the reformers of English versification at a time when it had become insufferably rugged and harsh. It is indeed on this latter side mainly that they possess historical importance. This is especially true of Waller. 'The excellence and dignity of rime,' said Dryden, 'were never fully known till Mr. Waller taught it; he first made writing easily an art; first showed us how to conclude the sense most commonly in distichs, which in the verse of those before him runs on for so many lines together, that the reader is out of breath to overtake it.' This reshaping of the heroic[10] couplet is Waller's principal claim to distinction. He brought into use that kind of heroic couplet which we know as the 'classic' or 'closed' form, in which the rule is that, instead of the sense being allowed to flow on from couplet to

---

[10]The epithet 'heroic' (derived from the common employment of this measure in 'heroic' poetry) is here used to denote that each line of the couplet is iambic pentameter, or composed (like the ordinary line of blank verse) of five accents (or ten syllables), the unaccented syllabic normally coming first and the accented syllable following; as in Pope's line:

'To érr | is hú | man, tó | forgivé | diviné.'

The reader must carefully note the distinction between the two contrasted types of heroic couplet—the 'classic', which is here immediately in question; and the 'romantic', which will come before us later.

couplet indefinitely, it should habitually close with the end of the second line; the metrical pause and the rhetorical pause thus coming together, Dryden (who, as will be observed, writes extravagantly in Waller's praise) is wrong in supposing that this closed couplet was actually that poet's invention. It had been used from time to time by many earlier writers. But when Waller began his work, the tendency was wholly away from it towards a kind of verse so loose as to be almost formless, and it is from him that the new movement may fairly be said to date. The classic couplet did not reach its final shape in his hands. As a specific form it evolved gradually, and it assumed perfection first in the work of its greatest master, Pope. But Waller led the way. Then Denham (now chiefly remembered for his descriptive poem, *Cooper's Hill*) followed. Of Waller and Denham together Dryden wrote: 'Our numbers [versification] were in their nonage till these last appeared.'

50. Dryden's Life. JOHN DRYDEN was born at Aldwinkle All Saints, Northamptonshire, in 1631; was educated at Westminster and at Trinity College, Cambridge, and settled in London about 1657. Soon after this he wrote his first poems of any importance, the *Heroic Stanzas on the Death of Oliver Cromwell* (1659), and (indicative of a rapid change of front) *Astraea Redux*, in celebration of the 'happy restoration' of Charles II. In 1663 he began to work for the stage, which was then the only profitable field for anyone who had to depend for his livelihood upon his pen; and for some fifteen years playwriting continued to be his chief occupation. In 1670 he was made poet laureate, and 1681 opened a new chapter in his career with the publication of the first of his great satires in verse, *Absalom and Achitophel*. This was followed by other works of the same character, and later by two theological poems, *Religio Laici* (1682), a defence of the Church of England, and *The Hind and the Panther* (1687), an elaborate argument in favour of Roman Catholicism, to which in the meantime he had been converted. In consequence of this change of religion the revolution of 1688 came upon him as a heavy blow. He lost his position of poet laureate, and, all hopes of official recognition now being destroyed, devoted himself for his remaining years to literature with praiseworthy courage and industry. He produced five more plays, translations of Juvenal, Persius, and Vergil, and a volume of *Fables* (or para-phrases from Homer, Ovid, Boccaccio, and Chaucer). These were published in November, 1699. Six months later—in May, 1700—he died.

51. Dryden's Poetry. Of Dryden's work in prose and the drama we shall speak in our next chapter. Here we have to deal only with his verse.

As a poet, he ripened very slowly. His first poem, an elegy on the death of young Lord Hastings, written at eighteen, is almost incredibly bad; his *Heroic Stanzas*, written at twenty-seven, though they contain a few fine lines and images, are crude and bombastic. For the time being he was greatly influenced by Cowley, whom he afterwards described as 'the darling of my youth', and as a result, all the characteristic absurdities of the metaphysical school abound in these early works. They survive even in *Annus Mirabilis* (1667), in which, writing of the two great events of the 'wonderful year'—the war with Holland and the Fire of London—he indulges from time to time in the most fantastic conceits; as when, for example, he depicts the Deity extinguishing the conflagration with a 'hollow crystal pyramid', precisely in the way in which himself was accustomed to put out his own candle. But though its faults are numerous and glaring, the masculine vigour and lucidity of the poem reveal an immense development in the writer's genius. For the full exhibition of his powers, however, we have to turn to the work of the last twenty years of his life, in which his emancipation from the false taste of the metaphysical writers is complete, and his style, no longer turbid and choked with all sorts of rubbish, flows clear and strong. This work, which marks the definite establishment of the classical school of poetry in England, may be dealt with under three heads—

(1) The political satires: *Absalom and Achitophel*, written amid the excitement following the alleged Popish Plot, to defend the king's policy against the Earl of Shaftesbury, and specially famous for its

powerful character-studies, as of Shaftesbury himself under the name of Achitophel, and of the Duke of Buckingham under that of Zimri; *The Medal*, a further invective against Shaftesbury; and *MacFlecknoe*, a scathing personal attack on a former friend, Thomas Shadwell, who had replied to *The Medal* in a poem filled with scurrilous abuse.

(2) The two great doctrinal poems, *Religio Laici* and *The Hind and the Panther.* These are not in the strict sense religious; there is nothing devotional or spiritual about them. They are theological and controversial; and written as they are from two opposed points of view, they are curiously interesting as exhibiting Dryden's mastery in the conduct of an argument in verse, and his extraordinary skill in making the most of whatever position he might for the moment adopt. His mental flexibility and agility gave him remarkable power as a special pleader.

(3) *The Fables.* These fine tales, written amid the anxieties of Dryden's fast years and under the increasing burden of age and ill-health, so far from suggesting any flagging of energy, rather show the poet almost at his best, and give him a title to rank among our best story-tellers in verse. The *Palamon and Arcite*, based upon the *Knightes Tale* of Chaucer, provides an opportunity for a most instructive comparison between the method and art of the fourteenth century, and those of the seventeenth century poet.

Dryden's poetry, alike in its limitations and in its merits, is thoroughly representative of the age. As a whole it is marked by a general want of what we are accustomed to call the essentially poetic qualities. It has little imaginative power, little depth of feeling, little spiritual glow or fervour; and except here and there, as in the two remarkable odes *To the Memory of Mrs. Anne Killigrew* and *Alexander's Feast*, it rarely touches a high lyrical note. On the other hand, it is characterised by splendid intellectuality and a manly vigour of style. If Dryden is seldom poetic (using the word in the sense which we attach to it when we are thinking, say, of Coleridge or Keats) he at least gives us many passages of wonderful strength and eloquence. It is therefore easy to see why he holds his own as a satirist and as a reasoner in verse. In both these fields, the author of *Absalom and Achitophel* and *Religio Laici* is still our greatest master.

It was Dryden's influence and example which lifted the classic couplet into the place it was to occupy for many years as the accepted measure of serious English poetry. When he began to write, he, like the literary world in general, was in a state of uncertainty in regard to the best form to adopt. Thus we find him fluctuating between the 'Gondibert'[11] stanza in the poem on *Oliver Cromwell* and in *Annus Mirabilis*, and the regular couplet in *Astraea Redux* and the *Panegyric* on the coronation. With *Absalom and Achitophel* he made his final choice of the latter form, and by his splendid use of it he proved its capabilities and assured its success.

52. Butler. Only one other poet of the period is important enough to detain us here, and he lives entirely on the strength of one work. This is SAMUEL BUTLER (1612–80), author of the famous *Hudibras*, the three parts of which were published in 1663, 1664, and 1678. A satire on the Puritans, *Hudibras* instantly hit the taste of the time, and by its popularity greatly stimulated the general reaction against the 'saints' and their cause. The machinery of the poem is obviously fashioned upon *Don Quixote*, for like that wonderful Spanish burlesque romance, it tells of the misadventures of a knight and his squire, and the knight's ill-fortunes in love. In the two central figures, the author holds up to our contempt two contrasted representatives of Puritanism: the Presbyterian Sir Hudibras himself being a military enthusiast who, though unconsciously a good deal of a hypocrite, is not consciously insincere; while his attendant, Ralpho, is a vulgar, canting impostor, who merely assumes the mask of virtue for his own profit. The story begins with an attempt of these two to put down a bear-baiting, which involves them in a tremendous conflict with the rabble, and leads to their being set by the heels in the parish stocks.

---

[11]So called because it was popularised by Dryden's friend and coadjutor in the drama, Sir William Davenant, in his poem entitled *Gondibert* (1651). It is the four-line, iambic pentameter stanza, rhyming *abab*, which we know best as that of Gray's *Elegy*.

This is the most amusing portion of the book. Other incidents follow which keep up the interest till well on into the second part; but after this the story lapses, and the rest of the poem is composed of odds and ends of epistles, digressions, and satiric tirades. To modern taste, *Hudibras* is far too long; some of its best passages suffer from prolixity; and too much space is given in it to the discussion of various points of Puritan casuistry. The local and temporary nature of its subject-matter is also a serious disadvantage in the eyes of the reader of today. Yet it is full of wit and vivacity, and even its doggerel metre and its astonishing double rhymes, though we tire of them after a while, are, as Dryden said, fitted to the spirit and purpose of the burlesque. It was Butler's intention to kill Puritanism by ridicule, and we can well understand that his poem delighted the court, and was the favourite reading of Charles II, who, by the bye, while he laughed over and praised it, nonetheless permitted the author to spend his last years in poverty. It need hardly be added, however, that we are not to take Butler's picture of Puritanism as complete and final. It is a mere caricature. He saw only the extravagance and the charlatanism which were of course often associated with Puritanism. But its greatness and strength—the elements which rendered it so important in the making of history—he could not or would not see, or at least, he gave them no recognition in his work.

12

The Age of Dryden:
Prose and Drama

53. The Rise of Modern Prose. 'The Restoration', says Matthew Arnold, 'marks the real moment of birth of our modern English prose. It is by its organism—an organism opposed to length and involvement, and enabling us to be clear, plain, and short—that English prose after the Restoration breaks with the style of the times preceding it, finds the true law of prose, and becomes modern; becomes, in spite of superficial differences, the style of our own day.' From the historical point of view the establishment of this modern prose is the greatest single fact in the literary annals of the Age of Dryden.

We can easily put Arnold's statement to the test by reading a page out of Milton's *Areopagitica*, and then a page out of Dryden, or Defoe, or Addison, and noting (as indeed no one can fail to note) the fundamental differences between them. Of Milton's style we instinctively say—'We should never for a moment think of trying to write like that'; of the style of Dryden, Defoe, Addison—'this, though in places a little archaic in manner, is after all very much our own way of writing.' The older prose—the prose of such men as Hooker, Milton, and, in Dryden's own time, of Clarendon and Jeremy Taylor—was, as we have learned, too intricate, involved, and cumbrous for general use; the sentences were long; parentheses were numerous; the construction adopted was often that rather of Latin than of English syntax. In the new prose all this is changed. The sentences are much shorter and simpler; the large straggling masses are broken up; the parentheses and classical inversions are cleared away. Such changes made, it is evident, for ease in writing and reading, and for directness and lucidity.

Many causes combined in the introduction and establishment of this new prose. The spread of the spirit of common sense and of the critical temper of mind, which was so injurious to the higher interests of poetry, had itself a good deal to do with it. The extending influence of science, which favoured clearness of thought and plainness of expression, must also be recognised. Then it must be remembered that a new kind of public was growing up which was far more miscellaneous and varied in character than that which hitherto had possessed the practical monopoly of literary interests; and the tastes and capacities of this increasingly large body of general readers had to be consulted by those who catered for them. In an age of unceasing political and religious excitement, there was an immense development of that sort of evanescent literature which we now class under the head of journalism; the general reader and the ready writer thus appeared together; each reacted upon the other; and this change of public necessarily meant that things which had formerly been treated in a dry, pedantic, and difficult way had to be made simple and pleasant. All those influences told in the transformation which our prose now underwent, and to these we have to add the further influence of French literature. In advance of all other European countries, France had already evolved a kind of prose which in its clearness, flexibility, and good taste was admirably adapted for all the purposes of ordinary exposition, discussion, and social intercourse. This prose provided just the model that the English writers needed for their guidance.

The establishment of the new prose was not quite so sudden as Arnold's statement might lead us to think, nor was it the work of any one man. But in a brief survey like this Dryden has his special claim upon our attention as the first of our really great prose writers in the modern style.

54. Dryden's Prose Work. Apart from a good deal of mere hack-work, which may of course be disregarded, Dryden's prose writings consist mainly of essays and prefaces dealing with a large range of questions connected with poetry and the drama. Here, again, we perceive the thoroughly representative character of his production. As the Restoration saw the rise of the new prose, so also it saw the real beginnings of modern criticism; for though, as we have noted, there had already been a certain amount of criticism in England, it was now for the first time that people addressed themselves systematically to the study of the principles and laws of literature. In this growth of criticism and of the corresponding tendency to check and guide production by line and rule, we have another illustration of the spirit of an age which was far stronger on the side of analysis than on that of imagination, and in which the intellectual predominated over the creative powers; and Dryden, our first great modern prose writer, is also our first great modern critic. In the course of his criticism he takes up and discusses, and from various points of view (for his judgment was subject to perpetual fluctuations) nearly all the topics which were of interest to the literary world of his time—the forms and methods of the drama, for example; the elements of heroic and epic poetry; the relations of art and nature; the qualities of the great writers of Greece and Rome; and so on. His work is thus of capital importance as a commentary upon the tastes and ideals of the rising classical school of literature. On the whole, his best criticism is to be found in his writings on the drama, and particularly in the earliest and most masterly of all of them, the *Essay of Dramatic Poesy*, in which he considers the respective principles and merits of the three chief types of drama—the classical drama of the Greeks and Romans, the neo-classical drama of the French, and the romantic drama of the English, and, among other matters, undertakes to justify the use of rhyme in place of blank verse on the stage and to 'vindicate the honour of our English writers from the censure of those who unjustly prefer the French before them'. Dryden often writes hastily and is habitually careless in detail; and as in general he accepted the limitations and prejudices of his age, a good deal of his criticism, while historically important, has but slight permanent value. At the same time, we can seldom fail to be struck by the sound good sense which he brings to bear upon almost every subject he touches. His sagacity and penetration are indeed remarkable; while his prose style is characterised by clearness, vigour, a wonderful felicity of phrasing, and a colloquial ease which (in contrast with that of some of the smaller contemporary writers) preserves a literary distinction, and rarely descends to the level of the slipshod or the commonplace.

55. Bunyan. The only other really great name in the prose literature of Dryden's age is that of JOHN BUNYAN (1628–88). The son of a tinker, whose trade he himself afterwards followed, Bunyan was born at Elstow, Bedfordshire; fought for a time in the civil war, though on which side is uncertain; was converted; married early; and in 1655 began to preach on village greens. Continuing the practice after the Restoration, he was soon convicted as 'a common upholder of several unlawful meetings and conventicles', and committed to the Bedford jail, where he remained twelve years. His autobiographical *Grace Abounding* was the work of his captivity; the first part of *The Pilgrim's Progress* belongs to a second imprisonment of six months in 1675. Meanwhile he had obtained a licence to preach, and had become the regular minister of the Baptist congregation, then meeting in a barn, at Bedford. In his later years he was also famous as a preacher in London. It was on a visit to London that he died; and he was buried in the old Dissenters' Burial Ground at Bunhill Fields, where Defoe and Isaac Watts were afterwards to be laid to rest. Bunyan wrote much; but his four great works are *Grace Abounding* (1660), *The Pilgrim's Progress* (1678–84), *The Life and Death of Mr. Badman* (1680), and *The Holy War* (1682), There are many things about Bunyan which make him a very important figure in literary history. His wonderful imagination gave him a place almost by himself (save for Milton, perhaps quite by himself) in an unimaginative age. He is the only man in our literature who has ever succeeded in writing a long prose allegory and in filling it throughout, without any sacrifice of the symbolism, with the absorbing interest of a real human story. The combined vividness and plainness of his writing is another remarkable feature of his work. Bunyan was not an educated man; he knew nothing of the classics; nothing about theories of literature; little or nothing, even, about English literature. But he had the Authorised Version of the English Bible by heart, and he was endowed by nature with a genius for style. Few writers, no matter what their training and accomplishments, have in fact ever shown a keener sense of the right word and the telling phrase. At this point the contrast with Milton becomes significant. Both were Puritans; yet as we have seen, Milton, the master of all the learning of the schools, was fed also by the Renaissance, while Bunyan, in the most unqualified sense of the term, was the child of Puritanism only. If therefore we are asked to name the greatest product of Puritanism in English literature, our choice should fall on *The Pilgrim's Progress* rather than on *Paradise Lost*. Finally, we must not overlook Bunyan's position in the evolution of English prose fiction. The controlling didactic purpose and the allegorical form prevent us from putting *The Pilgrim's Progress* into the class of regular modern novels; yet so well sustained is the interest of the narrative, the characters, and the dialogue, so great is the dramatic power, and so firm is the grasp of ordinary life, that it must at least be regarded as a forerunner of the novel.

56. Other Prose Writers of the Period. SIR WILLIAM TEMPLE (1628–99), who is best known through his relations with Swift, and who wrote letters and essays in a plain but polished style, and JOHN TILLOTSON (1630–94), who, abandoning the older tradition of the pulpit, introduced a similar style into religious oratory, have a certain importance in the establishment of the new prose. The great value of that prose in philosophic exposition and discussion was distinctly shown by JOHN LOCKE (1632–1704) in his *Essay on the Human Understanding, Treatise on Government,* and *Thoughts on Education*. But the most interesting minor prose writing of the time for the general reader is to be found in the work of the two diarists, JOHN EVELYN (1620–1706) and SAMUEL PEPYS (1633–1703). Evelyn's *Diary* is now read mainly as a record of contemporary events as seen from the point of view of a loyal, thoughtful, and high-minded royalist. It is written in a grave, simple style. Pepys's *Diary*, on the other hand, apart altogether from its historical value, is one of the most entertaining of books, and the most extraordinary thing of its kind in any literature. It covers a period of nearly ten years—from 1st January, 1660, to 31st May, 1669, when the writer's eyesight gave out—and therefore includes, among many other noteworthy occurrences, the Restoration, the Great Plague, and the Great Fire. But its principal interest lies in the vivid descriptions which it gives of the men and manners of the day, and the habits, fashions, and scandals of the 'Town', in its reproduction of the gossip of the streets, the coffee-houses, and the playhouses, and in its record of the personal life and doings, the domestic troubles, the jealousies, philanderings, successes and disappointments of the irrepressible diarist himself. Pepys did not write for the public eye, but for himself alone; he used a shorthand which was not deciphered till the early nineteenth century; and so certain was he of the inviolable secrecy of his journal, that he did not scruple to entrust it with his inmost thoughts and feelings. As a revelation of character from the inside, the *Diary* is unique.

57. Drama of the Age of Dryden. We need not give much space to this part of our subject. The theatre was now almost wholly the creature of the demoralised world of fashion, and it everywhere reflected the taste of its patrons. In the comedy of the time—the Comedy of the Restoration, as it is generally, though loosely, called— the chief names are those of WILLIAM WYCHERLEY (1640?–1716), WILLIAM CONGREVE (1670–1729), the most brilliant writer of the group, and one of our greatest masters of artificial comedy, SIR JOHN VANBRUGH (1664?–1726), and GEORGE FARQUHAR (1678–1707). The work of these men is as a rule wonderfully clever; it has dash and gaiety; and its wit is abundant and unflagging. But it is entirely lacking in truth to nature, while in its open and unabashed indecency it reveals at its worst the spirit of the society for whose amusement it was produced. Its grossness in the end drew down upon it a tremendous castigation from the REV. JEREMY COLLIER (1650–1726), whose *Short View of the Profaneness and Immorality of the English Stage* (1698), caused an immense sensation and had a salutary effect. Tragedy meanwhile, though it kept free from the profligacy of comedy, was equally artificial. For a time its most popular form was that of the Heroic Drama, in which love, gallantry, and courage were depicted on a gigantic scale with little reference to life, and the dialogue of which was filled with sonorous rant and bombastic extravagance. In these Heroic plays, rhyme, which it will be remembered Dryden advocated in his *Essay of Dramatic Poesy*, displaced blank verse. Dryden himself was the principal master of this form, which is shown in its perfection in his *Tyrannic Love, or The Royal Martyr* (1669) and the two parts of his *Conquest of Granada* (1670). The vogue of the Heroic Drama did not, however, last very long, and a reaction towards other forms set in. The Senecan or French school had its followers, as in the case of Congreve, whose one tragedy, *The Mourning Bride* (1697), is fashioned faithfully upon the regular classic model. In his *All for Love*, which is based on *Antony and Cleopatra*, Dryden, now weary of the Heroic style and of rhyme, reverted to Shakespeare and blank verse. No new dramatic lead of any value was, however, given, and the work now done for the stage possesses little value as literature. Nathaniel Lee (1653–92), who wrote first in rhyme and then in blank verse, and in whom we have a little fire and a great deal of smoke, and THOMAS OTWAY (1652–85), whose *Orphan* and *Venice Preserved* long kept their popularity with actors and playgoers alike, are the only other tragic poets of the period who need here be even named.

TABLE OF THE AGE OF MILTON (1625–60) AND THE AGE OF DRYDEN (1660–1700)

Historic Events	Poetry	Prose	Drama
Charles I 1625–49			Death of Fletcher, 1625
	Milton's *Nativity Ode*, 1629 Herbert's *The Temple*, 1631 Death of Donne, 1631	Death of Bacon, 1626	
	Dryden, b. 1631		
	Milton's L'*Allegro* and II *Penseroso*, 1633 *Comus*, 1634 *Lycidas*, 1637		Death of Jonson, 1637
	Denham's *Cooper's Hill*, 1642	Sir T. Browne's *Religio Medici*, 1642	The theatres closed, 1642
	Waller's *Poems*, 1645	Milton's *Areopagitica*, 1644	
	Cowley's *Mistress*, 1647		
Commonwealth, 1649	Herrick's *Noble Numbers* and *Hesperides*, 1648	Baxter's *Saints' Rest*, 1650 Taylor's *Holy Living*, 1650 Taylor's *Holy Dying*, 1651 Walton's *Compleat Angler*, 1653	

Death of Cromwell, 1659	Dryden's *Heroic Stanzas on the Death of Cromwell*, 1659		
Charles II, 1660–85	Dryden's *AstræaRedux*, 1660	Pepys's *Diary* begins, 1660	Reopening of the theatres, 1660
		Fuller's *Worthies*, left unfinished at his death, 1661	
		Defoe, b. 1661?	
	Butler's *Hudibras*, Part I, 1663; Part II, 1664		Dryden's first play, *The Wild Gallant*, 1663
The great fire of London, 1666			
	Dryden's *AnnusMirabilis*, 1667	Dryden's *Essay of Dramatic Poesy*, 1667	
	Paradise Lost, 1667 Death of Cowley, 1667	Swift, b. 1667	
			Dryden's *Tyrannic Love*, 1669
	Paradise Regained, and *Samson Agonistes*, 1671	Walton's *Lives*, 1670	*Conquest of Granada*, 1670
			Wycherley's Comedies, 1671–77
		Dryden's *Essay of Heroic Plays*, 1672	
		Addison, b. 1672	

	Death of Milton, 1674	Steele, b. 1672	
	Butler's *Hudibras*, Part III, 1678	*Pilgrim's Progress*, Part I, 1678	Dryden's *All for Love*, 1678
		Bunyan's *Mr. Bad-man*, 1680	Otway's *Orphan*, 1680
	Dryden's *Absalom and Achitophel*, 1681		
	Dryden's *Religio Laici*, 1682	Bunyan's *Holy War*, 1682	Otway's *Venice Preserved*, 1682
		Pilgrim's Progress, Part II, 1684	
James II, 1685–88	Dryden's *The Hind and the Panther*, 1687 Death of Waller, 1687		
The Revolution, 1688	Pope, b. 1688	Death of Bunyan, 1688	
William III and Mary, 1689		Richardson, b. 1689	Congreve begins to write for the stage, 1693
			Vanbrugh begins to write for the stage, 1697
		Collier's *Short View*, 1698	
	Dryden's *Fables*, 1699		Farquhar begins to write for the stage, 1699
	Death of Dryden, 1700		

13

The Age of Pope (1700–1745):
Verse

58. The Age of Pope. Though manners were coarse, politics scandalously corrupt, and the general tone of society brutal, the England of the early eighteenth century witnessed a resolute attempt in the direction of moral regeneration. As the reception accorded to Collier's *Short View* clearly proved, people were fast growing sick of the outrageous licence which in fashionable circles had followed the return of the Stuarts, and had begun once more to insist upon those elementary decencies of life and conduct which the preceding generation had treated with open contempt. The desire for improvement is, as we shall presently see, a marked feature of not a little of the literature of this half-century, and especially of the literature which emanated from middle-class writers, who were of course most strongly influenced by moral considerations. But, while revolting in this way against Restoration profligacy, the men of Pope's era were quite as hostile as their fathers had been to everything that savoured of Puritan fanaticism and religious zeal, and thus, though England now began to regain lost ground morally, it did not recover the high passion or the spiritual fervour of the Elizabethan age. In their dread of those emotional excesses which to them seemed almost as monstrous as the moral excesses of the roysterers, they fell indeed into the mood of chilly apathy. Virtue was recommended and preached, but any manifestation of earnestness even in the pulpit, would have been regarded as dangerously suggestive of what was called 'enthusiasm', and in shockingly bad taste. Good sense became the idol of the time; and good sense meant a love of the reasonable and the useful, and a hatred of the extravagant, the mystical, and the visionary. This is shown in the field of religion, in which the prevailing principles were rationalism and utility. In the great Deistic controversy which raged in England from the opening of the century to the death of Bolingbroke in 1751, the Deists, or advocates of a purely natural religion, kept up a persistent attack upon revelation and the miraculous, while far more noteworthy even than this is the fact that the orthodox defenders of Christianity themselves were just as rationalistic in spirit as their opponents. The assumption common to both parties was the supremacy of logic and reason. It was to the reason and to the good sense of their listeners that the greatest preachers appealed; they sought, not to stir the sluggish conscience through the feelings, but to convince the intellect; while on the whole religion was conceived by them more as something necessary to the well-being of society, like an effective system of police, than as a power over the individual soul. All the theological writings of the eighteenth century down to the beginnings of Wesley's evangelistic revival, are characterized by this rationalistic and utilitarian temper. The same temper marks the literature of the age, which exhibits a similar coldness and want of feeling, and a similar tendency towards shallowness in thought and formality in expression. It is a literature of intelligence (though of intelligence which rarely goes much beneath the surface of things), of wit, and of fancy, not a literature of emotion, passion, or creative energy; and in it spontaneity and simplicity are sacrificed to the dominant mania for elegance and correctness. This is true even of poetry, which seldom travelled beyond the interests of that narrow world of the 'Town', by which men's outlook was commonly circumscribed, and finding its public in the coffee-house and drawing-room, drew for its substance upon the politics and discussions of the hour. Such poetry, however clever, was necessarily more or less fugitive; it lacked inevitably the depth and grasp of essential things which alone assure permanence in literature; and the quest for refinement in style resulted too often in stilted affectations and frigid conventionalism.

The Age of Pope is sometimes called the Classic Age and sometimes the Augustan Age of English literature.[12] Neither of these terms can be commended, but they are so current that it may be well to explain the senses in which they should be understood. The epithet 'classic' we may take to denote, first, that the poets and critics of this age believed that the works of the writers of classical antiquity (really of the Latin writers) presented the best of models and the ultimate standards of literary taste; and secondly, in a more general way, that, like these Latin writers, they had little faith in the promptings and guidance of individual genius, and much in laws and rules imposed by the authority of the past. When in 1706 Walsh wrote to Pope; 'The best of the modern poets in all languages are those that have nearest copied the ancients', he expressed concisely the principle of classicism; and this principle Pope himself reiterated in some well-known lines in his *Essay on Criticism:*

' 'Tis more to guide than spur the Muse's steed;
Restrain his fury, than provoke his speed;
The winged courser, like a gen'rous horse,
Shows most true mettle when you check his course.
Those Rules of old discover'd, not devis'd,
Are Nature still, but Nature methodiz'd;
Nature, like liberty, is but restrain'd
By the same laws which first herself ordain'd....
Learn hence for ancient rules a just esteem,
To copy Nature is to copy them.'

---

[12]Both these phrases are also employed more broadly to cover the Age of Dryden as well as that of Pope, or, roughly, the whole period between 1660 and 1745.

The other epithet, 'Augustan', was applied in the first instance as a term of high praise, because those who used it really believed that as the Age of Augustus was the golden age of Latin literature, so the Age of Pope was the golden age of English literature. As this is not now our view, the original meaning of the word has disappeared. But we may still employ it as a convenient catchword, because it serves to bring out the analogy between the English literature of the first half of the eighteenth century and the Latin literature of the days of Virgil and Horace. In both cases men of letters were largely dependent upon powerful patrons. In both cases a critical spirit prevailed. In both cases the literature produced by a thoroughly artificial society was a literature, not of free creative effort and inspiration, but of self-conscious and deliberate art.

59. Characteristics of the Classical School of Poetry. To understand the course of English poetry during the eighteenth century, both along the main line represented by the work of the Augustans and their later adherents, and along the various lines of reaction against their influence, it is essential that we should have the salient features of the classical school clearly in mind. Though in the following epitome some repetition will be inevitable, this will be justified by the importance of the subject.

(1) As we have said, classical poetry is in the main the product of the intelligence playing upon the surface of life. On the side of emotion and imagination it is markedly deficient. It is commonly didactic and satiric—a poetry of argument and criticism, of politics and personalities.

(2) It is almost exclusively a 'town' poetry, made out of the interests of 'society' in the great centres of culture. The humbler aspects of life are neglected in it, and it shows no real love of nature, landscape, or country things and people.

(3) It is almost entirely wanting in all those elements which we rather vaguely sum up under the epithet 'romantic'. In the Age of Pope, with its profound distrust of the emotions, a hatred of the 'romantic' in literature was the logical accompaniment of a hatred

of 'enthusiasm' in religion; romanticism and enthusiasm alike cut across all its accepted notions of reasonableness and good sense. The critical taste of the time was distinctly unsympathetic towards the 'ruder' masters of our older literature—towards Chaucer, for example, and Spenser, and even Shakespeare; and it was especially hostile to everything that belonged to the middle ages with their chivalrous extravagance, their visionary idealism, and their strong religious faith. This critical antagonism to romantic literature and art is everywhere reflected in contemporary poetry.

(4) Extreme, devotion to form and a love of superficial polish led to the establishment of a highly artificial and conventional style, which presently became stereotyped into a regular traditional poetic diction. Classical embroidery of all kinds was employed in season and out of season till it was worn threadbare and made ridiculous by constant use. Simplicity and naturalness disappeared before the growth of a false conception of refinement, and grandiloquent phrases and pompous circumlocutions were substituted for plain and direct expressions even when the matter dealt with was of the most commonplace kind. Thus, when the classic poet undertook to refashion the crude stuff of an old ballad, he translated the downright 'God rest his soul' into the stilted 'Eternal blessings on his shade attend', and honestly thought that he was thereby turning a vulgar colloquialism into beautiful poetry. This is a good illustration of that 'gaudiness and inane phraseology' against which Wordsworth was presently to enter his emphatic protest.

(5) Classic poetry adhered to the closed couplet as the only possible form for serious work in verse. The supremacy of the closed couplet should therefore be carefully noted. A little attention will show that on account of its epigrammatic terseness this form lent itself admirably to the kind of poetry that was then popular. But it will be equally evident that in the long run it was bound to grow monotonous, and that it was too narrow and inflexible to be made the vehicle of high passion or strong imagination.

60. Pope's Life. ALEXANDER POPE, the greatest master of

this classic school, was born in London in 1688—the year of the Revolution and of Bunyan's death. His father, a prosperous linen-draper, was a Roman Catholic, and on account of his religion Pope was excluded from the public schools and universities. The result was that he picked up most of his knowledge in a haphazard way, and though he read widely he never became an accurate scholar. The want both of sound learning and of mental discipline is apparent in his work. Extraordinarily precocious (in his own famous words, he 'lisped in numbers for the numbers came') he published his *Pastorals* in 1709 and his *Essay on Criticism* in 1711. He lived with his parents first at Binfield, on the skirts of Windsor Forest, and then at Chiswick, till the completion of his translation of Homer, the financial success of which enabled him (1719) to buy a house at Twickenham. There he passed the remainder of his life, and there he died in 1744. Long regarded as the foremost man of letters of his day, he was petted and spoilt by admiring friends, and might have enjoyed a far fuller meed of general esteem than actually fell to his share but for the petty spitefulness of his nature, which perpetually turned friends into foes. As it is, the history of his relations with his contemporaries is a tangled record of miserable jealousies and quarrels. Our judgment upon him must nevertheless be tempered by recognition of the fact that his extreme irritability and peevishness were in large measure the consequence of chronic ill-health. As he puts it in his *Epistle to Dr. Arbuthnot* (his devoted physician) his life was one 'long disease'. Yet, despite his invalidism, he worked steadily almost to the last, and with a sincere love of literature for its own sake, which is the more noteworthy because it was very rare at the time.

61. Pope's Work. Pope's poetic career falls quite naturally into three periods—an early and a late period of original work divided by a period (1715–25) of translation.

(1) To the period before 1715 belong a number of miscellaneous poems, of which the most important are: *Four Pastorals*, short poems on spring, summer, autumn, and winter, closely fashioned on Virgil and in the most artificial manner of their class (cp. §25). *The Messiah*,

a poetic rendering of the Messianic passages in Isaiah, in imitation of Virgil's fourth eclogue. The noble impressiveness of the original is quite lost in the meretricious glitter of Pope's overwrought style, *Windsor Forest*, undoubtedly inspired by Denham's *Cooper's Hill*. In this it is easy to perceive the indifference of the classic school to the real beauties of nature. Pope's landscape is copied out of the Greek and Latin poets rather than painted from first-hand knowledge of what he professes to describe. The *Essay on Criticism*, which is certainly a very remarkable performance for a man of twenty-one. It is not original in conception, for it was inspired by Horace's *Ars Poetica* and Boileau's *L'Art Poétique*. Nor does it contain any fresh or independent thought, for, as Lady Mary Wortley Montagu cruelly said, it is 'all stolen'. But Pope had read with some care the standard critics of the time, especially the French critics, and he puts the ideas he had gathered from them into wonderfully terse, epigrammatic, and quotable verse. The poem is of great interest as a popular interpretation of the literary creed of the age. *The Rape of the Lock*, which may safely be called Pope's masterpiece. This was founded upon an incident which occurred in the Roman Catholic society in which he had many friends. A certain Lord Petre cut a lock of hair from the head of a young beauty named Arabella Fermor (the Belinda of the poem). This practical joke led to a quarrel between the two families, and Pope was appealed to by a common friend, John Caryl, to throw oil on troubled waters by turning the whole thing into jest. *The Rape of the Lock* was the result. Pope defines the poem as 'heroi-comical'. It is better to call it a Mock Epic. In Butler's *Hudibras* humorous matter had found appropriate setting in rough doggerel verse. Here, on the contrary, trivial occurrences are handled with all the dignity and seriousness which properly belong to the epic. This calculated and sustained discrepancy between theme and treatment is of the essence of this particular kind of parody; and the effect is further supported by the arrangement of the plot upon the regular epic plan, the employment of the 'supernatural machinery' which every epic was supposed to require, and the many passages in which scenes and phrases from the great epics are directly imitated and burlesqued. So admirably is all this managed that the *Rape* is the most perfect thing of its kind in our literature. By the general flippancy of its tone, and especially by its cynical attitude towards women, it shows us meanwhile something of that fundamental callousness of feeling which the superficial gallantry of Pope's age scarcely served even to veil.

(2) The translation of the *Iliad* and the *Odyssey*—the former made single-handed, the latter with much help from others—represents the labours of Pope's second period. His *Homer*, as the two parts are together popularly called, has never ceased to be enjoyed and praised; but it contains far more of Pope than of Homer. He took up the task with a very meagre equipment of scholarship, and had to depend much on former translations. But this disadvantage was slight. The real difficulty lay in the fact that neither he nor his age could understand or enter into the spirit of Homer or the Homeric world. His public, however, wanted neither a scholarly nor a faithful version of the Greek poems, but a readable, drawing-room rendering of them in accordance with the taste of their own time. This Pope gave them. As Gibbon afterwards said, his translation has every merit except fidelity to the original. It is, in fact, not Homer, but a very striking and brilliant piece of eighteenth century work.

(3) After the publication of his *Homer*, Pope confined himself almost wholly to satiric and didactic poetry. The principal works of this third period are: *Satires and Epistles of Horace Imitated*. The *Prologue* to these—the *Epistle to Dr. Arbuthnot*—is specially valuable as the most frankly personal of all Pope's writings. It contains among other well-known passages the famous character-study of Addison under the name of Atticus. *The Dunciad*, a long and elaborate satire on the 'dunces'—the bad poets, pedants, and pretentious critics—of Pope's day. The epic machinery of this was obviously suggested by Dryden's *MacFlecknoe*; but the inspiration is to be sought in Pope's innumerable quarrels with all sorts of people. While it is extremely clever, the utter obscurity of most of the dunces attacked destroys

much of its point for the modern reader. *The Essay on Man*, a poem in four epistles (portions only of a larger plan never carried out) in which Pope undertakes a defence of the moral government of the universe and an explanation of the physical and moral evil in it, on the optimistic postulate that 'whatever is, is right'. Unfortunately, Pope was not a philosopher, he had no natural leanings towards philosophy, and no training for it; it was simply the influence of others, and especially of his Deistic friend, Lord Bolingbroke, which induced him to dabble in it; and he certainly never thought out for himself the large and difficult questions with which he rashly set himself to deal. In consequence, the *Essay* is hopelessly confused and self-contradictory. No one today, therefore, would dream of using it as a treatise. But it contains many passages which are justly famous, and are still often quoted, for their rhetorical beauty and power.

Pope's merits and defects are those of the classical school. We can no longer regard him as a great poet. He had neither the imaginative power nor the depth of feeling without which great poetry is impossible. Nor was he a great thinker. His view of life was the narrow and shallow view so characteristic of his age. But he was the very embodiment of the kind of intelligence which was currently known as 'wit', and which that age cultivated and admired. He was also, within his limits, a marvellously clever and adroit literary craftsman, and the neat, compact, antithetic, and epigrammatic style of writing which was the classical ideal, assumed perfection in his hands. After Shakespeare he is the most frequently quoted of English poets, and such familiar lines as these, which are taken just as they come, will suffice to show his extraordinary power of condensed and happy phrasing:

'Who shall decide when Doctors disagree?'
'A little learning is a dangerous thing.'
'And fools rush in where angels fear to tread.'
'To err is human, to forgive divine.'
'The proper study of mankind is man.'
'The Right Divine of kings to govern wrong.'

'A wit's a feather, and a chief a rod;
An honest man's the noblest work of God.'

He is also the most consummate master of the classic couplet, which he trimmed of some of the licences which Dryden had permitted himself, confining the sense more rigorously than ever within the two lines. Pope's perfected model was followed with slavish fidelity by all other poets who used the couplet till the early nineteenth century.

62. Other Poets of the Period. I will here record the names of the more important verse writers who belonged to Pope's generation and to his school. Consideration of several most interesting younger men, though a portion at least of their work falls within the limits of Pope's age, will be deferred to a later chapter because they represent the beginnings of a change of taste.

In point of time, MATTHEW PRIOR (1664–1721) takes precedence even of Pope himself. He came into notice as a man of twenty-three when in collaboration with Charles Montague, afterwards Earl of Halifax, he wrote a parody of Dryden's *The Hind and the Panther*, entitled *The Town and Country Mouse*. He afterwards produced an imitation of *Hudibras* called *Alma*, and a long and very serious poem, *Solomon*. But his light society verses, which are not always very proper, but are generally lively and graceful, are the only portions of his work which now survive. Far better known than Prior, John Gay (1685–1732), an intimate friend of Swift and Pope, wrote *Fables* which still keep their place in anthologies; a series of six pastorals, *The Shepherd's Week*, which, though conceived in the spirit of burlesque, are much truer to the facts of rustic life than the sham pastorals of Pope; *Trivia*, a humorous description of the London streets; and a travesty of the then immensely popular Italian opera, *The Beggar's Opera*, which took the 'Town' by storm. Very different in character and genius was Edward Young (1683–1765), a most contemptible person, who wrote much in various styles, including satires in Pope's manner, and tragedies, but who long maintained a popularity far exceeding his deserts as the author of *Night Thoughts*, a gloomy and un-wholesome poem, full of copybook moralisings couched in florid and pompous verse, but with occasional passages of undeniable power. One point about it is historically significant; like another sombre production of the same 'churchyard' school, *The Grave*, by a Scotch poet, ROBERT BLAIR (1699–1746), it is written, not in the prevailing classic couplet, but in blank verse. A descriptive poem, *The Chase*, by WILLIAM SOMERVILLE (1675–1742) is another early specimen of the same form. The mock-heroic *The Dispensary* of SIR SAMUEL GARTH (1661–1719), a satire on the Society of Apothecaries, has little interest for us now, but it may be mentioned as an illustration of the taste of the age.

14

The Age of Pope:
Prose and Drama

63. Defoe. Taking the chief prose writers of Pope's age roughly in their chronological order, we come first to DANIEL DEFOE (1661–1731). This singular man was the son of a well-to-do butcher, who did business in the very heart of the city of London; was trained for the nonconformist ministry; abandoned divinity for practical life; and in the course of a long and adventurous career was hosier, tile factor, foreign trades-man, printer, volunteer trooper, confidant to the king, inmate of a Newgate cell, government spy, a fugitive from political prosecution and a hero in the pillory of a sympathetic mob. A born journalist and pamphleteer, he wrote with extra-ordinary facility and effect on an infinite variety of subjects, and though no complete list of his publications has ever been drawn up, they are said to number more than 250. He had the keenest sense of what the public wanted, and, keeping his eye on the market, he seized upon whatever promised to make good 'copy', and turned it to account while popular interest was still hot. At the same time he was avowedly a moral and social reformer, and aimed to correct and teach his age. He owes his importance in literature, however, mainly to his works of fiction which were simply the offshoot of his general journalistic enterprises. For many years he had been busy manufacturing lives of people who chanced for one or another reason to engage the public attention—of famous men who had just died, and of notorious adventurers and criminals. These so-called biographies were written at the moment for the moment, and were very loosely put together, with slight regard to accuracy. He had thus only to drop the framework of history to develop the special form of prose fiction in which at sixty he entered upon a new phase of his diversified career. As one of his critics has said—'From writing biographies with real names attached to them it was but a short step to writing biographies with fictitious names.' This step he took with the publication of *The Life and Adventures of Robinson Crusoe*, which is one of the books which everybody is supposed to have read. The success of this proved that he had opened up a profitable new vein, and after his habit, Defoe proceeded to work this vein with the utmost industry, producing *The Memoirs of a Cavalier*, *Captain Singleton*, *Moll Flanders*, *Colonel Jack*, and *Roxana*. His *Journal of the Plague Year*, though professedly the genuine record of an eye-witness, and long accepted as such, is in reality a fabrication, and must therefore also be classed as fiction. As this remarkable feat of pseudo-history reminds us, Defoe to the very last gave out his made-up stories as true stories, and took infinite pains to convince his readers of the authenticity of his narratives. It is for this reason that we may best describe them in the phrase used, as 'fictitious biographies', or, in Sir Leslie Stephen's words, as 'history *minus* the facts'. This detail is important, because, it helps us to understand Defoe's peculiar method and the characteristic quality of his work. His fictions were still thrown into biographical form, and no attempt was made towards the organisation of the materials into a systematic plot; and, since it was his object at all times to give to his inventions the air and sem-blance of truth, his stories are told as if they were stories of actual life, in the plain, matter-of-fact, business-like way appropriate to stories of actual life, and with a studious avoidance of everything suggestive of artifice. Hence the extraordinary minute realism which is recognised as an outstanding feature of his fiction. His homely, easy, colloquial style lent itself admirably to his purpose. Defoe's great importance in the history of the English novel is universally admitted, though there is some dispute as to the exact significance of his contribution to its development. On this question, however, we will say something when we come to deal in a later chapter with the establishment of the novel shortly after his death.

64. Swift. Next in sequence comes JONATHAN SWIFT (1667–1745), by far the most powerful and original genius of his age. His life was one of the most tragic in our literary annals. Born of English parents in Ireland, he became in 1689 confidential secretary to Sir William Temple at Moor Park, Surrey. In 1694 he was presented to the living of Kilroot, near Belfast. After two years he returned to Moor Park, and on Temple's death in 1699 became Vicar of Laracor in Ireland. He was soon a great power in politics, first on the Whig and then on the Tory side, and made his mark as a pamphleteer. Preferred to the Deanery of St. Patrick's, Dublin, in 1714, he espoused the cause of the Irish people, by whom he was so idolised that the Lord Lieutenant humorously complained that he governed Ireland only by Dr. Swift's permission. He had for many years suffered from recurrent attacks of a mysterious brain disease which made him the victim of fearful agony and even more fearful melancholia. In 1736 the disaster he had long foreseen occurred, and his mind began to give way; little by little he lost his memory completely; but he lingered on in almost unbroken misery for some years, till death at last brought him a merciful release. Mental disease had undoubtedly not a little to do with Swift's ferociously pessimistic temper, but we must also remember that he was an enormously ambitious man, the failure of whose ambitions filled him with bitterness of spirit. His relations with three women also had their part in his unhappiness. The most important of these was Esther Johnson, or Stella, as he called her, whom he first met at Temple's when he was a young man and she hardly more than a child. Whether or not a private marriage ever took place between them is one of the puzzles of an obscure love-story. But we know that he was passionately devoted to her, and that her death in 1728 was a blow from which he never recovered. His *Journal to Stella*, a narrative of his life in London during the time of his greatest political activity and influence, and never intended for publication, is a wonderful revelation of the real tenderness which lay concealed in the depths of his fierce and domineering nature.

Swift is one of the greatest of English prose writers. As a master of simple, direct, colloquial style—a style as far as possible removed from the ornate and the rhetorical—he has few rivals and no superior. His special field was satire and his favourite instrument irony, which is the art of saying one thing in order to convey another. The skill with which, nominally adopting a position entirely alien from his own, he proceeds gravely and without once dropping the mask, to pour ridicule upon the very cause he is apparently supporting, is simply amazing. An excellent illustration will be found in his *Argument to prove that the Abolishing of Christianity in England may...be attended with Some Inconveniences*, in which, writing ostensibly as one who admits that 'the system of the gospel... is generally antiquated and exploded', he makes a scathing attack both upon the free-thinkers and upon the insincere professors of the current religion. On a larger scale *The Battle of the Books* and *A Tale of a Tub* (both published in 1704, though written some years earlier) take rank among the finest prose satires in the language. The former grew out of a controversy, in which Sir William Temple had taken a prominent part, concerning the respective merits of ancient and modern literatures, and is chiefly occupied, not with the substantial issues involved, but with the discomfiture of Temple's personal opponents. The mock-heroic description of the great battle in the King's Library between the rival hosts, is a masterpiece of its kind. The *Tale of a Tub*, beyond all other books of the writer, contains the essence of his thought and style. It was designed to champion the Protestant Church against the pretensions of the Church of Rome and the extravagances of the dissenting sects, and to exhibit the corruptions of modern Christianity. This purpose is carried out under the form of an allegorical story, the principal figures in which are the three brothers, Peter, Martin, and Jack, standing respectively for the Roman Church, the English Church, and the Calvinists, or dissenters. Scarcely half the work, however, is connected with this central theme, the rest being composed of apologies, introductions, dedications, and digressions. But these subsidiary sections, dealing with the abuses of learning and other kindred subjects, contain some of Swift's most trenchant and characteristic writing. He himself said that the aim of the book was to reconcile divinity with wit; but the wit is so pungent and the satire so terrific that the general impression left is that of utter irreverence in the handling of sacred things. One other work of Swift stands in a sense apart—*Gulliver's Travels*—because, while the rest of his production is read by students only, these, like *Robinson Crusoe*, are amongst the enduringly popular things in English literature. As a matter of fact, however, in purpose and spirit the *Travels*, as he himself said, are of a piece with all his writings, and were erected upon the 'great foundations' of that misanthropy which was the basis of his thought. This most delightful of children's books, therefore, turns out on closer inspection to be one of the bitterest satires on mankind ever penned, and we note as a significant point, the deepening of the satire as we pass from each one to the next of the four parts of which it is composed. In the Voyage to Lilliput, which is largely concerned with the English politics of the time, we have an exposure of the infinite littleness and absurd pretensions of man. In the Voyage to Brobdingnag, in which Gulliver becomes the pigmy, the same moral is driven well home, while the contempt of the writer becomes more marked. In the Voyage to Laputa, Swift scornfully attacks philosophers, projectors, and inventors, and all who waste their energies in the pursuit of visionary and fantastic things. His incidental interpretation of history and the episode of the Struldbrugs—a race of wretched creatures doomed to immortality—show the darkening of his thought. Finally, in the Voyage to the Country of the Houyhnhnms and Yahoos, Swift tears away all the accessories and artifices of civilization and puts 'that animal called man' before us as he himself saw him, sunk so deep in degradation as to be little better than a brute. The *Travels*, like the rest of Swift's work, reveal him as essentially a man of his time in his want of spiritual quality, in his distrust of the visionary and the extra-vagant, and in his thoroughly materialistic view of life. At one most important point, however, he stands out as an exception. His age was an age of flippant and shallow optimism— the optimism of the *Essay on Man*. Swift, on the contrary, was a profound pessimist.

65. Addison and Steele. The names of JOSEPH ADDISON (1672–1719) and SIR RICHARD STEELE (1673–1729) are always associated on account of their collaboration in the periodical essay. Just of an age, they met as boys at the Charterhouse, and afterwards as young men at Oxford. Then Steele went into the army, later threw himself with characteristic ardour into politics, and after many ups and downs and much buffeting by fortune, died in Wales, having, as Thackeray says, 'outlived his places, his schemes, his wife, his income, his health, and almost everything but his kind heart'. Addison meanwhile gained a high reputation for classical scholarship, made the Grand Tour of Europe as a preparation for diplomacy, entered the House of Commons, was Chief Secretary for Ireland and for a year Secretary of State, and died ten years before his friend. Their characters were curiously contrasted. Steele was a thorough Bohemian, easy-going, thriftless, careless, but full of generosity and sympathy and with an honest love of what is pure and good. Addison was an urbane and polished gentleman, of exquisite refinement of taste and lofty ideas of rectitude and piety, but shy, self-conscious, and a little remote and austere. These striking differences of temperament and outlook, however, were of the greatest value to both, when they came to join forces in the field of the periodical essay. Outside that field, both men did a good deal of miscellaneous work. Of Steele's comedies and Addison's one tragedy, however, we will say a word presently, while of the latter's once famous poem, *The Campaign*, which was written to celebrate the victory at Blenheim, and proved to be its author's passport to political advancement, it is enough to record that the praise once lavished upon it seems absolutely ridiculous now. For the moment, then, we are concerned with Addison and Steele as essayists only. Here Steele, who was always the more originative genius, led the way by the foundation of *The Tatler*, the first of the long line of eighteenth century periodical essays. This was followed by the most famous of them, *The Spectator*, in which Addison, who had contributed to his friend's former enterprise, now became the chief partner. It began on March 1, 1711, was published daily, Sundays excepted, and ran till December 6, 1712; though some eighteen months later it was revived by Addison alone, and issued three times a week from June 18 to December 20, 1714. In its complete form it contains 635 essays. Of these Addison wrote 274 and Steele 240, the remaining 121 being the work of various friends.

The ethical importance of what Addison and Steele together did through the medium of the periodical essay could not well be overstated, while their method too is highly significant. They set themselves as moralists to break down two opposed influences—that of the profligate Restoration tradition of loose living and loose thinking on the one hand, and that of Puritan fanaticism and bigotry on the other. Their method was admirably adapted to their purpose. They did not indulge in sweeping condemnations and unqualified invectives, as, greatly to the damage of their cause, the Puritan moralists habitually did; they wrote good-humouredly, met all classes of readers on their own ground, and made ample allowance for the ordinary failings of humanity; but at the same time they consistently advocated the claims of decency and sound sense. It was, moreover, by their use of wit, humour, and satire that they scored most. In post-Restoration literature these had commonly been employed in the service of vice and to make decency and sound sense look ridiculous. Addison and Steele turned the tables upon the scoffers, and got the laugh on the other side; and the gain was enormous. Thus they did much to set the conscience of their time right on the fundamental questions of social and domestic conduct, and for this reason they occupy a high place in the history of English manners during the first half of the eighteenth century. Nor is this all. They wrote with an educational as well as with a purely moral aim, and it was always one of their objects to extend and popularise general culture. Thus they discussed (always in a light and engaging way) art, philosophy, the drama, and poetry, and sought in so doing not only to interest the general reader in such subjects, but also to guide and develop his taste. It was in *The Spectator*, for example, that Addison first published his series of eighteen papers on *Paradise Lost*, by which he helped to spread among English people a better appreciation of Milton and his work. In particular, they addressed themselves avowedly and directly to women; and at a time when women in society were as a rule immersed in the mere trivialities of existence, they did their best to draw them into the currents of the larger intellectual life.

One other aspect of *The Spectator* deserves attention. When Addison and Steele wrote their daily miscellany, no lively picture had appeared in our literature (outside the drama) of men and manners in the ordinary social world of their time. In the many papers in which they dealt with the leading figures of the Spectator Club, and especially, with the eccentricities of the delightful Tory squire, Sir Roger de Coverley, our essayists painted such a picture, and painted it admirably. For more than a century before this, satirists in verse and prose had been cultivating what is known as 'character writing', taking the *Characters* of the Greek Theophrastus as their model.[13] These formal studies of types were often clever, but they were mere lay figures, without reality or life. In the hands of Addison and Steele,

---

[13]The *Characters* of Sir Thomas Overbury (1581–1613), the *Characters of Virtues and Vices* by Joseph Hall (1574–1656), and the *Microcosmographie* of John Earle (1601?–65) are the principal examples of this sort of writing. Such detailed portraits as those, for instance, in Dryden's satires are really 'characters' of this kind, set in a framework and individualised.

the seventeenth century character study became personal and vital; instead of catalogues of qualities, we have actual men moving amid real scenes and taking part in various incidents. Though in the scattered papers of the *Spectator* we cannot look for that sustained interest which is essential to a novel, this large development in characterisation must still be regarded as a stage in the evolution of the genuine novel. It is scarcely too much to say that in many of the *Spectator* papers, in which scenes from the life of Sir Roger are described, we have the modern novel in germ.

66. Other Prose Writers of the Period. The Age of Pope was richer in prose than in verse, and in general its prose is much more interesting. Among writers of the second rank the most attractive is Pope's friend, JOHN ARBUTHNOT (1667–1735), a distinguished physician, and a kind as well as witty man. As testimony to his personal character it will suffice to quote Swift's declaration that if the world possessed but a dozen Arbuthnots he would burn his *Gulliver's Travels.* He wrote among other things a very clever satire, *The History of John Bull,* which is noteworthy, if only because it created that now traditional type of the true-born Englishman. Another of Pope's friends, Henry St. John, Lord Bolingbroke (1678–1751), wrote on politics and philosophy in an agreeable though rather showy style. Francis Atterbury (1662–1732) was also one of Pope's intimate associates, and, though his sermons and miscellaneous writings are now forgotten, he figures prominently through his relations with others in the literary history of the time. The lively COLLEY CIBBER (1671–1757), the hero of the second version of Pope's *Dunciad,* must properly be classed among the playwrights, but may be mentioned here on the strength of his entertaining *Apology,* or autobiography. ANTHONY, third LORD SHAFTESBURY (1671–1713), the grandson of Dryden's Achitophel; GEORGE BERKELEY (1685–1753), and JOSEPH BUTLER (1692–1752), belong to the special literature of philosophy and theology; but the influence of the Deistic Shaftesbury's *Characteristics* in popularising the optimism which was later expressed in the *Essay on Man* was so great, while the reputation of Berkeley's *Principles of Human Knowledge* and of Butler's *Analogy of Religion*, is so high, that they could hardly be passed over without a word.

67. Drama. The drama of Pope's age is of slight importance, and the little that has to be said about it here will have reference only to its broad historical interest. From the literary point of view the most noteworthy work in tragedy was done by ADDISON in his *Cato*, which was an attempt to introduce to the English stage the decorous and rhetorical drama of the French School. It contains a few rather fine passages, but its versification is stiff, its declamations chilling, and its characters lifeless. The most significant thing about the comedy of the time as a whole is its well-marked determination to purify itself from the licentiousness of the Restoration drama. This effort is associated with the names of COLLEY CIBBER, whose constant coarseness does not altogether hide his moral intentions; MRS. CENTLIVRE (1667–1723); and particularly STEELE, whose four plays (the best of which, *The Constant Lovers*, was his last performance of any moment) are in fact so over-weighted with ethical purpose as to be, in spite of their occasional humour, insipid and dull. Forgetting that the first business of comedy is to amuse and not to preach, Steele turned his stage into a sort of lay-pulpit, and became the founder of that highly genteel, didactic, and vapid kind of play which is known as Sentimental Comedy and which long kept possession of the boards. Here we have a capital illustration of the general truth that strong reactions always tend to extremes. With this Sentimental Comedy we may connect the experiment of GEORGE LILLO (1693–1739), in his *London | Merchant, or History of George Barnwell*, and *Fatal Curiosity*, to establish a 'domestic drama', or form of tragedy the characters and incidents of which were to be taken from common life instead of from history or romance. Lillo was a tradesman and a nonconformist, and his didactic stress (which we may trace directly to his Puritanism) is another sign of the power of that middle-class moral spirit which we have marked elsewhere in the literature of the period under review.

TABLE OF THE AGE OF POPE

Verse	Prose	Drama
		Steele's *The Funeral*, 170
		Steele's *The Lying Lover*, 1703
Addison's *The Campaign*, 1704	Swift's *Battle of the Books* and *Tale of a Tub*, 1704	
	Traherne, d. 1704	Steele's *The Tender Husband*, 1705
Pope's *Pastorals*, 1709	*The Tatler*, 1709–11	
	Berkeley's *Principles of Human Knowledge*, 1710	
Pope's *Essay on Criticism*, 1711	*The Spectator*, 1711–12 and 1714	
	Shaftesbury's *Characteristics*, 1711	
Pope's *Rape of the Lock*, 1712	Arbuthnot's *History of John Bull*, 1713	Addison's *Cato*, 1713
Gay's *Shepherd's Week*, 1714		
Gay's *Trivia*, 1715		
Pope's *Homer*, 1715–25		
Prior's *Poems*, 1718		
	Death of Addison, 1719	
	Defoe's *Robinson Crusoe*, Part I, 1719	
	Defoe's other novels, 1720–25	
Young's *Universal Passion* (satires), 1725		Steele's *The Conscious Lovers*, 1722

Thomson's *Seasons*, 1726–30	Swift's *Gulliver's Travels*, 1726–27	
Gay's *Fables*, 1727		
Pope's *The Dunciad*, 1728 (4th edition, 1742)		Gay's *Beggar's Opera*, 1728
	Death of Steele, 1729	
Pope's *Moral Essays*, 1732–35	Death of Defoe, 1731	Lillo's *The London Merchant*, 1731
Pope's *Essay on Man*, 1732–34		
Pope's *Imitations of Horace*, 1733–37		
Pope's *Epistle to Arbuthnot*, 1735		
	Butler's *Analogy*, 1736	
Young's *Night Thoughts*, 1742		
Blair's *The Grave*, 1742		
Death of Pope, 1744		
	Death of Swift, 1745	

15

The Age of Johnson
(1745–1798):
General Prose

68. The Age of Johnson. We do not advance far into the history of the second half of the eighteenth century before we become aware that profound changes are taking place in the spirit of English society. We have seen that in their moral reaction against the licence which had followed the Restoration, the men of Pope's time had settled down into formalism, taking as their guiding principle the rule of reason and good sense. So deeply had they come to distrust the emotions that the whole atmosphere of their lives and writings became hard and dry. Their dread of earnestness and enthusiasm also gave a tone of flippancy and often of cynicism to their thought. Pope's ridiculous optimism expresses the easy-going mood of a self-complacent age; the kindly, but thin and superficial, social criticism of Addison and Steele reveals the same temper in a different form; while the fierce misanthropy of Swift, striking a discordant note, is in part at least to be interpreted as the measureless scorn of a strong man for that petty world about him, which had none the less bound him down as his own Gulliver had been bound down by the Lilliputians. The new generation now in its turn reacted against the smug self-complacency, the chilliness, and the aridity of the preceding age. They found themselves discontent with the way in which their fathers had looked at life, with their formalism, their narrowness of sympathy, and their controlling ideals. Weary of the long-continued artificiality, they began to crave something more natural and spontaneous in thought and language. They awoke to a sense that in a world of wonder and mystery there were many things undreamt of in the shallow philosophy of the Augustan school. In particular, they were quickened into fresh activity by the renaissance of the feelings. This is perhaps beyond all others the one capital fact in the history of this period of transition. The emotions, long repressed, were now reinstated, and all life was modified in consequence. We see this in the case of religion. In Pope's time, as we have noted, religion itself, partaking of the general tendencies of contemporary society, had been formal, utilitarian, and unspiritual. In the great evangelistic revival, led by Wesley and Whitefield, the old formality was swept away, the utilitarianism abandoned, and a mighty tide of spiritual energy poured into the church and out among the masses of the people. The preachers of the last age, as we have said, had sought rather to convince by argument than to move by feeling, and their discourses had been carefully written essays, characterised by decorum, reserve, and a thorough recognition of the proprieties. The evangelists, on the contrary, made their appeal directly to the emotional nature and in extemporaneous discourses, and by their impassioned tones and gestures they showed that they cared nothing for decorum and the proprieties where the eternal destiny of the soul was at stake. The immense success of Handel's *Messiah* on its first London performance in 1743, may be taken as another index of the coming change.

A natural accompaniment (part cause, part effect) of this revival in religion was a widening and deepening sympathy with man as man. The spread of the humanitarian spirit, and the increasing frequency and vigour of the protests which were now made not only against the brutality of society, but also against its general callousness, are historically of much importance. But all these things were simply aspects of one great comprehensive movement—the rapid growth of democracy. More than ever before, the individual man was now recognised in his essential manhood and the stress laid upon those qualities of character which have nothing to do with factitious associations of birth and breeding. As the century ran its course, social and political unrest became more and more marked. All sorts of new and explosive ideas filled the air. People became increasingly familiar with the notions of liberty, equality, and the rights of man, and increasingly alive to the countless absurdities and evils of the existing social state. The passionate attacks of the great French writer, Rousseau,[1] upon civilisation and all its idols, and his fiery gospel of 'back to nature', sent a strange thrill through the whole European world. Turn where we may in these closing decades of the century, signs of vast upheaval are apparent. Across the Atlantic a new Republic springs into being, the foundation principle of which is that men are born free and equal. Only a little later, the great storm which had long been gathering over France, bursts in the Revolution.

[1] Rousseau was born at Geneva, but he is always classed among French writers.

That the literature of such a half-century will reveal in many ways the conflict of old ideas and new, the steady triumph of the new, and the profound changes of mood which resulted, must of course be obvious. Looking at this literature from the more purely literary point of view, we may also expect to find that it exhibits a struggle between the powerful traditions of the Augustan age and various opposed theories, and, with the gradual failure in prestige of the classic school, the establishment of a literature essentially different from this in respect alike of matter, spirit, and form. Though in the history of the literature of the Age of Johnson there is much which at first sight seems confusing, we shall not, I think, find it difficult to mark out the main lines of its evolution.

69. Johnson. The greatest English man of letters between Pope and Wordsworth, SAMUEL JOHNSON was born at Lich-field in 1709. From his father, a bookseller, he inherited his huge, unwieldy, unhealthy frame, and that 'vile melancholy' of disposition which was to throw a gloom over so much of his life. The elder Johnson died on the verge of bankruptcy; Samuel acted for a time as a school usher; did some translation for a Birmingham publisher; married a widow twenty years his senior; and, having sunk what little money she brought him in a futile attempt to establish a school of his own, resolved to try his fortunes in London. He reached the metropolis in 1737 with twopence halfpenny in his pocket, having as his companion one of his late pupils, David Garrick, presently to be famous as the greatest actor of his time. In 1738 he published a poem called *London,* and formed a connection with *Cave's Magazine,* to which for a number of years he regularly contributed the parliamentary reports, though he himself was never in the gallery of the House, and merely worked up his debates from the notes of others. Amid much miscellaneous drudgery, during the next few years he produced the *Vanity of Human Wishes* (1749) and a tragedy, *Irene* (1749), on the neo-classic model; and in March, 1750, started a periodical, *The Rambler,* in imitation of *The Spectator,* which appeared on Tuesdays and Saturdays till March, 1752; all save five numbers being from his own pen. This was followed later by two other series—*The Adventurer* and *The Idler.* Meanwhile he was occupied for eight years (1747–55) by an immense task—*A Dictionary of the English Language,* in which he undertook not only to define, but also to illustrate his definitions by quotations taken from the whole range of English literature. Though weak in etymology and philology (subjects which were then in their infancy), this work laid the foundation of English lexicography. Johnson's magnificent letter to Lord Chesterfield, to whom he had addressed his prospectus, and who neglected him entirely till his labours were near completion, dealt the deathblow to the whole eighteenth century system of patronage. The *Dictionary* made him independent, and when somewhat later he received a pension of £300 a year, his struggles and anxieties were over. He now became the acknowledged Dictator, or as Smollett called him, 'the Great Cham' of literature, and night by night in the famous club founded by him in 1764, and in which he sat surrounded by such men as Goldsmith, Sir Joshua Reynolds the great painter, Burke, Gibbon, Sir William Jones the orientalist, Garrick, and Boswell, he had ample opportunity for the exercise of his unmatched conversational and controversial powers. He published his didactic tale, *Rasselas,* in 1759; an edition of Shakespeare in 1765; an account of his tour to the Hebrides with Boswell under the title of *Journey to the Western Islands of Scotland* in 1775, and his largest and also his greatest work, *The Lives of the Most Eminent English Poets with Critical Observations on their Works* in 1779–81. He died in 1784, and was buried in Westminster Abbey.

In one particular the case of Johnson is peculiar. As Macaulay put it, 'the memory of other authors is kept alive by their works, but the memory of Johnson keeps many of his works alive.' Though with one or two exceptions his writings are today commonly neglected, no other English author is so intimately known to us. This is because he lives in the pages of his biography by his hero-worshipping friend, James Boswell (1740–95), the greatest book of the kind in our own or any other literature. Every detail of his oddly compounded but powerful personality is there portrayed for us; his countless eccentricities of behaviour; his fits of moroseness and downright brutality; his tenderness and warmth of heart; his wonderful shrewdness and wisdom; his fine mental honesty and hatred of all forms of cant; his bigotry, intolerance, and childish prejudices; his prodigious memory; his quickness of grasp and repartee; his extraordinary genius for talk. Yet, though it may be admitted that Johnson owes his present fame mainly to Boswell, it is a mistake to ignore his own books, for he was a very great writer. Though at each point we have to recognise his well-marked limitations, he was great both as a critic of literature and as a critic of life. As a critic of literature he is almost always penetrating and stimulating, though he sometimes allowed his strong prejudices to interfere with his judgment; as when he failed to appreciate the value of Milton's poetry, because of his antipathy to Milton's politics and religion. In all his tastes and standards he was a thorough-going conservative, holding fast to the principles of the Augustan school of poetry, and stoutly resisting every movement of revolt against what he regarded as the orthodox literary creed. But to this matter we shall have to return later, when we shall also have something to say about the technical side of his own poetry. As a moralist he is characterized by remarkable sanity and massive commonsense. Broadly speaking, he is a pessimist. 'Life', he declared, 'is a progress from want to want, not from enjoyment to enjoyment'; we are stirred into activity by a feeling of its 'vocabulary, we speed our energies for the most part in the pursuit of chimerical pleasures; and when our desires are gratified, the usual result is satiety. He develops these views in many of his miscellaneous writings, and most notably in two of his finest works, the *Vanity of Human Wishes* and *Rasselas*. The former (an adaptation of the tenth satire of Juvenal) is an impressive sermon on the text which is stated in the title, and which is supported by a number of typical illustrations taken from history. The latter, which is historically significant as a reply to the flimsy optimism of Shaftesbury and Pope, tells of a young Abyssinian prince who sets out to discover the perfect way of life, and from his varied experiences among all kinds of people learns at length that the happiness which they all seek is nowhere to be found. But, while the tone of Johnson's philosophy is thus profoundly sad, there is nothing debilitating about it. Throughout his life he made a most heroic fight against the besetting melancholy which was one consequence of his chronic ill-health, and the steady courage of his own manhood pervades his work. The essence of his teaching is that we should face the facts of existence honestly, and not talk sentimental nonsense about them (as Pope had certainly done), while we bear the evil uncomplainingly and make the most we can of the good. Moreover, as the conclusions of *The Vanity of Human Wishes* and *Rasselas* show, he was saved from utter hopelessness by his strong religious faith.

As a prose writer Johnson did not follow the lead of the Augustan masters, and in place of the easy grace of Addison and the vigorous idiomatic colloquialism of Swift, he gives us a style which is highly

Latinised in vocabulary and in sentence structure is marked by elaborate balance and antithesis. Most readers now feel that his way of writing (or 'Johnsonese', as Macaulay called it) is pompous and heavy. But it is never obscure, and at its best it has great strength, nobility, and dignity.

70. Goldsmith. In the literature of the Johnsonian era the writer who stands nearest to Johnson himself, both in personal and in historical interest, is OLIVER GOLDSMITH. The most eccentric of an eccentric family, Goldsmith was born in 1728 at Pallas, Co. Longford, Ireland, where his father was a Protestant clergyman. In early life he gained an unenviable reputation for wildness and stupidity, and after just contriving to take his degree at Dublin he spent some years in idleness before he was sent by his relatives to Edinburgh to study medicine. From Edinburgh, where his Bohemianism developed unchecked, he went to Leyden, and at Leyden, while nominally pursuing his medical studies, he earned a little money by teaching and lost it all at the gaming tables. Then in 1755 he set out to make the Grand Tour of Europe with one clean shirt, a guinea in his pocket, and his favourite German flute as his equipment. He went through Flanders to Paris, thence to Switzerland, across the Alps, down into Italy as far as Padua (then celebrated for its medical school), and back through France. How he managed to pay his way is still something of a mystery; but for information regarding this question, as well as for details of his experiences, it is probable that we are safe in turning to his poem, *The Traveller,* and to the account of George Primrose's continental wanderings in *The Vicar of Wakefield*. In 1756 he reached London penniless and friendless, and after acting for a time as an apothecary's assistant, and as usher in a Peckham school, he obtained an introduction to Richardson (see §74), became corrector for the press, and so at thirty drifted into literature. His career was mainly that of a hackwriter, and the larger portion of his output belongs to the class of what are popularly known as 'pot-boilers'; though even these have much of the charm of his personality and style. His more substantial work, done meanwhile in the intervals of drudgery, consists of two poems—*The Traveller* (1764) and *The Deserted Village* (1770), one novel, *The Vicar of Wakefield* (1766), and two comedies—*The Good-Natured Man* (1768) and *She Stoops to Conquer* (1773). To these should be added a number of essays, including a series entitled *The Citizen of the World* (1760–62). His friendship with Johnson dates from 1761 or even earlier, and he was one of the original members of the famous Club. The warm relations between the two men, so entirely different in mind and temper, and yet so sympathetic, throws an interesting light on both. It is specially noteworthy that, though Johnson often bullied Goldsmith, he would allow no one else to do so, and that it was Goldsmith who said about Johnson's roughness of manners, that there was nothing of the bear about him but his skin. Slow in conversation and with a perfect genius for blundering, Goldsmith was the laughing-stock of the wits of London's literary world; but he was loved by such men as Burke and Reynolds; and, as Garrick in a mock-epitaph said of him, he 'wrote like an angel' even though he 'talked like poor Poll'. His struggles and vicissitudes continued to the end of his life, and when he died in 1774, he was still deeply in debt. Poor Goldsmith was capricious, vain, and improvident, but he was so large-hearted, sympathetic, and humane that we forget his faults and think of him always with the tenderest affection. As a man of letters he was, in the words of Johnson's Latin epitaph in Westminster Abbey, 'a gentle master' who 'left scarcely any kind of writing untouched, and touched nothing that he did not adorn'.

Goldsmith's work is very miscellaneous in character, and it is as a matter of convenience only that we place him here among general prose writers. Of his one novel and of his poems we will speak elsewhere; but as the drama of the Johnsonian age is hardly important enough in the mass to merit a separate section, we may at once deal with his contributions to the literature of the stage. His two admirable comedies, the later of which still holds its own as an excellent acting play, are historically interesting because they mark a reaction against the dull and vapid moralisings of Sentimental

Comedy, and a return to real humour and life. In this revival of the true comic spirit an equal part was played by Gold-smith's fellow-countryman, RICHARD BRINSLEY SHERIDAN (1751–1816), with his brilliant comedies, *The Rivals* (1775) and *The School for Scandal* (1777).

A striking feature of Goldsmith's original writings (and we must here distinguish between these and his mere compilations) is the strong personal element in all of them. Their peculiar charm is therefore fundamentally the charm of the man himself. More than most men he projected into what he wrote not only his temperament but also his experiences; and a large portion of his imaginative work is really reminiscence, either, as in many passages in *The Citizen of the World* and *The Vicar of Wakefield*, under the thinnest possible disguise, or, as in the case of his two great poems, under no disguise at all. Thus it is easy to discover the originals of most of his best-known characters in his relatives or himself; Dr. Primrose, for example, is certainly his father; the good priest in *The Deserted Village*, his brother Henry; Moses in *The Vicar of Wakefield*, young Honeywood in *The Good-Natured Man*, and Tony Lumpkin in *She Stoops to Conquer*, humorous studies of himself. Yet, though he keeps so near to actual life, he is in no sense a realist. His temperament was, on the contrary, so essentially poetical that everything he takes out of experience undergoes idealisation in his hands. As a critic and theorist he was, if possible, even more consistently conservative than Johnson, and stoutly maintained the supremacy of Pope. This fact will receive further emphasis presently in connection with his poetry. For the moment we may in passing note that his admiration of the Augustan age was shown even in his prose style. Uninfluenced by the more elaborate rhetoric which Johnson had brought into vogue, he wrote in an easy, informal way which, though of course entirely his own, may nonetheless be said to carry on the traditions of Addison and Steele.

71. Other General Prose Writers of the Period. Some of the best prose work of Johnson's age was done in history, a field which was now indeed cultivated with greater success and in a more artistic spirit than ever before in England. DAVID HUME (1711–76), who is even better known as a sceptical philosopher, wrote a *History of England*, which is characterized by polished clearness of style, but greatly marred by carelessness in regard to facts and by strong Tory bias in favour of the Stuarts and against the Puritans. Following the lead of Voltaire, he combined with his political narrative much information concerning civilisation and manners. WILLIAM ROBERTSON (1721–93), a more careful if less brilliant writer, made a great mark with his *History of Scotland*, *History of Charles V*, and *History of America*. But incomparably the greatest historian of the time was EDWARD GIBBON (1737–94), whose *History of the Decline and Fall of the Roman Empire* remains one of the acknowledged masterpieces of historical literature. The origin of this monumental work may be given in the author's own words: 'It was at Rome, on the 15th October 1764, as I sat musing amongst the ruins of the Capitol, while the bare-footed friars were singing vespers in the Temple of Jupiter, that the idea of writing the decline and fall of the city first started to my mind.' Gibbon's record begins with the reign of Titus, a.d. 98, and closes with the capture of Constantinople by the Turks in 1453. He thus built a 'Roman road' through fourteen centuries. In the execution of this vast design he united laborious research, painstaking accuracy, and the most wonderful power of organizing enormous and chaotic masses of material into a well-ordered whole. The only serious faults which can be found with him are, that he lacks feeling and sympathy, that (partly in consequence of this) he deals inadequately with the religious aspects of his subject and especially with the whole question of Christianity, and that his style is too monotonously laboured and grandiose. But, as a recognised authority, the late E. A. Freeman said of him, Gibbon 'remains the one historian of the 18th century whom modern research has neither set aside nor threatened to set aside'.

As Gibbon's is the great name in the historical prose of the period, so its great name in political prose is that of EDMUND BURKE (1729–97). A man of noble nature and extraordinary breadth of outlook, Burke carried into political controversy passionate moral earnestness, vivid imagination, and splendid logical powers, while his rich and highly wrought rhetorical style gave a gorgeous colouring to everything he wrote. His principles were those of philosophic conservatism, and a profound sense of historical continuity was one of the central elements of his thought. He supported the cause of the American colonies in his speeches *On American Taxation* (1774), and *On Conciliation with America* (1775), and bitterly opposed the French Revolution in his *Reflections* (1790), *Letter to a Noble Lord* (1790) and *Letters on a Regicide Peace* (1796–97). The first of these was answered by THOMAS PAINE (1737–1809) in his *Rights of Man*. But the *Thoughts on the Present Discontents* may perhaps be regarded as the most permanently interesting of Burke's political writings. His early *Inquiry into the Origin of our Ideas of the Sublime and Beautiful* (1757) is the first important English treatise on aesthetics. Burke was also at one time suspected of writing the seventy letters, filled with fierce invective against the government, which appeared, between 1768 and 1772 over the signature 'Junius', and which, though the mystery of their authorship has never been completely cleared up, are now generally attributed to SIR PHILIP FRANCIS (1740–1818). If Burke was the great English representative of the conservative attitude towards the French Revolution, its most conspicuous philosophical supporter was WILLIAM GODWIN (1756–1836), whose *Inquiry concerning Political Justice,* setting forth the most extreme revolutionary ideas with all the calmness of a mathematical demonstration, exercised, as we shall see later, an enormous influence upon the younger generation.

During Johnson's age there was also great activity in the literature of theology, philosophy, and political economy, but the work done in these fields was too special in character to be included here. In lighter prose the most important names are those of the letter-writers, for letter-writing was at this time assiduously cultivated both as a pastime and as an art. Of these, three call for mention—LADY MARY WORTLEY MONTAGU (1689–1762), PHILIP DORMER STANHOPE, EARL OF CHESTERFIELD (1694–1773), and HORACE WALPOLE (1717–97). The letters of Lady Mary cover a period of nearly half a century, and are almost equally readable throughout, but they are perhaps particularly interesting when they deal in the author's characteristically vivacious way with her varied experiences abroad. Those of Chesterfield, addressed to his son, were intended as a manual in polite behaviour for the young man's guidance, and their tone is that of the typical man of the world. Those of Walpole are exceedingly amusing as a lively chronicle of social doings, politics, personalities, scandals, and small talk, in the charmed circles in which that dilettante trifler played his part; but their flippancy, their triviality of style, and their frequent spitefulness, give us a rather poor impression of his character. His name will come up again presently in connection with the novel.

# 16

The Age of Johnson:
The Novel

72. Prose Fiction in England before Richardson. Though it is impossible to dogmatise, and useless to quarrel about the actual beginnings in England of that particular kind of prose fiction which we now call the novel, it is quite safe to say that its firm establishment and assured popularity date from the age of Johnson, and may indeed be accounted the greatest achievement of that age. It may also be fairly contended that it was with Richardson that prose fiction passed definitely into its modern form. We will here, therefore, take his work as a fresh point of departure. But a rapid survey of the evolution of English fiction before his time is necessary, in order that we may place him in his proper historical position.

We have seen that a certain amount of prose fiction had been produced during the age of Shakespeare, notwithstanding the fact that imaginative energy had then found its chief outlet in the drama. Most of this fiction had been purely romantic, as with Sidney, Lodge, and Greene; or didactic, as with More, Lyly, and Bacon; but a slight tendency to realism had been shown in the picaresque work of Nash. A little later, the long-winded Heroic Romance—a strange compound of sham chivalry, sham pastoralism, pseudo-history, and the extra-vagant gallantry of a sophisticated society—was imported from France, where for the moment it was immensely popular, and, along with many other French fashions, enjoyed a temporary vogue on English soil. Then, in reaction against the terrible prolixity and absolute unreality of this type, Aphra Behn (1640–89), and several other women-writers, began to cultivate a form of story which was marked by brevity and concentration of treatment, and which, while still radically conventional in matter and method, showed by contrast, a certain desire to get back to truth and nature. Meanwhile a number of extraneous influences were at work, all contributing, as we can now see, to the transformation of prose fiction into something which, despite all superficial similarities, was to be essentially unlike any of its previous varieties; among them, as we have noted, the work of the Character-writers, and, much more important, of Addison and Steele in the periodical essay. Moreover, Bunyan's marvellously effective use of fiction as allegory has to be recognised, and emphasis must also be laid upon the increasing popularity of biography, the forms and methods of which, it is evident, could very easily be carried over from historical into fictitious narrative. This is a matter which, as we remember, is of special interest in connection with the tales of Defoe; and here the question, already touched upon, definitely confronts us, of the place which Defoe occupies in the evolution of fiction. That by rejecting as he did all the fantastic conventions of romance, and adopting with studious preciseness the manner and tone of actual biography, he came very near indeed to the genuine novel, cannot be denied. Yet, nonetheless, it may still be maintained that he just missed his way. His tales are so far removed from normal life and character, they deal so largely with strange adventure and crime, and the picaresque element in them is so strong, that, speaking strictly, it would seem that they should be classed rather as romances than as novels. This indeed is a question of mere nomenclature, and no great importance needs to be attached to it. But recognition of the qualities of Defoe's art will at least help to bring the peculiar character of Richardson's work into relief. Before him, a good deal had been done in prose fiction along many lines. But no one, not even Defoe, had yet written a novel of contemporary social and domestic life, the interest of which should depend upon the doings of ordinary people in a familiar setting. Such a novel Richardson produced in *Pamela*; and it is in view of the fresh movement which he thus initiated that he may not unjustly be called the father of the modern novel.

73. Historical Significance of the Novel. Before we turn to Richardson, however, we may fittingly pause to lay stress upon the great historical significance of the novel from both the literaral and social points of view. The following points should be carefully considered. In the first place, the popularity of the novel, like that of the periodical essay which immediately preceded it, coincided with, and very largely depended upon, the growth of a miscellaneous reading public, and of a public in which women were becoming increasingly numerous and influential. Secondly, as practically a new form of literary art, the novel was a sign that literature was beginning to outgrow the cramping limitations of classicism, and to abandon the doctrine that modern genius was bound to go in the leading-strings of tradition. In the epic and the drama it was impossible as yet that men should reject altogether the authority of antiquity. In the novel that authority could be ignored. There was indeed, as notably in Fielding's case, some discussion of technical questions from the classicist standpoint and an occasional parade of classical learning. But, in general, the novel offered a fresh field, in which modern writers were able to work independently. Thirdly, the rise of the novel was one result of the democratic movement in eighteenth century England. The romance, like tragedy, had been almost consistently aristocratic in the range of its interests and characters; and even Defoe, while he repudiated romantic conventions in this as in all other respects, still, as we have said, held aloof from the ordinary social world, merely substituting adventurers and criminals for princes and Arcadian shepherds. The comprehensiveness of the novel, its free treatment of the characters and doings of all sorts and conditions of men, and especially its sympathetic handling of middle-class and low life, are unmistakable evidences of its democratic quality. It was not by accident, therefore, that it appeared at a time when, under Sir Robert Walpole's firm rule, this country was settling down after a long period of military excitement, and when, with the consequent growth of commerce and industry, the prestige of the old feudal nobility was on the wane, and the middle classes were increasing steadily in social and political power. As Lord Morley has said of *Pamela*, it was the 'landmark of a great social, no less than a great literary transition, when all England went mad with enthusiasm over the trials, the virtues, the triumphs, of a rustic lady's maid'. Finally, as the form of the novel gives a far wider scope than is allowed by the corresponding form of the drama for the treatment of motives, feelings, and all the phenomena of the inner life, it tended from the first to take a peculiar place as the typical art-form of the introspective and analytical modern world.

74. Richardson. SAMUEL RICHARDSON (1689–1761), a prosperous printer, and an embodiment of all the proprieties, had reached the age of 50 without realising any vocation for authorship, and then drifted by mere accident into the production of an epoch-making book. Two friends of his who were publishers asked him to prepare for them 'a little volume of letters in a common style', as models for 'country readers who were unable to indite for themselves', and at his suggestion—for moral considerations were always uppermost in his mind—guidance in conduct was to be combined with instruction in the art of composition. He had hardly embarked upon his task when a true story he had heard many years before came to his mind, and he conceived the idea of using this as a thread upon which to string his letters. Then the thought occurred to him that such a story (I quote his own words), 'if written in an easy and natural manner, suitable to the simplicity of it, might possibly introduce a new species of writing,...turn young people into a course of reading different from the pomp and parade of romance writing, and...tend to promote the cause of religion and virtue.' So the proposed ready letter-writer was for the moment set aside, and *Pamela, or Virtue Rewarded* came into being (1740). The story itself is very slight. It tells of a young girl, a lady's maid, who is for a long time persecuted by the addresses of the libertine son of her mistress, now dead, and successfully resists all his arts and intrigues, until at length, his heart being softened towards her, he makes her his wife. But despite its simplicity of subject, it was so fresh in character and interest that it scored an instant and sensational success. Of its moral teaching, upon which Richardson himself laid the chief emphasis, and which was praised from the pulpit, perhaps the less said the better, for it seems to us today to the last degree sordid and mercenary. As a piece of art it is mainly interesting from the historical point of view, and because it presents in a rather crude form the peculiar methods which were afterwards used with a much surer hand and with much finer effect in its two successors, *Clarissa, or The Adventures of a Young Lady*—generally known as *Clarissa Harlowe* (1747–48), and *Sir Charles Grandison* (1753). *Clarissa* is Richardson's masterpiece; it gave him a European reputation; and it is still regarded as, in its own way, one of the greatest of eighteenth century novels. It is also noteworthy as containing Richardson's most remarkable character-study in the scoundrel, Lovelace, whose name has become proverbial. It is difficult for us now to do justice to Richardson, in part because of profound changes in thought, in part because of the immense development of the art of prose fiction, since his time. His books are extremely long, and are incumbered with endless repetitions and masses of unimportant detail. His stories drag; and their machinery is very clumsy. They are all written in the form of letters which pass among the characters; and while this epistolary method has its advantages in bringing us into intimate touch with the writers themselves, it tends to the scattering of interest, and, involving as it does the initial postulate of everlasting correspondence in and out of season, it leaves us with a disturbing sense of the extreme artificiality of the whole fabrication. But for patient, microscopic analysis of motive and passion, Richardson still holds a pre-eminent place. This is some justification of his remorseless prolixity. His is the art of the infinitely little, and his effects are built up out of thousands of small and seemingly trivial things. In many of its fundamental characteristics his genius was rather feminine than masculine; from boyhood up he had sought by preference the society of women; and it is a point of importance that in general he succeeded best in the delineation of female characters. His first-hand knowledge of the world was small, and his view extremely narrow, and the moral element in his work (and he wrote primarily as a moralist) suffered greatly in consequence. He carried on the ethical traditions of Addison and Steele, and in his own pragmatic fashion undoubtedly did good work in the purification of society and manners. But his moralising is apt to sink into wearisome twaddle, and his sentiment is often overstrained and mawkish. In general, the atmosphere of his books is too much like that of a hot-house to be entirely pleasant or wholesome.

75. Fielding. The second of our eighteenth century novelists, and by far the greatest of them all, HENRY FIELDING (1707–54), was a man of very different type. His was a virile, vigorous, and somewhat coarse nature, and his knowledge of life, as wide as Richardson's was narrow, included in particular many aspects of it from which the prim little printer would have recoiled shocked. There is thus a strength and a breadth in his work for which we look in vain in that of his elder contemporary. Richardson's judgment of Fielding—that his writings were 'wretchedly low and dirty'—clearly suggests the fundamental contrast between the two men. Moreover, for some ten years before he took up the novel, Fielding had been busy writing plays, and this long training in the drama had taught him many valuable lessons in the art of construction. Unlike Richardson, therefore, he started with a good preliminary preparation in technique.

Oddly enough, his own first experiment in the novel was a direct offshoot from the first experiment of Richardson. In 1740 all England was in raptures over *Pamela*. Fielding did not share the general enthusiasm. The underlying absurdities of the story appealed to his quick sense of humour; he was struck by the downright artfulness of the little heroine, whose virtues were paraded with so much satisfaction; and the author's overwrought sentimentalism disgusted him. The happy idea, therefore, occurred to him to take advantage of the popularity of the book, and at the same time to raise an honest laugh against it, by turning it into burlesque. This was the origin of *The Adventures of Joseph Andrews* (1742). Fielding began by reversing the initial situation in *Pamela*. As Richardson's heroine had been tempted by her master, so his hero (who is supposed to be Pamela's brother) is tempted by his mistress; and he keeps up the parody till his tenth chapter. After this, carried away by his own invention, he discards his first design, and the story becomes an 'epic of the highway', full of adventures, horseplay, and not too decent fun. This was experimental work only, but it helped Fielding to find his proper way. It was followed in 1749 by *The History of Tom Jones*, the greatest novel of the eighteenth century. Here Fielding takes an enormous canvas, and crowds it with figures. His hero is a foundling, who is brought up in the west of England by a squire named Allworthy, with whom, however, he presently quarrels; after which he tramps up to London in quest of fortune. Country men and manners fill the first part, metropolitan men and manners, the second part, of the book, which as a whole gives us our fullest and richest picture of English life about the middle of the eighteenth century. Fielding's third great novel, *Amelia,* appeared in 1751. In this, as the title indicates, the interest centres in the character of a woman, and thus Fielding, probably of set purpose, met the author of *Clarissa* on his own ground. The story tells of the courage and patience of a devoted wife and of the ill-doings of her weak-willed husband. It is far sadder, far less vigorous, and far less humorous, than its predecessors; and, despite the excellence of some of its character-drawing, it exhibits unmistakable signs of failing power.

Fielding was much concerned about the structural principles of prose fiction, a matter to which neither Defoe nor Richardson had given much attention. To him the novel was quite as much a form of art as the epic or the drama. Hence the interest of his preface to *Joseph Andrews* and of the introductory chapters to the successive books of *Tom Jones*, which are in fact a skilled craftsman's essays on various questions connected with his craft. His own success in construction was not indeed nearly so great as is commonly supposed, and the praise which Coleridge and Thackeray lavished upon the plot of *Tom Jones* must be dismissed as wildly extravagant. But he still deserves the fullest credit for what he did by both theory and practice to carry over into the novel those ideas of unity and balance which are essential to any work of art. While we are now often repelled by his grossness and animality, we must also remember that Fielding was, like Richardson, in his own way avowedly a moralist, though he repudiated root and branch Richardson's pinched ideas of conduct, and the spirit of smug respectability which pervades his work. As a social satirist and teacher, his place is close beside his friend, Hogarth, whom he resembled in his total want of squeamishness, the limitless freedom which he assumed in depicting vice, and the downright honesty and sincerity with which he sought, in his own words, 'to expose some of the most glaring evils, as well public as private, which at present infect the country'. There are weak points in Fielding's ethics, and he touches certain matters with a laxity which we may deplore. But, on the whole, as he was a much greater artist than Richardson, so his treatment of life and the tone of his writings are both truer and healthier than his.

76. Smollett. A third writer, TOBIAS SMOLLETT (1721–71), is usually associated with Richardson and Fielding in the history of the eighteenth century novel, but it must be distinctly understood that his work is on a much lower level than theirs. In early life Smollett spent some years as surgeon on a man-of-war, and thus gained that first-hand knowledge of the sea, of sailors, and of the appalling conditions of the naval service, which he afterwards turned to good account. He settled in London with the intention of practising his profession, but medicine failing, like Goldsmith, he turned to literature. As a bookseller's hack, again like Goldsmith, he produced a large amount of miscellaneous work, including a *History of England*, which was a publisher's opposition venture to Hume's. The success of Richardson and Fielding naturally prompted him to try his hand in fiction, and he wrote half a dozen novels, the most important of which are—*The Adventures of Roderick Random* (1748), *The Adventures of Peregrine Pickle* (1751), and *The Expedition of Humphry Clinker* (1771). Smollett conceived the novel as 'a large diffused picture' of life, and, unlike Fielding, made little attempt to organise his materials into an artistic whole. His stories are simply strings of adventures, and such unity as they possess is given to them only by the personality of the hero; while his one object is to keep the reader's interest alive by a perpetual succession of incidents. His fertility of invention and animation are undoubtedly remarkable; but we soon weary of mere incident when it is not related to the interest of character; and Smollett's characters are generally very crudely drawn. Alike in the looseness of his composition, in his dependence upon action, and in the nature of his subjects, he reverts to the picaresque type of fiction. Though he still has his admirers, the enjoyment of his novels requires stronger nerves than most of us today possess. The world as he depicts it is a dirty and dingy place, and its inhabitants for the most part are very sorry and disagreeable fellows; he loves to dwell upon the most foul and nauseating phases of life; and he gives us little that is really cheerful to relieve the prevailing gloom, for even his humour is commonly of the coarse physical kind. An exception must indeed be made in favour of *Humphry Clinker*, which is far finer in tone and richer in genuine comedy and character interest than its predecessors; but in regard to these it can only be said that, while they often carry us along by the zest of their narrative, they have in them much to disgust even the least fastidious reader. It has, however, to be remembered that Smollett wrote expressly as a satirist and reformer, and that his purpose was to paint the monstrous evils of life in their true proportions and colours that he might thus drive them home upon the attention of the public; and we must certainly set it down to his credit that the sickening realism of the ship scenes in *Roderick Random* led directly to drastic changes for the better in the conditions of the naval service. While in general he compares very unfavourably with his two forerunners, he also did something to enlarge the scope of fiction. He was the real creator of the English novel of the sea and of sailors, and the first of our novelists to exploit systematically and successfully the national peculiarities of Irish, Scotch, and Welsh.

77. Other Novelists of the Period. Of the innumerable works of fiction which now flooded the market, the vast majority are no longer remembered today even by name. We have here to glance only at the productions of a few writers who, whether by the intrinsic excellence or the temporary importance of what they did, have a recognised position in literary history.

It is natural to speak first of GOLDSMITH'S one excursion into the field of fiction, *The Vicar of Wakefield*. In structure this shows that, like Smollett, Goldsmith had learned little of the art of the novel from the precepts and practice of Fielding, for its plot is ill-concocted, full of glaring improbabilities, and huddled up in the most ludicrous manner at the close. But as we are willing to make the amplest allowance for the writer's personal weaknesses, so we are ready to make a similar allowance for the technical defects of his work, because it is instinct with his peculiar charm and tenderness, and because its materials are handled with that transfiguring power which touches the simplest details with idyllic beauty. Its humour is perennially delightful; and, while much of its characterisation is purely conventional, no praise would be excessive for the subtlety with which the good Dr. Primrose and his family are portrayed. Its spirit is that of quiet, manly piety, without the slightest suggestion of the 'goody-goody'; and the large sympathy which is conspicuous in many of its descriptions—notably in the prison scenes towards the end—shows that in human feeling and real social insight alike Goldsmith was ahead of most of the professional preachers and teachers of his time. The novel had been didactic in the hands of his predecessors, but he made it directly humanitarian.

Reference must next be made to the strange work of a very strange man, the REV. LAURENCE STERNE (1713–68), whose *Life and*

Opinions of Tristram Shandy, Gentleman appeared in nine volumes from 1759 to 1767. This can hardly indeed be called a novel. It is rather a medley of unconnected incidents, scraps of out-of-the-way learning, whimsical fancies, humour, pathos, reflection, impertinence, and indecency. Sterne's method was that of deliberate oddity and carefully cultivated caprice; and his work has so little backbone that, had he lived ten years longer (for he left it incomplete at his death), he could easily have written nine more volumes on the same plan and without advancing in the least towards any real conclusion. He owes his rank as a novelist to the wonderful power of his characterdrawing in the elder Shandy and his wife, Corporal Trim, and Uncle Toby, who are among the most living figures in eighteenth century fiction. In one other way, he also counts much historically. We have spoken of the reinstatement of the emotions as a chief fact in the life of the period now under review. Considering the general conditions of the time, it is not surprising that in the reaction against the dry intellectuality of the preceding generation, the feelings should run riot, and a new mood—the 'melting' mood of heightened sensibility—should arise in consequence. A fresh type of man—the 'man of feeling'—now appeared upon the scene, whose nature was exquisitely attuned to the pathos of things, and who found a curious satisfaction in the cultivation of melancholy; and as people at large began to discover that there was a peculiar and delicate kind of pleasure to be extracted from overwrought emotional states, those who catered for their entertainment naturally addressed themselves to the task of inducing such states. There is a good deal of this new emotionalism in Richardson; but Sterne was our first English writer—as Rousseau was the first writer on the Continent—to employ it as part of his regular literary stock-in-trade; and with him it becomes so much of a habit that it fills his pages with a kind of mildew. He also appears to have discovered the proper name for it. In a letter, about 1740, to a friend, Miss Lumley, he reminds her of the 'sentimental' repasts they had enjoyed together. This is the first known use of the epithet in the sense now attached to it, and Sterne himself presently made the word classic and current in his record of continental travel, the *Sentimental Journey*. He was not, of course, the creator (no one man was the creator) of this tearful mood, but his work fell in with a fast-growing fashion, which it therefore helped to stimulate and spread. Among his direct followers one has some distinction— HENRY MACKENZIE (1745–1831), whose principal novel, *The Man of Feeling*, carries its significance in its title. Possessing nothing of Sterne's other qualities, Mackenzie exaggerated his high-pitched emotionalism, and his book is from beginning to end a perfect welter of tears. As has been well said, at least it is not a dry book. I should take it, on the contrary, to be one of the dampest books in English literature.

In later life Mackenzie opposed the French Revolution, but his earlier writings reveal many traces of the influences of that general spirit of revolt which gained strength rapidly in England during the second half of the eighteenth century. This leads us to note that, as we might expect, writers who had a message to deliver soon began to perceive that the novel could be used with great effect as a means of popularising their political and social ideas. Thus, to take one instance only, WILLIAM GODWIN (see §71) wrote his powerful *Caleb Williams, or Things as They are* (1794), in order (in the words of the original preface) to give 'a general review of the modes of domestic and unrecorded despotism by which man becomes the destroyer of man'.

It is an interesting feature of the growth of the novel that almost from the first women began to take part in it. But though a number of women had been writing fiction before FRANCES BURNEY (1752–1840), her *Evelina, or The History of a Young Lady's Entrance into the World*, laid the real foundations of the woman's novel. Published in 1778, twelve years after the *Vicar of Wakefield*, when 'little Fanny' (as Johnson affectionately called her) was only twenty-six, this was reckoned the greatest success since *Clarissa*. In many ways it belonged entirely to the eighteenth century school.

It clearly owed much to Richardson, whose epistolary method and tone of sensibility it adopts; while, in broad humour, its strongest point, it follows the tradition of Fielding and Smollett, but without their coarseness. At the same time, as the first novel in which a woman wrote of life quite frankly from the woman's point of view, it was really a new thing. We may therefore regard Miss Burney as the founder of the 'tea-table school' of fiction. Her second book, *Cecilia*, was more ambitious, but lacked the freshness of its predecessor. Her later novels were failures.

78. The Revival of Romance. While the eighteenth century novel arose as a picture of men and manners, the favour which it enjoyed made it inevitable that it should soon expand in many directions under the various influences of the time. One important new movement was thus initiated when it began to respond to that growing interest in the middle ages which, as we shall learn more fully later, was a prominent feature in the great changes which were then coming over popular taste. A revival of romance was the result. In this revival the most conspicuous name is that of Horace Walpole, who has already been mentioned as a letter-writer. A busy trifler, who in the course of a long life as man of fashion and virtuoso dabbled in many things, Walpole among other fads took up medievalism. As early as 1747 he bought a small house or 'villakin', near Twickenham, which little by little he transformed into a miniature Gothic castle. In this he installed with great satisfaction his collection of curiosities and art treasures, suits of armour, illuminated missals, specimens of stained glass, and other miscellaneous articles of the same general description. His 'Gothic' romance, as he called his *Castle of Otranto* (1765), was simply the expression in fiction of the peculiar tastes already manifested architecturally in this toy Castle of Strawberry Hill. Inspired, according to his own account, by a dream of 'a gigantic hand in armour', this extraordinary book impresses us today as a mere jumble of childish absurdities, and we only smile when we should be amazed and awed by its crude supernaturalism—by the picture which descends from its frame, for example, and the statue which bleeds at the nose. But the point to emphasise is that it broke new ground. It was taken very seriously at the time and by readers of the next generation; for Gray was so frightened by it that he dreaded to go upstairs to bed, Byron called it 'the first romance in the language', and Scott praised it with his usual reckless generosity. Its popularity, of course, bred imitations, one of which, CLARA REEVE'S *Old English Baron* (1777), also described as 'a Gothic story', is specially important because it is avowedly an attempt (though not a very successful one) to create romantic interest with machinery less violent and implausible than that which Walpole had employed. Sensationalism of the most extravagant kind was, however, the general characteristic of the romantic fiction which was produced in enormous quantities during the closing decades of the eighteenth century. Most of this has gone into the lumber heap of forgotten things; but the works of two writers have still a faint historical interest. ANN RADCLIFFE (1764–1823) gained an immense public by her *Romance of the Forest* (1791), *The Mysteries of Udolpho* (1794), and *The Italian* (1797)—books which are very long, very complicated in plot, full of thrilling situations, and so compact of horrors that though the author was in fact a very quiet, commonplace kind of woman, the story got about that she had actually gone insane in writing them. MATTHEW GREGORY LEWIS (1775–1818), now best remembered for his personal relations with Scott, achieved a great success on somewhat similar lines with his first book, *Ambrosio, or The Monk*. Published when he was only twenty, this owes much to *The Castle of Otranto* and *The Mysteries of Udolpho*, though it outdoes both in the wild sensationalism of its machinery and effects. There is little in the productions of either of these writers to interest us much today. But we must note the historical significance of their return to the romantic middle ages, and of their appeal to the imagination by the free use of the mysterious and the supernatural; and we must remember that they did much to stimulate and fertilise the genius of Scott.

17

The Age of Johnson:
Verse

79. General Characteristics. Broadly viewed, the history of our later eighteenth century poetry is, as we have said, the history of a struggle between old and new, and of the gradual triumph of the new. On the one hand, there were writers who followed the general practice of the school of Pope, and aimed to produce the kind of verse which Pope had brought to perfection and made popular. In the works of these men, therefore, we recognise the continuance of what we may here call the Augustan tradition. On the other hand, there was a marked tendency among writers of the rising generation to abandon the practice of the school of Pope, respond to a different range of influences, and seek fresh subjects, fresh forms, and fresh modes of feeling and expression. In the works of these men, therefore, we may recognize the breaking up of the Augustan tradition. When in his *Essay on Pope* (1756) Joseph Warton took the ground that Pope was a great 'wit', but not a great poet, since his work lacked those imaginative and emotional qualities which are essential to true poetry; when in his *Conjectures on Original Composition* (1759), addressed to Richardson, Young maintained that poets should leave off imitating classic models and depend upon nature and the promptings of individual genius, it is evident that the change of taste is beginning to express itself in open protest against the principles of the reigning fashion.

Thus the Age of Johnson, in respect of its poetry, is obviously an age of transition, innovation, and varied experiment. It must, however, be borne in mind that the great general movement from old to new was the result of many forces and resolves itself under analysis into a number of different movements following many lines. At this juncture the reader should return to the epitome of the chief characteristics of the classical school of poetry already given (§59). As was there shown, classical poetry (1) was mainly the product of the intelligence, and was strikingly deficient in emotion and imagination; (2) it was almost exclusively a 'town' poetry; (3) it was conspicuously wanting in romantic spirit; (4) it was extremely formal and artificial in style; and (5) it adhered rigorously to the closed couplet. At all these points reaction set in. (1) Emotion, passion, and imagination invaded poetry to the destruction of its dry intellectuality, and the old narrow didactic principles were discarded. (2) Poetry ceased to concern itself exclusively with the 'town', and began to deal with nature and rustic life. A most important feature in it is the growth of the sense of the picturesque. (3) The romantic spirit revived, and this revival brought with it great changes in the themes and temper of verse. (4) Efforts were now made to break away from the stereotyped conventions of 'poetic diction', and to substitute for these simplicity of phrase and the language of nature. (5) The supremacy of the closed couplet was attacked, and other forms of verse used in its place.

These lines of reaction are sometimes independent of one another, sometimes they run together, and sometimes they cross; and the resulting complexity is so great that to follow the history of our later eighteenth century poetry in detail would be impossible within the limits of a brief sketch like this. A few matters of outstanding importance only can be here touched on. In the interests of simplicity we will first deal with the continuance of the Augustan tradition; then we will consider some aspects of the breaking up of that tradition;

and finally we will speak of a few individual poets whose work is sufficiently significant, either on the personal or on the historical side, to justify separate mention.

80. The Continuance of the Augustan Tradition. Neglecting many minor men, we may here associate this with the names of two most important writers—JOHNSON and GOLDSMITH.

Emphasis must first be laid upon a point already noted, that both Johnson and Goldsmith were strong conservatives in literary theory. In an epoch of change, they held fast to the immediate past. Johnson 'took it for granted', as Macaulay said, 'that the kind of poetry which flourished in his own time' and 'which he had been accustomed to hear praised from his childhood' was the best kind of poetry; and he not only upheld its claims by direct advocacy of its canons, but also consistently opposed every experiment in which, as in the ballad revival (see §84) he detected signs of revolt against it. Goldsmith was equally convinced that the writers of the Augustan age provided 'the true standard for future imitation'; for him, in Masson's words, 'Pope was the limit of classic English literature'; and at all important points, as in his aversion to blank verse, he showed himself fundamentally hostile to change. We shall thus be prepared to find that the creative work of both these writers is avowedly classical in matter and manner. Johnson's two chief poems, *London* and *The Vanity of Human Wishes,* belong entirely to the preceding generation; not indeed in their pessimistic tone, for that is the expression of the poet's personal character, but in their didacticism, their formal, rhetorical style, and their adherence to the closed couplet. The same may be said of Goldsmith's two important poems, *The Traveller* and *The Deserted Village,* for these, also, as versified pamphlets on political economy, are stately didactic; they are written in the closed couplet, of which indeed they provide admirable examples; and they are often marred by the stilted and pompous phraseology which was then deemed effective. They may, therefore, be fairly described as the last great works of the outgoing artificial eighteenth century school. Yet when we examine them more minutely we realise that, as Goldsmith put himself and his own poetical temperament into everything he wrote, these poems, though they nominally follow the Augustan tradition, mark in various ways a rupture with it. While they are didactic and philosophical, the thesis is often an excuse for digressions of the purest poetry, and the argument a mere thread upon which the writer hangs pictures, reflections, and reminiscences. The tender feeling which pervades them and gives them so much of their peculiar charm, is also remarkable; Goldsmith greatly disliked sentimentalism, yet he was himself touched by its growing power. Their treatment of nature and rural life must also be noted. The poet, looking back at past experiences through a haze of memory, recalls what he has himself seen and known, and writes of that; and though his landscape and his peasants are undoubtedly rather conventionalised, his descriptions have nonetheless an unmistakably personal quality. It is clear, therefore, that conservative as Goldsmith was, he yielded more than he realised to the influences at work about him; while, as for Johnson, it is particularly instructive to remember that, though he was incomparably the strongest individual force in the literary world of his time, he was still unable to check the encroachments of the new spirit which he abhorred.

81. The Reaction in Form. In considering some aspects of the reaction against the Augustan tradition, we may conveniently begin with the change in form, though, as this was very generally associated with changes in other directions, it cannot of course be dealt with exhaustively by itself.

The main feature of this reaction in style was the abandonment of the Popean couplet for experiments in other kinds of verse. It is probable that these experiments were in part prompted by natural impatience of a single monotonous form, and a corresponding desire for change. But the direct influence of reviving interest in long-neglected pre-Augustan writers has also to be recognised. Growing admiration of Milton, for example, was the principal immediate cause of the rise and spreading popularity of blank verse. The first important piece of eighteenth century blank verse, Thomson's *Seasons*, to which further reference will be made later, was obviously fashioned on Milton's. Other examples of the same form belonging to the closing years of the Age of Pope are, as already mentioned (see §62), Somerville's *The Chase,* Young's *Night Thoughts,* and Blair's *The Grave*; and to these may now be added Dyer's *The Ruins of Rome* (1740) and Akenside's *The Pleasures of the Imagination* (1744). The use of blank verse greatly increased during the Age of Johnson, and the language of Goldsmith in regard to it, in the dedication to *The Traveller* and elsewhere, proves that, much to that writer's annoyance, it was then firmly established side by side with the couplet. An equal interest attached to what is known as the Spenserian revival. This began quite early in the century with a number of attempts, none of them very serious or important, to reproduce the Spenserian stanza (see §26), and even Spenser's archaic diction, and the immense vogue which such experiments presently obtained is shown by the fact that over 50 poems in this stanza were published between 1730 and 1775. Johnson's emphatic protest in *The Rambler* (May 14, 1751) is conclusive evidence of the extending power of this particular movement. 'The imitation of Spenser', writes the Great Cham, 'by the influence of some men of learning and genius seems likely to grow upon the age'—a circumstance which he goes on to deplore. We speak of the Spenserian revival here, because at the outset it was purely formal. But little by little the spell of the *Faery Queene* fell upon those who read and imitated, and thus Spenser helped to open up for the new generation the wonder-world of chivalry, knight-errantry, and medieval romance. The general course of the movement may perhaps be indicated by a comparison of the three principal Spenserian poems of the century. *The Schoolmistress* (1742, revised 1750) of WILLIAM SHENSTONE (1714–63), in which we have a delightful picture of an old village dame school, uses the language and style of Spenser expressly for purposes of burlesque; nothing, the author declares, would ever induce him to take Spenser seriously. Thomson's *Castle of Indolence* (1748) adopts much of the Gothic machinery of the *Faery Queene,* and reproduces many of its essential characteristics. *The Minstrel* (1771–74) of JAMES BEATTIE (1735–1803) rejects the mere formal imitation of Spenser entirely, except in respect of the stanza, but the larger influence of the master is sufficiently attested in the reasons which the poet assigns for his choice of this: 'it pleases my ear,' he says, 'and seems, from its Gothic structure and original, to bear some relation to the subject and spirit of the poem.'

Two points in connection with the general reaction in form must be made clear. In the first place, in technical quality and aesthetic effect, both blank verse and the Spenserian stanza are the very antithesis of the terse, epigrammatic closed couplet, and appealed to the new generation both by contrast with this, and by their elasticity and the opportunity they afforded for the free movement of the poet's mind. Secondly, while many writers now rejected the couplet, the couplet itself was allowed to remain intact in the particular shape which it had finally assumed in the hands of Pope. In other words, until well on in the nineteenth century, when poets used the couplet at all, it was still the classic couplet which they adopted. It was not until the days of Leigh Hunt and Keats, as we shall see presently, that the reaction in form extended to the couplet itself, and the loose romantic type was substituted for the long supreme Popean kind.

82. The Growth of the Love of Nature in Eighteenth Century Poetry. The growth of a love of nature and of a feeling for the picturesque is one of the most marked and interesting general features in the history of English poetry between Pope and Wordsworth. It is true that even in the thoroughly metropolitan literature of the Restoration period and the Age of Anne, we occasionally catch a breath of fresh air which seems to blow straight from the woods and fields. To say nothing of Milton and Marvell, who were survivors of 'the giant race before the flood', we must remember that THOMAS PARNELL (1679–1718) and LADY WINCHILSEA (*circa* 1660–1720) show a genuine sense of natural beauty and the charms of rural life. But these were exceptions, and speaking in general terms, we are quite justified in saying that our English Augustan poetry was a poetry of city life. The muse of the time loved best to frequent the coffee-house and the drawing-room; solitude she despised; and if, once in a while, she wandered out into the country, it was seldom farther than Richmond Hill or Windsor Forest. Nature in its wilder and more rugged aspects shocked the refined taste of a generation which had been trained to prefer the trim garden to the unspoilt hillside. According to the artificial conception then prevalent, nothing could be beautiful save what had been reduced to symmetry by rule and line. In the words of a typical and authoritative exponent of these ideas, Addison, 'we find the works of nature still the more pleasing the more they resemble art.'

In dealing with the poetry of the fifteenth century (see §16) we noted the fact that, while the landscape of the English writers of that time was wholly bookish and conventional, that of their Scottish contemporaries was often painted directly from reality and with great care and accuracy; and we asked the reader to bear this in mind, since we should presently learn that Scottish poets 'did much to bring the love of nature into later English literature'. The truth of this statement we are now in a position to appreciate. It was in the writings of a Lanarkshire man, ALLAN RAMSAY (1686–1758), that the reviving love of nature first became conspicuous. Drawing his inspiration largely from the popular songs and ballads of his own peasantry, Ramsay produced in *The Gentle Shepherd* (1725), a real pastoral poem, the characters in which are genuine shepherds and shepherdesses, and not the traditional shadows of a mere literary Arcadia. But the stream which he here set flowing reached our London public and became an influence in our English literature through the works of another Scotsman, whose name has already been mentioned—JAMES THOMSON (1700–48). His *Seasons*, a descriptive poem in four parts (1726–30) belongs in many ways to the Augustan school; it is charged with didacticism in the approved manner; its vocabulary is highly Latinised; the conventions of 'poetic diction' abound in it; its style is in consequence often frigid and bombastic; its descriptions frequently impress us as 'got up'. Yet Thomson gives us real landscape; he writes largely from personal knowledge; and many of his incidental touches are marked by great precision and sympathy. However we may now judge his performance, we must at least recognize its historical claims as the first really important poem in which nature, instead of being subordinated to man, is made the central theme. While less influential than the *Seasons,* we must still name with them the contemporary work of a Welshman, JOHN DYER (1700–58), who has already appeared in connection with the reaction in form, and whose descriptive *Grongar Hill,* a piece of vigorous landscape painting, which owes much to Milton, but more to nature itself, was published in the same year as Thomson's *Winter.* From this time on the love of nature became increasingly prominent in our poetry. We find it, for example, in William Collins and William Blake; in Goldsmith, as we have said; and, as we shall presently see, in Gray, Burns, and Cowper.

83. The Development of Naturalism. With this steady growth of a love of nature we may conveniently associate that general 'return to nature' (as it is broadly called) which pro-foundly affected later eighteenth century poetry in subject, tone, and style. This 'return to nature' meant something more than an increasing feeling for the picturesque and for the charms of the country. It meant a rising sense of all that is implied in the contrast between nature and civilisation, and a deepening belief that, as the cramping conventions of our artificial social system prevent the free development and expression of individuality, and give birth to many evils, the only way of salvation for men and nations lies through a radical simplification of life. This resulted in poetry in the quest for more elementary themes, which of course had to be sought among the unsophisticated country-folk rather than amid the complexities of the recognised centres of culture and refinement, and for more natural modes of treatment. Greater simplicity in the subject-matter chosen, in the passions described, and in the language employed, were thus among the principal objects aimed at by many poets of the new generation. In considering the various lines of reaction against the artificial poetry of the Augustan school, the utmost stress must therefore be laid upon the attempt to bring poetry back to nature and reality.

As the development of naturalism, so conceived, was due to the co-operation of many influences, literary and social, so its effects have to be looked for now in one direction and now in another, and they are in general so intimately bound up with other features of the new poetry that it would be impossible to isolate them for separate study. One or two points must, however, be indicated.

On the side both of matter and of style, simplification was much aided by the spread of an interest in old ballad literature. Of the ballad revival in its other aspects I shall speak in the next section. Here we have only to note its connection with the development of naturalism. Augustan of the Augustans though he was, Addison had perceived that the informality and spontaneity of *Chevy Chase* and *The Babes in the Wood,* childish as they seemed to him to be, gave them a wonderful power of appeal; and this power of appeal now came to be more and more fully realised. The old ballad phrase, 'God rest his soul', had, as we remember, been 'improved' and 'refined' by the Augustans into 'Eternal blessings on his shade attend'. Despite Johnson's ridicule of the old ballads in general, people now began to discover that the simpler form is much better and more poetical than the translation, and this discovery led to a change of taste, which in the long run was bound to prove fatal to all the theories of the Augustan school about elegance and effect. At first the movement towards simplicity was slow and halting; even Bishop Percy (see next section) 'polished' some of the old ballads in his collection as a concession to the extreme refinement of his age. But it gained ground, and, as it did so, it made writers and readers alike increasingly conscious of the superiority of what is natural and spontaneous in poetry to all the carefully cultivated conventional mannerisms of the long-accepted school of art.

At this point mention may be made of the work of WILLIAM BLAKE (1757–1827). A mystic and a visionary, whose apocalyptic effusions were inspired, as he himself declared, by the desire to restore the golden age, and who was also much influenced by the medieval revival, Blake might indeed find a place also among our early romantic poets. But I speak of him here, because in that part of his poetry which really concerns all readers—in his *Poetical Sketches, Songs of Innocence,* and *Songs of Experience*—the love of the country, of simple life, of childhood and home, marks him out as a leader in that naturalistic kind of poetry—the poetry of ordinary things—which Wordsworth was a little later to bring to perfection. Meanwhile, another and curiously contrasted phase of naturalism was being exemplified by Blake's contemporary GEORGE CRABBE (1754–1832), in whose works—*The Village, The Newspaper, The Parish Register, The Borough, Tales in Verse,* and *Tales of the Hall*—it took the form of extreme and uncompromising realism. Himself a child of poor parents, and for many years a hard-working parish clergyman, Crabbe knew the life of the poor, with all its penury, misery, and discontent, from the inside, and it is this life, as he had seen it, that he sets himself to depict in his verse. His programme is unflinching fidelity to facts: 'I sing the cot,' he announces, 'as truth will paint it, and as bards will not'; and he holds so resolutely to his principle that he never relieves the heavy gloom of his pictures by a single idealising touch. It is singular that, though he lived through the years of its splendid activity, Crabbe remained to the end of his long life entirely uninfluenced by the romantic movement. His regular employment of the closed couplet is also a point of connection with the outgoing classic school. But his plain and realistic handling of materials taken from actual life, and his total repudiation of all the pastoral conventions which had long stood between the poet and the world of reality about him, give him special importance in the naturalistic reaction against the Augustan tradition.

84. The Romantic Revival. Even more important than this development of naturalism was the general revolt which went on at the same time against the hard temper, the dry intellectuality, the hatred of the fantastic, the visionary, and the mystical, which, as we have seen, were among the chief characteristics of the Augustan school. This revolt we call the romantic movement. To find a definition of 'romantic', which shall be at once sufficiently broad and sufficiently exact, is extremely difficult. The word is so loosely employed even by critics that it is often taken to cover everything anti-Augustan, including naturalism. This is a mistake against which the student should be carefully on his guard, since naturalism, though contemporary with romanticism, and like this, a movement of reaction against Augustan ideals, was a reaction on entirely different lines. Perhaps the points already indicated will serve to show the origin, direction, and fundamental meaning of this particular movement. By romantic we connote (1) the principle of spontaneity in literature, which implies the assertion of individuality against the conventions of the schools, the rejection of that critical code which had bound poetry down to the so-called rules of art, and the belief that poetic genius is really inspired, and should be a law unto itself. Romanticism was thus a part of the general later eighteenth century movement for the emancipation of the individual, and that is why the great French writer, Victor Hugo, described it as 'liberalism in literature'. (2) A particular mood and temper, of which strong passion, sensibility, aspiration, and melancholy are widely recognised component elements. It is this aspect of it which is specially brought out in Mr. Watts-Dunton's definition of the romantic revival as 'the renaissance of wonder and mystery'. (3) A love of the wild, fantastic, abnormal, and supernatural. And (4) as a result of the combined influences of all these things, a fondness for a particular kind of subject-matter which was quite a fresh kind in the middle of the eighteenth century, and which gave free play to individual genius, stimulated the mood in question, and appealed to the newly awakened taste for the marvellous. Perhaps a few concrete examples will help to make these points clear. Thus, then, we call the couplets of Keats's *Endymion* romantic because they are 'free', in the sense that they repudiate the formal canons of the Augustan form. We speak of the spirit of Gray's *Elegy* as romantic melancholy, and of the fierce emotion of Byron's eastern tales as romantic passion. We use the same epithet to describe the fantastic narrative of Scott's *Lay of the Last Minstrel* and the supernaturalism of Coleridge's *Ancient Mariner.*

Now, as the middle ages were, from all points of view, essentially romantic ages, it was natural that the imagination of men of the temper and tastes specified should turn back to them in search of inspiration and themes. Hence a very important phase of the romantic movement (in part a cause, and in part the effect of it) was the medieval or Gothic revival, to which, as we have seen, a certain stimulus had early been given by the renewed study of the writings of Spenser. The results of this medieval revival in prose fiction have already been noted. About the time of the production of *The Castle of Otranto* its influences became equally conspicuous in poetry. Its significance is shown in a most interesting way by the critical theories of a writer of this period, RICHARD HURD (1720–1808), who in his *Letters on Chivalry and Romance* (1762) boldly maintained that 'Gothic manners' provide far better material for poetry than classical mythology (now, it must be remembered, worn threadbare and reduced to lifeless convention by constant repetition). 'May there not', asks Hurd, 'be something in the Gothic Romance particularly suitable to the views of a genius, and the ends of poetry? And may not the philosophic moderns have gone too far in their perpetual ridicule and contempt of it?' And, again, in opposition to the Augustan principle that the poet should 'follow nature' in the sense that he should keep to the well-beaten tracks of experience: 'The poet has a world of his own, where experience has less to do than consistent imitation. He has, besides, a supernatural world to range in.... In the poet's world all is marvellous and extraordinary.' These ideas will help us to connect the medieval revival with the general movement of reaction against the Augustan tradition, and with the transformation which the whole conception of the nature, place, and functions of poetry was now undergoing.

As in the development of naturalism, so in this revival of the romantic past, a powerful influence was exerted by the spread of an interest in ballad literature, which, formerly cultivated only by a few antiquaries here and there, now became increasingly popular with general readers. The most important ballad book of the eighteenth century was Bishop Percy's *Reliques of Ancient English Poetry; consisting of old Heroic Songs and Other pieces of our Earlier Poetry; together with Some Few of Later Date* (1765). These volumes contained the collections of many years, and their publication was in the first instance suggested by Shenstone (see §81). Though Percy himself little anticipated such a result, the *Reliques* proved a great power in spreading romantic tastes, and, as we shall presently see, his first reading of them made an epoch in the intellectual development of Scott. An *Essay on the Ancient Minstrels,* which the editor prefixed as an introduction to the ballads themselves, also counted in the same direction. It was, for example, the immediate inspiration of Beattie's *Minstrel* (see §81).

A name of extraordinary fascination in the history of the medieval revival is that of THOMAS CHATTERTON, 'the marvellous boy', who was born at Bristol in 1752, and died by his own hand in a London garret in 1770, before he had quite completed his eighteenth year. Chatterton's poems fall into two groups, but those which he published in his own name, and in which the Augustan tradition in matter and form is largely preserved, are of far less importance to us here than those which he gave out as the work of a certain Thomas Rowley, a mythical Bristol priest of the fifteenth century. The medieval fiction, which the boy invented, and by means of which he endeavoured to palm off his fabrications upon the world as ancient originals, is in its own way as remarkable as the poems themselves. The fact that for a time he contrived to deceive many critics, including Walpole, proves how little real knowledge of fifteenth century English then existed, for his attempted reproduction of the language and style of the age he sought to revive is full of glaring blunders and anachronisms. We are now able to follow the actual processes by which he concocted his 'Rowley' dialect. But the value of such poems as *Aella* and the *Ballad of Charity* is as great as ever, both because they are probably the most wonderful things ever written by a boy of Chatterton's age, and because they are another clear indication of the fast-growing curiosity of critics and the public regarding everything belonging to the middle ages.

This medieval revival was accompanied by a further spread of interest in the romantic past, and especially by the opening up of the heroic and legendary world of the north—the world of Celtic antiquity. The *Ode on the Popular Superstitions of the Highlands of Scotland considered as the Subject of Poetry,* written by WILLIAM COLLINS (1721–59), as early as 1749, though not published till 1788, reveals its broad significance in its very title. But for the full meaning of this phase of the romantic movement we have to turn to what are known as the Ossianic poems. In 1760 a young Scotch schoolmaster, JAMES MACPHERSON (1736–96) published a small volume of *Fragments of Ancient Poetry collected in the Highlands of Scotland and translated from the Galic* [sic] *or Erse Language.* These were offered as literal versions of 'genuine remains of ancient Scottish poetry'. They gave rise to an immense amount of curiosity and speculation, and Macpherson started on a literary pilgrimage through the Highlands in quest of fresh material of the same general character. As a result he produced *Fingal, an Epic Poem in six books,* in 1762, and *Temora, an Epic Poem in eight books,* in 1763. Public interest both in Edinburgh and in London was now at fever heat, and a fierce controversy broke out between those who supported Macpherson's assertion that these poems were the actual work of a Gaelic bard of the third century named Ossian, and those (Johnson among the number) who denounced them as gross and impudent forgeries. The questions at issue cannot yet be regarded as definitely settled, and it is still impossible to decide how much of the substance of the poems is really ancient and how much in them, as they stand, is to be referred to the manipulation of the editor and compiler, who undoubtedly treated his materials with a very free hand. Fortunately, we need not enter into the discussion in order to appreciate the epoch-making character of Macpherson's work. In the loosely rhythmical prose which he adopted for his so-called translations he carried to an extreme the formal reaction of the time against the classic couplet. In matter and spirit he is wildly romantic. These Ossianic poems are filled with supernaturalism, steeped in melancholy, and tremulous with that highly-wrought sentimentalism which, as we have seen, was then invading literature from every side. The world they depicted, too, was a world of heroic simplicity set in a landscape of mountains and mists; and thus, while they exhibited a striking development in the treatment of nature, they also made a specially potent appeal to the imagination of men who were beginning to feel themselves cramped by the narrow and petty conventions of social life, and were fast growing weary of the well-bred tone of the drawing-room poetry which had long been fashionable. The desire to get 'back to nature' is a conspicuous feature of these poems. To us their note is hopelessly falsetto. But to the readers of their own time they seemed a genuine voice out of the strong, unspoilt, primitive past, when men were unsophisticated, natural, and great. In seeking to account for their enormous vogue and influence both in England and on the Continent—for a wave of Ossianic enthusiasm swept over Europe, and in revolutionary France boys and girls still bore the names of Ossian's heroes and heroines—we must always keep their social significance well in view. They captivated readers of all classes, touched their sympathies, and set their hearts aflame, not merely because they stood for a change in the style of literature, but also, and far more, because they fell in with the rising mood of revolt against the evils bred by an artificial society and an over-ripe civilization. In this case, therefore, we see how the influences of naturalism and romanticism ran together, and are able to trace both back to those social forces which moulded and directed the literature of the age.

It is interesting to observe that the whole movement for the revival of the romantic past came to its head in the decade between 1760 and 1770. To this decade belong Hurd's *Letters on Chivalry and Romance*, *The Castle of Otranto*, Percy's *Reliques*, the poems of Chatterton, Macpherson's *Ossian*, and, as we shall see in a moment, the most romantic work of Gray. It will therefore be evident that those who, like Scott and Coleridge, were born in the first years of the decade following, grew into boyhood just in time to feel the full force of the influences which these writers had brought into literature.

85. Gray, Burns, and Cowper. To deal in any detail with the writings of these three specially important poets of the age of transition would carry us beyond the limits of our sketch, but enough must be said about each of them to make his historical position clear.

THOMAS GRAY (1716–71), a man of poor physique, a great scholar, and a recluse, produced but little poetry, but what he wrote is not only exquisite in quality and finish, but is also curiously interesting as a kind of epitome of the changes which were coming over the literature of his time. Among his first poetic efforts (apart from a Latin poem on Locke's philosophy) was a poem on *The Alliance of Education and Government,* belonging to the Augustan school and written in the closed couplet. Gray never succeeded in finishing it. His first publication was the ode *On a Distant Prospect of Eton College* written in 1742 and published anonymously by Dodsley in 1747. Next year appeared in the first three volumes of Dodsley's collection his Eton *Ode,* the *Ode to Spring,* and the poem *On the Death of a Favourite Cat.* These are conventional in thought and diction and contain little to suggest the new spirit. The *Elegy written in a Country Churchyard* was published by Dodsley in 1751, when it quickly went through fifteen editions and was often pirated. With this (perhaps the most famous of all English poems) a great change appears, and many features make it historically very important. There is, first, the use of nature, which, though employed only as a background, is still handled with fidelity and sympathy. There is, next, the churchyard scene, the twilight atmosphere, and the brooding melancholy of the poem, which at once connect it (as we have said) with one side of the romantic movement—the development of the distinctive romantic mood. The contrast drawn between the country and the town—the peasants' simple life and 'the madding crowd's ignoble strife'—is a third particular which will be noted. Finally, in the tender feeling shown for 'the rude forefathers of the hamlet' and the sense of the human value of the little things that are written in 'the short and simple annals of the poor', we see poetry, under the influence of the spreading democratic spirit, reaching out to include humble aspects of life hitherto ignored. Thus, despite the poet's continued use of the Augustan trick of personification and capital letters, the *Elegy* marks a stage in the evolution of Gray's genius. Yet it was only a stage, for as he grew older he became increasingly romantic. The two great odes, *The Progress of Poesy* and *The Bard,* are filled with the new conception of the poet as an inspired singer rather than an' accomplished artist—in the terms of the eighteenth century antithesis, an 'enthusiast' rather than a 'wit'; while the short poems on northern and Celtic themes, like *The Fatal Sisters* and *The Descent of Odin,* take their place (as we have already pointed out) in the history of the revival of the romantic past. The interest of Gray's development as a poet should now be clear. He began with versified pamphlets in Pope's manner; passed on through conventional lyrics to the *Elegy*; and ended with experiments which are fundamentally romantic in character.

Gray, though a man of very pure poetic feeling, was singularly unprolific. ROBERT BURNS (1759–96) was endowed with a marvellously spontaneous power of genius and an almost unrivalled gift of song. Absolute sincerity to himself and his surroundings was, however, the ultimate basis of his strength; a Scottish peasant, he wrote frankly as a peasant, and became the poetic interpreter of the thoughts and feelings, the racy humour, the homespun philosophy, the joys, sorrows, passions, superstitions, and even sometimes the lawlessness and the debaucheries, of the class from which he sprang. Of all these things he sang with an entire freedom from everything suggestive of mere literary mannerism and affectation. It is indeed quite a mistake to regard him as an unlettered plowman. He read widely and critically. But standard English literature affected him but little, though it may be noted as a detail that his most ambitious poem, *The Cotter's Saturday Night,* is in the Spenserian stanza. His poetic ancestry was in fact Scottish, and the chief literary influences behind his own work, vernacular poetry as represented by the songs and ballads of the Scottish peasant folk. Perhaps more than any other poet of the later eighteenth century he helped to bring natural passion back into English verse. Another important point about his writings is their strong democratic quality. He was keenly responsive to the revolutionary spirit of his age. We feel this spirit when, in *The Cotter's Saturday Night,* he contrasts the homely life and the simple piety of the peasant and his family with the wealth and vulgar ostentation, the luxury and the artificial refinements of the fashionable world; and when he sings that

'The rank is but the guinea's stamp—
The man's the gowd for a' that,'

prophesies of the coming time when all over the world men will be brothers, and reminds us that it is 'man's inhumanity to man' which 'makes countless thousands mourn', he constitutes himself the mouthpiece of the growing faith of his time in Liberty, Equality, and Fraternity.

No contrast could be greater than that between this full-blooded, robust Ayrshire plowman, and the delicate, sensitive, morbid WILLIAM COWPER (1731–1800), yet in the movements of literary history the two men stand close together. Cowper began to write poetry late in life, and as a means of keeping his mind from preying upon itself and from brooding over those torturing religious anxieties which more than once turned his melancholy into positive madness. He was not a student of poetry; he gave little or no attention to poetry as an art; he wrote just to express his own ideas in his own way. In his satires indeed he follows the conventional model of Pope, but in his principal poem, *The Task,* he abandons tradition entirely and pursues an independent course. This long blank verse poem is in one sense as much the poetic masterpiece of later eighteenth century evangelicalism as *Paradise Lost* is the masterpiece of the militant Puritanism of the seventeenth century. But, though it contains much of the narrow religious teaching of Cowper's sect, it contains a great deal, too, which transcends all mere sectarian limitations. It is extremely discursive and rambling, and is wholly wanting in any structural backbone. Yet, if it exhibits no organic unity, it possesses a unity of motive and meaning. Its real text, as Cowper himself said, is praise of retirement and of country life as favourable to religion and virtue; the philosophy of life expounded in it is expressly hostile to all the evils attendant upon the march of civilisation; and the oft-quoted line—'God made the country and man made the town'—shows how far Cowper was unconsciously at one with the revolutionists who were preaching the gospel of 'back to nature' and the simplification of life. In the sympathetic treatment of nature and landscape he comes nearest of all eighteenth century poets to Wordsworth; while, despite occasional lapses into 'poetic diction', he comes nearest to him, too, in the unaffected directness of his language. *The Task* also overflows with the spirit of humanitarianism, and, notwithstanding the poet's personal fastidiousness, his hermit-like existence, and the selfish character of his religion, it is also strongly impregnated with the ideas of liberty. Its denunciation of such abuses as militarism and the slave-trade is noteworthy; and even more so, the powerful passage in which the Bastille is attacked as the symbol of tyranny and irresponsible authority. It is an interesting point to remember that this passage was published in 1785, and that only four years later the Bastille fell.

Some critics have seen in Cowper a premonition of Wordsworth; others, of Byron. In a sense, he foreshadowed both. In his love of nature, his emotional response to it, and his sympathetic handling of humble rural life, he certainly antic pates Wordsworth; but, strangely enough, considering the character of the man and his creed, his poetry is filled with indications of social unrest, and thus in a rough way points forward to Byron. The most important figure in English poetry between Pope and Wordsworth, his life serves to connect the age of the former with that of the latter. When he was born, Pope was at the height of his power. When he died, Burns had been four years in his grave and the *Lyrical Ballads* two years before the world.

Meanwhile, a writer unlike all others of the period had been producing poetry which is now regarded as being on a much higher level than his contemporaries thought it to be. CHRISTOPHER SMART (1722–71) was educated at Cambridge, but he spent most of his later life in poverty, was for a while insane, and towards the end of his life went into a debtors' prison. Yet his *Song to David* (1763) is one of the greatest among English religious poems, and Robert Browning's *Saul* owed much to it. Smart's most remarkable work, *Jubilate Agno*, was left as a jumble of manuscript, which the editor of an edition published in 1954 has endeavoured to arrange in proper order. Even though, as a whole, *Jubilate Agno* is difficult to interpret, it contains much that is worth pondering; while the sections addressed to 'my Cat Jeoffrey' delight every lover of cats as well as every poetry lover.

TABLE OF THE AGE OF JOHNSON

General Prose	The Novel	Verse	The Drama
	Richardson's *Pamela*, 1740		
	Fielding's *Joseph Andrews*, 1742		
		Pope, d. 1744	
		Akenside's *Pleasures of the Imagination*, 1744	
	Richardson's *Clarissa*, 1748	Thomson's *Castle of Indolence*, 1748	
	Smollett's *Roderick Random*, 1748	Thomson, d. 1748	
	Fielding's *Tom Jones*, 1749	Johnson's *The Vanity of Human Wishes*, 1749	Johnson's *Irene*, 1749

Johnson's *Rambler*, 1750–52	—*Amelia*, 1751 Smollett's *Peregrine Pickle*, 1751 Richardson's *Sir Charles Grandison*, 1753	
Hume's *History of England*, 1754–61	Fielding, d. 1754	Crabbe, b. 1754
Johnson's *Dictionary*, 1755		
Burke's *Essay on the Sublime and Beautiful*, 1756		
Robertson's *History of Scotland*, 1758		Blake, b. 1757
	Johnson's *Rasselas*, 1759 Sterne's *Tristram Shandy*, 1759–61	Burns, b. 1759
	Richardson, d. 1761	Macpherson's *Ossian*, 1760–63 Smart's *Song to David*, 1763 Chatterton's *Poems*, 1764–70 Goldsmith's *Traveller*, 1764

	Walpole's *Castle of Otranto*, 1765	Percy's *Reliques of Ancient English Poetry*, 1765	
	Goldsmith's *Vicar of Wakefield*, 1766		The Drama Goldsmith's *Good-natured Man*, 1768
	Sterne, d. 1768		
Letters of Junius, 1769–72		Goldsmith's *Deserted Village*, 1770 Wordsworth, b. 1770 Chatterton, d. 1770	
	Smollett's *Humphry Clinker*, 1771 Smollett, d. 1771 Mackenzie's *Man of Feeling*, 1771	Beattie's *Minstrel*, 1771–74 Gray, d. 1771 Scott, b. 1771 Smart, d. 1771	
Goldsmith, d. 1774		Coleridge, b. 1772	Goldsmith's *She Stoops to Conquer*, 1773
Burke's *American Taxation*, 1774 —*Conciliation with America*, 1775 Gibbon's *Decline and Fall of the Roman Empire*, 1776–88		Southey, b. 1774	Sheridan's *Rivals*, 1775 —*School for Scandal*, 1777
	Burney's *Evelina*, 1778		

Johnson's *Lives of the Poets*, 1779–81		Crabbe's *Village*, 1783
		Blake's *Poetical Sketches*, 1783
Johnson, d. 1784		Cowper's *Task*, 1785
		Burns' first poems, 1786
		Byron, b. 1788
		Blake's *Songs of Innocence*, 1789
Burke's *Revolution in France*, 1790	Radcliffe's *Romance of the Forest*, 1791	
Paine's *Rights of Man*, 1791–92		
Boswell's *Life of Johnson*, 1791		
Godwin's *Political Justice*, 1793		Clare, b. 1793
Gibbon, d. 1794	Godwin's *Caleb Williams*, 1794	Blake's *Songs of Experience*, 1794
	Lewis' *The Monk*, 1795	Burns, d. 1796
Burke's *Regicide Peace*, 1796–97		
Burke, d. 1797		*Lyrical Ballads*, 1798
		Cowper, d. 1800

18

The Age of Wordsworth (1798–1832):
The Older Poets

86. The Age of Wordsworth. The Age of Wordsworth is the age of the Revolution in the history of politics and of what is broadly called the romantic triumph in that of literature; though, when we speak in this way, we have to remember that the triumph of romanticism was accompanied by that of naturalism (see §83). Now it is most important for us to understand that the movement in literature was only one aspect of a comprehensive general movement, another aspect of which is to be found in the Revolution. At bottom both the political and the literary movements were inspired by the same impatience of formulas, traditions, conventions, and the tyranny of the dead hand, by the same insistence upon individuality, and by the same craving for freedom and the larger life. In the doctrines of the new poetry, as in the teachings of the revolutionary theorists, there was indeed much that assumed the shape of challenge and attack. The long-accepted rules of art, in fact prescribed rules of any kind, were treated with open contempt; the reaction against Pope and the Augustan school became aggressive; and the principle of spontaneity was everywhere thrust to the front. Here and there, it is true, conservative critics endeavoured to make a stand against these, to them, wild and dangerous ideas; as when Lord Jeffrey wrote in an early number of the *Edinburgh Review*: 'Poetry has this much in common with religion, that its standards were fixed long ago by certain inspired writers, whose authority it is no longer lawful to call in question.' But such a conception of things did not represent the dominant spirit of the age. That spirit was rather expressed by Keats when he wrote: 'The genius of poetry must work out its own salvation in a man. It cannot be matured by law and precept, but by sensation and watchfulness in itself. That which is creative must create itself.' A comparison of this passage with the couplet from Pope which we have already quoted:

> 'Those rules of old discovered, not devis'd,
> Are Nature still, but Nature methodis'd,'

will suffice to show the fundamental difference in principle between Augustan and romantic poetry.

We are not of course to imagine that the political and the literary movements necessarily met in the same persons, or that a man could not be an adherent of the one without sympathising with the other. The error of such a supposition is at once exposed by the case of Scott, who was a romanticist and a Tory, and whose particular form of romanticism was indeed, as we shall see, a part of his Toryism. We are speaking only of movements; and the vital connection between these is denoted by the fact that the keynote of both was emancipation.

We have, however, to go further than this, and to consider the intimate association of English poetry with the various stages of the French Revolution and with the striking changes in the temper of European society which these produced. The great outburst of 1789 sent a thrill of fresh life through the whole civilised world. It came as the prophecy of a new day, and for the moment it seemed as if, leaving behind it all the evils of the past, humanity at large was to pass forward immediately into an era of realised democratic ideals—of liberty, brotherhood, and the rights of man. A wonderful humanitarian enthusiasm and gorgeous dreams of progress and perfection were thus kindled in ardent young souls; and in England, quite as much as in France itself, men of generous natures were ready to catch fire by contact with the passions which the French cause aroused because, as our later eighteenth century literature shows, there had been in England a steady growth of many of the principles which the political revolution now promised to translate out of abstractions into living facts. As Wordsworth afterwards wrote:

> 'But Europe at that time was thrilled with joy
> France standing on the top of golden hours,
> And human nature seeming born again;'

and once more:

> 'Bliss was it in that dawn to be alive,
> But to be young was very heaven.'

But as the progress of the French movement soon proved, the glorious promises of '89 were destined to remain unfulfilled. The excesses of the reign of terror; the sensational rise of Napoleon; the establishment of a military despotism; the long strain of the Napoleonic wars; the restoration of the Bourbons; the determined attempt made by the crowned heads of Europe after Waterloo to destroy democracy and popular government—all these things were naturally productive of vast disturbances in thought and feeling. Reaction set in; the principles of the Revolution were discredited; and the failure of the great effort which France had made to initiate a new and better order of things resulted in a general collapse of faith and hope. The age of buoyancy and expectation passed away. The age of unrest and disillusion succeeded. Thus we may expect to find an enormous difference in tone between the poetry of the earlier and that of the later revolutionary period.

87. Wordsworth's Life. WILLIAM WORDSWORTH was born in 1770 at Cockermouth, Cumberland, and spent much of his boyhood among the shepherds and dalesmen of his native county. The influence of these early surroundings was, as he afterwards said, profound and lasting; for rough and rugged as they were, these simple peasant folk were types of the homely virtues of manhood and womanhood untainted by contact with the corruptions of civilisation, and from his familiar intercourse with them he learned faith in humanity and reverence for the elemental things of life. He was educated at Hawkeshead School, Lancashire, and at Cambridge. Then came two visits to France (1790 and 1791–92). In 1793 he published *An Evening Walk* and *Descriptive Sketches,* in which the regular classic couplet is used, and which are otherwise curiously reminiscent of Pope, Goldsmith, and Crabbe. A small legacy left by a friend made him so far independent that he was able henceforth to devote himself entirely to poetry. His friendship with Coleridge, which began about 1796, did much to stimulate his genius. Two years later Coleridge joined him in the publication of that epoch-making little book, the *Lyrical Ballads.* In 1802 he married Mary Hutchinson, and with his devoted sister Dorothy as a third member of his household, settled first at Grasmere and later at Rydal Mount, both in that Lake District with which his name is now always associated. Though he continued to write steadily, he failed for many years to catch the public ear, while the critics almost unanimously treated him with contempt. But little by little he won his way, and readers of the new generation began to perceive greatness and meaning in his poetry to which their fathers had been blind. The general change of opinion regarding him was shown in 1843, when, on Southey's death, he was made poet laureate. He died in 1850.

Some knowledge of his relations with the revolutionary movement is an indispensable preliminary to the study of his work. These relations are described in detail, together with other formative influences of his life, in his autobiographical poem, *The Prelude.* On his first visit to France during his vacation tour in 1790, he was delighted to find 'benevolence and blessedness spread like a fragrance everywhere'; but, though his attitude towards the popular cause was sympathetic, he was for the time being only an onlooker. During the thirteen months of his second visit his position was very different. At Orléans, where the greater part of his time was spent, he formed an intimacy with an officer of Girondist views named Beaupuis, with whom he freely discussed the iniquities of the old order and speculated on all the golden promises of the new; and he now became such an enthusiastic supporter of the Revolution that on his arrival in Paris in October, 1792, just after the September massacres, he was on the point of throwing in his lot with the Girondist party. Fortunately for him, he received a peremptory call from relatives in England and returned in time to escape the disaster which overwhelmed that party in the Reign of Terror. In England he found conservative opinion running strongly against the Revolution, the defence of which he accordingly undertook in an open letter to the Bishop of Llandaff. The outbreak of war between France and England, however, precipitated a crisis in his thought. At first he held fast to the French cause. Then came the Terror, and his faith was rudely shaken. It revived for a moment on the fall of Robespierre, only to be destroyed for ever by the rise of Napoleon and the events which followed. Then reaction set in, and this reaction led him first to rupture with France then to the repudiation of the abstract principles behind the Revolution, and finally to the complete recantation of all his youthful progressive ideas. Thus Wordsworth, who began as an adherent of the Revolution, ended as an extreme conservative. Even during his residence in France he had deplored the fact that the cause of progress entailed the destruction, together with the evils of the past, of so much that was sacred through age and association. The sense of the sanctity of the past now became a prominent element in his thought, and made him an earnest supporter of English institutions and traditions. Yet, despite the apparently complete collapse of all his revolutionary ideals, Wordsworth's work remained to the end a part of the great general democratic movement of his time. We shall understand this on turning to his theory of poetry.

88. The Lyrical Ballads and Wordsworth's Theory of Poetry. I have spoken of the *Lyrical Ballads* as an epoch-making little book, and it is universally admitted that a new chapter in the history of English poetry opens with its publication. The explanation of this is to be found in the fact that it marks the full development of both romanticism and naturalism. As Coleridge afterwards explained, the design of the collaborators was to include in it two different kinds of poetry; in the one, 'the incidents and agents were to be, in part at least, supernatural;' in the other, 'subjects were to be chosen from ordinary life.' Romanticism was represented by Coleridge's single contribution, *The Ancient Mariner*, naturalism by Wordsworth's *Goody Blake, The Thorn, The Idiot Boy,* and other similar productions.

In his preface to the second edition of the *Ballads,* Wordsworth further sets forth his aims. 'The principal object, then, proposed in these poems was to choose incidents and situations from common life, and to relate or describe them throughout in a selection of the language really used by men, and at the same time to throw over them a certain colouring of imagination, whereby ordinary things should be presented to the mind in an unusual aspect'; and he goes on to say that 'humble and rustic life was generally chosen because in that condition the essential passions of the heart find a better soil in which they can attain their maturity, are less under restraint, and speak a plainer and more emphatic language'. In this declaration three points call for comment. In the first place, there is Wordsworth's choice of subject; in search of themes he goes straight to common life, and by preference, for the reasons assigned, to humble rustic life. This was throughout his habit in his narrative and descriptive poems, of which *Michael* may be mentioned as a typical example. Secondly, in the treatment of such themes, he sets out to employ the appropriate language of actual life in place of the pompous and stilted circumlocutions of eighteenth century writers. This brings us to his famous attack upon the whole practice of the Augustan school and its 'gaudiness and inane phraseology'. To this attack we have more than once had occasion to allude. In connection with it, it should here be noted that in seeking to obliterate the difference between the language of poetry and that of good prose Wordsworth pushed his theories much too far; that, save in his early experiments, he did not himself adhere to his own principles; and that nonetheless his arguments were of immense service in helping to destroy the prestige of the long-accepted hackneyed and conventional diction and to substitute a simple and natural style in poetry. Thirdly, Wordsworth specially guards himself against the accusation of absolute realism by emphasising his use of imagination in the poetic transformation of his materials. This is a protest against the hard, literal, unimaginative treatment of life to which naturalism had led, as in the case of Crabbe.

It will now be seen why we are justified in describing Wordsworth's work as part of the general democratic movement of his time. His comprehensive sympathies, his insistence upon the primary and essential qualities of human nature as distinguished from the merely external and factitious, his firm belief in natural manhood, his deliberate selection of homely materials as the best for poetic purposes—all these features connect him with the radical tendencies of the revolutionary age. The whole trend of his writings was, moreover, towards the simplification of life, and in this way again he was in harmony with the revolutionary spirit. Even his theory of poetic diction is only another aspect of his general effort to pierce down through artifice and convention to nature and reality.

89. Characteristics of Wordsworth's Poetry. As Pope is our greatest poet of the town and of artificial life, so Wordsworth is our greatest poet of the country and of natural life. As an interpreter of nature he still holds the first place unchallenged. His love of nature was boundless, and his knowledge of nature was equal to his love. He wrote always (in his own words) with his eye 'steadily fixed upon his object'; nothing was too small to escape his attention; and his controlling purpose was to render with absolute fidelity what he had seen. He has been called, and rightly, 'the keenest eyed of all modern poets for what is deep and essential in nature,' and it has justly been said that in all his descriptions 'every touch is true, not the copying of a literary phrase, but the result of direct observation'.

Yet love, knowledge, and fidelity are not, after all, the most specific and personal qualities in Wordsworth's nature poetry, but rather the profound religious feeling which pervades it. As he shows us again and again in many of his poems—in the *Lines written above Tintern Abbey,* for example, and the *Ode on the Intimations of Immortality*—nature was for him the embodiment of the Divine Spirit; and when he insists (and this is a fundamental principle in his philosophy) that nature is the greatest of all teachers, he means that between the indwelling Soul of the Universe and the soul of man, which is akin to it, spiritual communion is possible through which we may gain constantly in power, peace, and happiness.

While, however, Wordsworth is essentially the poet of nature, he is not the less the poet of man, and in what he writes about human life his greatness as a moralist is specially apparent. This greatness results largely from his firm hold upon the central facts of conduct and duty, and his abiding sense of the supremacy of the moral law. His emphasis is everywhere thrown upon those spiritual forces within us which give us power over ourselves and the ability, if we exercise them alright, to lift ourselves through conscious and patient effort, above the reach of circumstance and the flux of external things.

The limitations of Wordsworth's genius are very obvious. He had no humour and little passion, and was singularly deficient in dramatic power. Even those who revere him most are bound to acknowledge that he wrote more uninspired and unpoetic verse than any other poet of equal rank. In his statedly philosophical poetry particularly, and notably in *The Excursion,* he often indulges for hundreds of lines together in prolix moralisings of the dullest and most prosaic kind. There is indeed an immense amount of perishable matter in his collected works, and beyond most great poets, therefore, he gains by judicious selection. But if what is best and really vital in his voluminous output is relatively to the total bulk of it small in amount, it comprises some of the finest treasures in English poetry, and suffices to give him a high place among those of whom he himself writes:

'Blessings be with them, and eternal praise,
Who gave us nobler loves, and nobler cares—
The Poets, who on earth have made us heirs
Of truth and pure delight by heavenly lays.'

90. Coleridge. Wordsworth's friend, SAMUEL TAYLOR COLERIDGE (1772–1834) was a boy at Christ's Hospital when the Bastille fell. The Revolution instantly appealed to him, and he welcomed it in some youthful verses. He carried his enthusiasm with him to Cambridge, where, however, he suffered much from ill-health and anxiety about debts. In 1794 he met Robert Southey (afterwards his brother-in-law) and with a few other congenial spirits the two young men entered into a scheme, which Coleridge christened Pantisocracy, for the establishment of an ideal society on the banks of the Susquehanna River in America. This Utopian plan, a direct product, of course, of revolutionary zeal, came to nothing; but meanwhile Coleridge gave poetic expression to his political aspirations in *Religious Musings,* the *Destiny of Nations,* and *Ode to the Departing Year* (1796). But the change in thought which soon came is shown in his splendid *France: an Ode* (1798), which he himself called his 'recantation'. After this, like Wordsworth, he went through all the stages of reaction, and before long allied himself definitely with the conservative cause. The subsequent story of his life is a story of aimless wanderings, of plans made and abandoned, of failure and the bitter sense of failure. A man of gigantic genius, he was absolutely wanting in will-power, and his slavery to opium, which lasted many years, helped still further to paralyse his energies. So the divinely gifted Coleridge shambled through life, dreaming great dreams and projecting great books; but the dreams were never realised, and the books were never written. All his work is fragmentary; yet his was so original and seminal a mind that in theology, philosophy, and literary criticism (to which he gave much time in later years) he exercised an influence out of all proportion to the bulk and apparent importance of his writings.

What is best in Coleridge's poetry is very small in amount, but that little is of rare excellence. His personal poems, like *Dejection: an Ode* and the poem, *Work without Hope,* have a pathetic interest in connection with the tragedy of ineffectiveness which made up so much of his life. But his historical importance is due mainly to such poems as *The Ancient Mariner* and *Christabel,* which represent the triumph of romanticism as fully as Wordsworth's narrative poems represent the triumph of naturalism. We have already seen that Coleridge took the supernatural as his particular province, and far beyond any writer before him he treated the supernatural in a purely poetic way. It will be remembered that Wordsworth saved naturalism from the hard literalism to which it was tending by naturalism from the coarse sensationalism then in vogue by linking it with psychological truth.

91. Scott. Romanticism found a less subtle but far more popular and influential interpreter in WALTER SCOTT, in whom may be said to have culminated the whole movement for the revival of the romantic past. A descendant of families whose names had figured prominently in the annals of Scottish chivalry, Scott was born in Edinburgh in 1771, and spent much of his childhood at his grandfather's home at Sandy Knowe, in the Border country, where he learned to love the wild, rough landscape, and where his boyish imagination was stirred by the stories which relatives there told him of Border battles in which forebears of his own had taken part, and of later Jacobite risings in support of Prince Charlie. A chance reading, when he was thirteen, of Percy's *Reliques* (from that time on one of his favourite volumes) aroused a passionate interest in ancient ballads, which he soon began to collect on his own account. While reading for the Bar, and during his early practice, he made several long vacation excursions into the Highlands, the inspiring purpose of which was always romantic and antiquarian; and, as to go into the Highlands in those days meant to step right out of the present into the feudal past, he gathered rich stores of material for future use.

A born Tory, whose sympathies were entirely with the feudal and chivalrous order, he was little affected by the Revolution, which, save that it served to deepen his hatred of democracy and to throw him back with fresh ardour upon history and romance, was only an incident in his career. But, meanwhile, he had become interested in German romantic literature, and the translating of some German ballads led him to independent experiments of the same kind. In these he was encouraged by Lewis. Then, still inspired by Percy, he turned his large collections of many years to good account in his first important publication, *The Minstrelsy of the Scottish Border* (1802–03). Out of this grew his first long poem, *The Lay of the Last Minstrel* (1805), a sort of extended ballad full of Border incidents, fighting, and enchantments. There was an eager public for just such a complete revelation of the interest of medieval story, and the *Lay* scored a success which surprised no one more than Scott himself. It was followed by other romances in verse, of which the most important are *Marmion* (1808), *The Lady of the Lake* (1810), and *Rokeby* (1813). Then the gradual exhaustion of the vein opened up by the *Lay* and the dangerous rivalry of Byron, who just then took the British public by storm, compelled Scott to seek a fresh outlet for his genius, and with the production of *Waverley* (1814) the romantic poet entered upon a new and even more brilliant career as the romantic novelist. Of his work in prose fiction I shall speak in another chapter. Here I may add that financial ruin overtook him in 1825; that unspoilt by long good fortune, he now showed himself heroic in adversity; that despite fast-failing health, he kept up to the last his splendid struggle to wipe off his immense indebtedness by the labours of his pen; and that he died in 1832.

Scott's poetry is just the kind of poetry we should expect from a man of his character and training. He rejected altogether the classic epic as his model, and his 'romantic tales in verse', as he called them, represent a natural development of the old ballad and medieval romance. In style, he is vigorous, free and rapid, but often careless, diffuse, and commonplace. He can tell a story admirably, and is particularly successful with scenes of stirring action and, above all, with his battle pieces. In the large, bold treatment of landscape he is also a master. But he wrote too fast, and his wonderful facility was often fatal. He has nothing of the mystical quality and the spiritual power of Wordsworth and Coleridge; he rarely takes us beneath the surface of things; he carries no weight of thought; and, while his tone is eminently healthy, his moralising is of the tritest.

92. Other Poets Contemporary with Wordsworth. With Wordsworth, Coleridge, and Scott I will here associate the more important poets who were born in their decade, or earlier, that is, before 1780. Taken in their chronological order, they are as follows: William Lisle Bowles (1762–1850); Samuel Rogers (1763–1855); James Hogg (1770–1835); Robert Southey (1774–1843); Walter Savage Landor (1775–1864); Thomas Campbell (1777–1844); and Thomas Moore (1779–1852).

Though little known today, Bowles deserves a word of kindly recognition, because his *Sonnets* ('written chiefly in Picturesque Spots during a Journey', as the title-page says, and first published in 1789), helped the growth of a love of nature in poetry in the years immediately preceding the *Lyrical Ballads*. Coleridge testified to the great influence they had upon him when he read them as a youth, and they were much admired abo by Wordsworth.

ROGERS, who was a successful banker as well as a poet (a rare combination), lived well on into the Victorian age, yet remained practically untouched by the spirit of the Revolution and by the new movements in literature, of which he witnessed the rise and triumph. His *Pleasures of Memory* (1792) is written in the orthodox closed couplet and in the 'correct' Augustan style; and, though his guide-book poem *Italy* (1822) is in blank verse, it maintains the tradition of artificial elegance. Rogers belonged to the past, but did not possess the strength of genius to initiate a reaction.

HOGG, nicknamed 'the Ettrick Shepherd', is better known today through his friendship with some of Edinburgh's famous literary men, including Scott, than for his own work, though he wrote much in prose and verse. Some of his ballads keep an honourable place in Scottish vernacular literature, while his longer poems, *Kilmeny* and *The Queen's Wake,* have a certain amount of fancy and power. After Burns (though a long way after) he is the truest poet who has ever sprung direct from the Scottish peasantry.

 SOUTHEY deserves a somewhat fuller notice. Like Wordsworth and Coleridge he fell as a youth under the spell of the Revolution, and gave vent to the most violent radical ideas and to his impatience of all the evils that are done under the sun, in an epic, *Joan of Arc* (written 1793, published 1796), a drama, *Wat Tyler* (1794), and a number of minor poems. The overthrow of the Girondist party was the turning-point in his political history, and ultimately, like Wordsworth and Coleridge, he repudiated all his early ideas and became a Tory of the Tories. He was a man of prodigious industry in verse and prose; his poems alone filling a volume of 800 pages of fine print in double columns. Little of this enormous output, however, now really lives, except some of his ballads, which are excellent, and such delightful lyrics as *After Blenheim, The Holly Tree,* and *The Scholar.* His *Joan of Arc* and *Wat Tyler* are full of all the extravagances which we should expect in the work of a raw, high-spirited youth; his ill-advised and ludicrous eulogy of George III, *A Vision of Judgment,* is remembered only through Byron's scathing satire upon it. His immense narrative poems (they can scarcely be called epics), on which he staked his poetic reputation—*Madoc, Thalaba the Destroyer, Roderick, The Curse of Kehama*—though greatly admired at the time by men like Scott, Landor, and Shelley, must now be regarded as monuments rather of their author's learning and industry than of real poetic inspiration. Yet their historical importance is considerable. They show the tendency of the romantic movement to carry the poet further and further afield in quest of fresh, striking, and picturesque objects, and two of them mark an extreme reaction in form against the regularity of eighteenth century versification. *Thalaba* is in unrhymed verses of varying length and metrical structure. *Kehama* preserves the metrical irregularity, though with the addition of rime. The verse of *Thalaba* was Shelley's model in *Queen Mab.*

 LANDOR wrote poetry all through his long life, his first volume appearing in 1795, his last in 1863; but while he gained an 'audience fit though few', he never became popular. He may be described as a classic writing in a romantic age, but his classicism was of the genuine Greek kind, and had nothing in common with the pseudo-classicism of the eighteenth century. Whether he deals with classic themes, as in his *Hellenics,* or with romantic, as in *Gebir,* he writes in the same restrained, severe, and sculpturesque manner. As Sir Henry Taylor said of him, he 'lived in a past world of heroic thought, unaltered by the events of common life; he passed nearly through the most eventful century of the world without learning from experience, and almost without adding to his ideas'.

CAMPBELL'S case was different. His early work shows little sign of rupture with the Augustan tradition in thought or form. His *Pleasures of Hope* (1799)—a much better thing than Rogers's *Pleasures of Memory*—belongs in matter and style to the outgoing school, and, like *Theodoric* many years later, is written in the closed couplet. But beneath the conventional surface of its diction there is a good deal of revolutionary feeling. Later, Campbell reflected the new poetical influences of his time, and in *Gertrude of Wyoming* (in which the Spenserian stanza is used) he is almost romantic. Some of his shorter poems—*Lochiel, Lord Ullin's Daughter,* and *The Last Man,* among them—are really striking; but he is chiefly known today for his vigorous war lyrics—*Ye Mariners of England, Hohenlinden, The Battle of the Baltic*—which rank among the best things of the kind in the language.

Of all the writers named in this section it is probable that Moore is now most attractive to the general reader. It is true that his once famous *Lalla Rookh*—an oriental tale in the style for which his friend Byron had prepared the public taste—is sadly faded. But it is not to this ambitious work that we should turn if we want to know what Moore can do at his best. It is rather to his *Irish Melodies.* He has been called the last of our minstrels, and the description is not inapt. He had a genuine lyric gift, and if his verse often lacks depth of feeling and is pervaded by a sentimentalism which has not worn well, there is enough that is really living in it to ensure him a permanent place among the poets whom we classify as singers.

19

The Age of Wordsworth:
The Younger Poets

93. The Later Revolutionary Age. The close of the French Revolution did not mean the end of the revolutionary movement, even in the field of politics. The people of Europe had been aroused, and were not now to be crushed or pacified. Hence repeated disturbances in Spain, Portugal, Italy, Greece, and much dangerous discontent in England. But meanwhile, as we have seen, a strong conservative reaction had set in; many of the older generation abandoned their early faith, and for a time the principles of progress and popular government suffered eclipse. The complacency of toryism, however, was impossible to many of the more fiery spirits among the younger men. Growing into manhood just in time to realise the full meaning of what seemed to be the failure of the democratic cause, they found themselves in a world which had emerged from the long strain of revolutionary excitement, exhausted but not satisfied. The old enthusiasms and hope had gone, and their collapse was followed here by apathy and indifference, there by the cynicism which often results from exploded idealism, and there again by the mood of bitter disappointment and aimless unrest. Such were the conditions which naturally weighed heavily upon the English poets who were born into the later revolutionary age. Yet every man will respond to the influences of his time in accordance with the peculiarities of his own genius and character; and, though the three chief poets of our younger revolutionary group, Byron, Shelley, and Keats, breathed the same atmosphere, and saw the same forces at work about them, nothing could well be more striking than the contrast between each and each in the quality and temper of their poetry.

94. Byron. The eldest of the three, GEORGE GORDON, LORD BYRON, is in the largest sense also the most thoroughly representative, because more than any other English writer he expressed that spirit of rebellion, at once comprehensive, passionate, and impotent, which was one of the salient features of his age. His own temperament and stormy life helped him to become its mouthpiece. Born in 1788, he sprang from a wild unruly stock, and from his father and mother inherited that irritable and volcanic character which repeatedly brought him into conflict with men and things. Hardly more than a boy, he published a little volume of verse, *Hours of Idleness,* which was ferociously attacked by the *Edinburgh Review.* To this attack he replied in a vigorous satire, *English Bards and Scotch Reviewers.* A tour on the Continent in 1809–11 furnished the materials for the first two cantos of *Childe Harold's Pilgrimage,* in which descriptions of the places he had visited were combined with historic memories and much melancholy meditation upon the instability of human grandeur and power. Published in 1812, these two cantos scored an immense success. 'I woke up one morning', said Byron, 'and found myself famous.' Then for a time he was the idol of the brilliant and dissipated society of the Regency, and amazed and delighted his thousands of readers with the fierce emotion and highly coloured scenery of his romances in verse—*The Giaour, The Bride of Abydos, The Siege of Corinth, The Corsair.* In 1815 he married; a year after, he and his wife separated; scandal broke out; he was execrated and denounced as a monster of iniquity by the very public which had lately loaded him with extravagant adulation; and he left England an embittered man. The remainder of his life was spent on the Continent, and it was during these years of exile that he produced his greatest work—*Manfred, Cain,* the third and fourth cantos of *Childe Harold,* and the unfinished *Don Juan.* In the end, weary of everything—of fame, of poetry, even of himself—he threw himself into the cause of Greece then struggling for freedom against the Turks, took the field, and died in 1824 of a fever at Missoionghi, before he had completed his thirty-seventh year.

Byron wrote with almost incredible facility, and his work is not only very voluminous, but also—including as it does lyrics, satires, narrative poems serious and serio-comic, regular tragedies and dramatic poems—apparently very varied. But the variety is only apparent; for Byron was a supreme egotist, and, no matter what the form adopted, rarely travelled outside himself, the result being that the final impression left by his poetry is an impression not of variety but of monotony. As a critic and theorist, he proclaimed himself an adherent of the Augustan school; admired Pope; cared little for Wordsworth or Coleridge; and compared the poetry of the eighteenth century with a Greek temple, and that of his own time with a barbarous Turkish mosque. Yet, as he himself admitted, no one had done more than himself to substitute the mosque for the temple; for, whatever his principles, the entire weight of his practical influence was on the side of romanticism. Lapse of time and changes both of feeling and of taste have played havoc with his poetry as a whole; much of it that held its first readers spellbound now seems tawdry and commonplace; he is often noisy and declamatory rather than poetical; and at times at least he is guilty of pose. But with all his carelessness and his many faults, he has amazing vitality and power, and in his most impassioned moods his verse rushes on like a torrent. He is at his best in description, especially when he blends description with meditation. As a poet of nature he is most at home with nature's wilder aspects; he loves mountains and storms, and he glories in the sea, because of its utter indifference to man. It must be added that as a satirist (as in the *Vision of Judgment* and *Don Juan*) he is incomparably the greatest of modern English poets.

His place in the literature of his age has already been indicated.

It is suggested by the very word Byronism, which we still use to denote the spirit of gloom, satiety, and unrest which is characteristic of most of his writings. As a revolutionary poet he represents the destructive side of the revolutionary movement only. Of its utopianism and social aspirations he knows nothing. He had no faith in the older order, and in many places, as in the brilliant *Vision of Judgment* (his reply to Southey's foolish poem of the same name) he pours merciless ridicule upon the spent forces of the ancient feudalism and monarchy. But he had no new faith to offer the world in place of the old, and his philosophy ends in blank negation. Vanity of vanities is the key-note of it. He is an apostle of liberty, but he conceives liberty in terms of pure individualism. The heroes of his romances are pirates, corsairs, outlaws, Ishmaels; in his *Childe Harold, Manfred, Cain, Don Juan,* he idealises all who are in revolt against society. Nor does he stop with his attack upon society. If society is rotten, the whole universe too is out of joint. He is therefore a rebel against the very conditions of human life—against what men have called the ways of providence and the moral order. In *Don Juan* he turns the batteries of his satire upon the conventions and hypocrisies of society. In *Cain* he produces a terrific indictment of God's dealings with men as interpreted by the current theology of his time.

95. Shelley. Byron, then, is our great interpreter of revolutionary iconoclasm. PERCY BYSSHE SHELLEY, on the contrary, is our revolutionary idealist, and our one poetic prophet of faith and hope in a world which for the moment had lost both. He was the son of a Tory squire; was born in 1792; and after some unhappy years at Eton, where he was nicknamed 'the mad Shelley', went up to Oxford, whence, however, he was soon expelled for publishing a pamphlet on *The Necessity of Atheism*. An ill-advised marriage with a mere school-girl, Harriet Westbrook, led to open rupture with his family, and Shelley found himself adrift. After the tragic death of his young wife, he married Mary, the daughter of William Godwin (see §71), whose influence on his mind was already immense. This second union proved a very happy one, for in Mary he had an intellectual companion, and a comfort and stay amid all the troubles arising from quarrels with his relatives, law suits about his property and his children, and his own highly strung temperament and fragile health. In 1818 he left England for Italy, and in 1822 was drowned while sailing across the Bay of Spezzia.

In the body of Shelley's writings two poems stand outside any general classification that can be made. One is *Adonais,* a splendid elegy on the death of Keats; the other, *The Cenci,* a romantic drama on a subject really too horrible for treatment, which nonetheless rises in places to a height of tragic intensity which we can parallel only by going back to some of the greatest things of the Elizabethan stage. Apart from these, his poems fall into two divisions. There are in the first place, his personal poems. Shelley's genius was essentially lyrical, and his moods, impressions, thoughts, and emotions embodied themselves naturally in verse. As a lyric poet, he ranks with our very greatest, and no praise would be excessive for the ecstasy of feeling, the lightness and grace, the felicity of phrase and the verbal magic of such poems, for example, as *The Skylark, The Cloud, The Sensitive Plant,* the *Ode to the West Wind,* and *A Lament.* In the second place there are the impersonal poems. Dreamer of dreams as he was, Shelley yet conceived it to be part of his poetic mission to become the inspirer and guide of men. He had, as he confessed, a passion for reforming the world, and this passion blazes out again and again in his poetry, in flames that are now fiercely lurid and now matchlessly pure. As he explained in the preface to *The Revolt of Islam,* he believed that the reaction which had followed the Revolution, though inevitable with those who did not look beneath the surface of things, would prove to be a temporary reaction only; already, he thought, the gloom and misanthropy which it had bred were passing away; and thus, despite the surrounding darkness, he held that the dawn of a new day was at hand. Such was the faith to which he clung steadily through all the doubts and disappointments of his time; such was the faith by which all his humanitarian poems were inspired. In *Queen Mab,* which he wrote at eighteen, his revolutionary creed had not yet passed beyond the destructive stage. Based on Godwin's *Political Justice,* whole passages of which are simply turned into verse, this violent and aggressive poem proclaims an individualistic philosophy of the most uncompromising kind. All institutions are condemned—kings and governments, church, property, and marriage, while Christianity falls under the same sweeping censure. Yet even this extravagant diatribe is redeemed by that fine passion for humanity which formed the basis of Shelley's religion. *The Revolt of Islam,* which followed in 1817, is a long rambling narrative in Spenserian stanzas, and is charged with the young poet's hopes for the future regeneration of the world. As a story it is confused and almost unintelligible, but it is very important as helping us to understand the fundamental difference between Shelley and Byron as interpreters of the Revolution. Byron's heroes—his Lara, Manfred, Childe Harold, Don Juan, and the rest of them—are self-engrossed egotists, and, as I have said, mere rebels against society. Laon, the hero of *The Revolt of Islam,* on the other hand, is filled with Shelley's own magnificent and unselfish enthusiasm, his one abiding purpose is to be the saviour of society, and in the end he becomes a willing martyr for the cause of man. But the fullest and finest expression of Shelley's faith and hope is to be found in his superb lyrical drama, *Prometheus Unbound.* In this re-adaptation of the famous old Greek myth, the Titan stands forth as the prototype of mankind in its long struggle against the forces of despotism, symbolised by Jupiter, and the allegory closes with a magnificent choral outburst over the consummation of the divine purpose in a regenerated world.

96. Keats. In JOHN KEATS (1795–1821), the last and youngest of the later revolutionary group, we have a remarkable contrast both with Byron on the one side and with Shelley on the other. Keats was neither rebel nor Utopian dreamer. Endowed with a purely artistic nature, he took up in regard to all the movements and conflicts of his time a position of almost complete detachment. He knew nothing of Byron's stormy spirit of antagonism to the existing order of things, and he had no sympathy with Shelley's humanitarian zeal and passion for reforming the world. According to his conception of it, poetry should be, not the vehicle of philosophy, religious teaching, or social and political theories, but the incarnation of beauty. The famous opening line of *Endymion*—'A thing of beauty is a joy for ever'—strikes the key-note of his work. 'I have loved', he declared in one of his later letters, 'the principle of beauty in all things'; and as the modern world seemed to him to be hard, cold, and prosaic, he habitually sought an imaginative escape from it, not like Shelley into the future land of promise, but into the past of Greek mythology, as in *Endymion, Lamia,* and the fragmentary *Hyperion*, or of medieval romance, as in *The Eve of St. Agnes, Isabella,* and *La Belle Dame Sans Merci*. In his treatment of nature this same passion for sensuous beauty is still the dominant feature. He loved nature just for its own sake and for the 'glory and loveliness' which he everywhere found in it, and no modern poet has ever been nearer than he was to the simple 'poetry of earth'; but there was nothing mystical in the love, and nature was never fraught for him, as for Wordsworth and Shelley, with spiritual messages and meanings.

Keats died of consumption before he had completed his twenty-sixth year, and is therefore, in Shelley's phrase, one of 'the inheritors of unfulfilled renown'. Allowance must thus always be made for the immaturity and experimental character of much of his work. His genius was ripening steadily at the time of his premature death, and we can measure his moral and spiritual as well as his artistic growth during the few years of his manhood by comparing his first little volume of verse published in 1817, or *Endymion* which appeared the next year, with the contents of his third and last volume—the volume of 1819—and especially with the great odes *To Autumn, To a Nightingale,* and *On a Grecian Urn*. But, even as it is, his place is assured, as Shelley prophesied, 'with the enduring dead.' Historically, he is important for three reasons. First, on the side of form and style he is the most romantic of the romantic poets, handling even his Greek themes with a luxuriance of language and a wealth of detail as far as possible removed from the temperance and restraint of Hellenic art. Here, in particular, we note his entire rejection of the classic couplet, for which, following the lead of his friend Leigh Hunt (see next section) he substituted couplets of the loose romantic type (see §49). Secondly, more than any other great poet of his time, he represents the exhaustion of the impulses generated by the social upheaval and the humanitarian enthusiasms of the Revolution. With him poetry breaks away from the interests of contemporary life, returns to the past, and devotes itself to the service of beauty. It is for this reason that he seems to stand definitely at the end of his age. Finally, his influence was nonetheless very strong upon the poets of the succeeding generation.

97. Other Poets of Later Revolutionary Age. This was a period of great poetic activity, and only a few of the minor poets can be mentioned here. Among them, special interest attaches to James Henry Leigh Hunt (1784–1859), because of his close relations with Shelley and Keats. It was in his *Story of Rimini* (1816) that the classic couplet was first rejected in favour of the freer form which had been employed by some of the pre-Augustan poets. In this innovation he was followed not only by Keats, as we have seen, but also by Shelley, though it should be added that in Keats's early experiments, as in the 'slip-shod' *Endymion,* freedom was carried to a degree of licence, which Hunt himself did not approve. The best of Hunt's work is in prose, but of this we shall speak later. Another poet on our list, THOMAS or TOM HOOD (1799–1845) is remotely connected with Keats, for he married a sister of Keats's most intimate friend, John Hamilton Reynolds. Hood's life was one protracted struggle against poverty and ill-health, and of the work which he did under constant pressure of necessity during some twenty-four years of hack-writing, at least one-half may be set aside as valueless. He is perhaps chiefly remembered for his humorous poems, in which he proved himself to be our greatest master of verbal wit and punning. But his serious poetry should not be neglected, for he was a true poet if not exactly a great one. He wrote some superb ballads and lyrics, like *The Dream of*

Eugene Aram, *The Song of the Shirt*, *The Bridge of Sighs*, *Fair Inez*, 'I remember, I remember'; his ode *To Melancholy* and his sonnet *Silence* are amongst the finest things of the kind in the language; the *Plea for the Midsummer Night Fairies* is full of graceful fancy; *The Haunted House* is wrought with splendidly sustained imaginative power; while *Miss Kilmansegg* is a masterpiece in a very difficult form of poetry, the gruesome grotesque. With Hood we may associate WINTHROP MACKWORTH PRAED (1802–39), a writer of admirable society verses, and RICHARD HARRIS BARHAM (1788–1845), whose ever-delightful *Ingoldsby Legends* are a burlesque development of the mediaevalism which Scott and others bad made so popular. In *The Bride's Tragedy* and *Death's Jest-Book* of THOMAS LOVELL BEDDOES (1803–49), we have a strange revival of the morbid and fantastic spirit of the later Elizabethan drama. Two women poets, FELICIA DOROTHEA HEMANS (1793–1835) and LETITIA ELIZABETH LANDON, known as L.E.L. (1802–38), must also be named. They both wrote much fluent and graceful verse, which caught the romantic and sentimental taste of the time, and assured them a wide public. But they were both wordy and rather weak, and in the case of L.E.L. particularly there was a marked tendency to mere gush. Few people would now think of reading the longer works of either of these writers; but they possess a rather faint sort of historical interest, while some of Mrs. Hemans' shorter effusions still enjoy popularity in children's books.

A stranger but finer poet was JOHN CLARE (1793–1864), who wrote much of his best verse while confined in the mad-house at Northampton where he died. Born poor and poor all his life, he was the last of the genuine peasant poets, writing of English country scenes at all seasons, and of the land he had know as a farm-hand before insanity afflicted him. He also continued for long years to compose affecting love poems to a girl who was perhaps more imagined than recollected. The several volumes of poems published in his lifetime are represented in *Selected Poems* (ed. Grigson, 1950) and the same editor has collected *Poems of Clare's Madness* (1949).

20

The Age of Wordsworth:
General Prose

98. General Characteristics. An important feature in the history of prose literature during the Age of Wordsworth was the rise of the modern review and magazine. First came the *Edinburgh Review*, established in 1802 by Jeffrey, Brougham, Sydney Smith, and other prominent men of letters of the Whig party. Seven years later, the *Quarterly* was started as a Tory counterblast. William Gifford was its first editor, and on his retirement in 1824 he was succeeded by Scott's son-in-law, Lockhart. These were followed by two important magazines, the range and interest of which, as the name implied, were intended to be broader and more varied than was the case with the regular review—*Blackwood's Edinburgh Magazine,* a Tory monthly launched in 1817 by Wilson, Lockhart, and Hogg; and shortly afterwards, as its rival, *The London Magazine,* which included among its early contributors Lamb, Hazlitt, De Quincey (who was also a '*Blackwood's* man'), Tom Hood, Allan Cunningham, and Carlyle. Another well-known periodical of the same general type, *Fraser's,* was founded in 1830.

Nearly all the men who are to be mentioned in this chapter were regular periodical writers, and some of them gave the whole of their time and energies to this practically new form of literature. It is well, therefore, to realise the influence which this form exerted upon prose literature in general. Two points may be emphasised. In the first place, it gave great encouragement to essay-writing, and for this reason we find that most of the prose writers of the time were essayists rather than makers of books. Secondly, it offered a fresh field for criticism, and especially for the criticism of contemporary literature. In this literature of criticism considerable space was naturally devoted to the discussion of the respective principles and merits of the old school and the new, and thus the critics of the age divided, roughly speaking, into two groups—the conservative or classical, and the radical or romantic.

It should also be noted that fundamental changes now appear in the form and temper of prose, and that these changes are parallel with those which had come over verse. We have seen how modern prose arose at the time of the Restoration (see §53), and with what effect it was employed in the eighteenth century by masters like Addison and Goldsmith. Yet this prose was a characteristic product of its age in its limitations as well as in its excellences; it had lucidity, grace, and charm, but it was wanting in variety, warmth, and colour; nor was it the sort of prose in which one could express strong passion or deep feeling. Now the romantic movement brought with it strong passion and deep feeling, and a love of variety, warmth, and colour. We shall not be surprised, therefore, to learn that many of the prose writers of the early nineteenth century discarded entirely the eighteenth century tradition, and sought richer harmonies and greater complexity of structure. This new movement in prose, like the corresponding movement in verse, was in part connected with the revival of interest in our pre-Augustan authors.

As a matter of convenience, we may arrange the writers with whom we have to deal in three groups, taking first those who were chiefly associated with the two great Edinburgh periodicals; secondly, the London men, who were largely, if not entirely, journalists and miscellanists; and lastly, such writers as do not naturally fall under one or other of these two heads.

99. The Edinburgh Men. FRANCIS JEFFREY (1773–1850), called by his admirers the 'Archcritic', and by his victims 'Judge Jeffrey' (in reference to the notorious 'bloody judge' of the seventeenth century) contributed some 200 articles to the *Edinburgh,* and may be regarded as the most influential though not the greatest critic of his time. On the whole, as our quotation in §86 will have shown, he represents the conservative side in criticism. He was not indeed consistently opposed to the romantic movement, nor was he a blind supporter of the Augustan tradition; but his general influence was on the side of authority and against innovation. Today his criticism seems in general unsatisfactory. He lacked breadth of sympathy and flexibility of judgment; his object was not to interpret, but to arraign and, if possible, to condemn; he was often brutal; he cared little for subject-matter and fixed his attention on form and style; and he had no feeling for the large human aspects of literature.

His chief coadjutor, SYDNEY SMITH (1771–1845), was an exceedingly clever clergyman, who is now better known for his witticisms than for his literature. He contributed some 65 articles to the *Edinburgh,* and produced a considerable body of other work, including a brilliant satire on the Irish question, *Peter Plymley's Letters* (1807). His writings labour under the disadvantage of having dealt for the most part with dead abuses and forgotten controversies. For this reason they are now little read, which is a pity, for they are full of good things.

Of the '*Blackwood's* men' the most famous in his own day was JOHN WILSON (1785–1854), better known under his pen-name of Christopher North. A man of powerful physique, a wrestler and boxer, and a devotee of the prize ring while he was Professor of Moral Philosophy in the University of Edinburgh, he carried his high spirits and his boisterous energies into nearly everything he wrote. His output was enormous, and comprised stories, poems, and a vast number of magazine articles on all sorts of subjects. His best work is to be found in his *Noctes Ambrosianae* (or Nights at the Ambrose Tavern in Edinburgh), which appeared in *Blackwood* at irregular intervals, and ran to 70 numbers in all. They are in the form of dialogues, and are full of conviviality, reckless humour, and dashing criticism of literature and politics. But their interest was largely local and temporary, and their broad Scotch makes it additionally difficult for the southern reader to appreciate them. In regard to prose style, Wilson was entirely with the romantics.

Though he wrote for the *London Magazine* as well as for *Blackwood,* we may here find place for a personal friend of Wilson, and a man of far greater importance in literature—THOMAS DE QUINCEY (1785–1859). He, too, was essentially a magazinist, and the 17 volumes of his collected works consist mainly of essays on a large variety of subjects. His writing is often marred by glaring defects; he had a habit of abusing his extraordinary learning and of sinking thereby into obscurity and pedantry; in argument, while wonderfully subtle, he was frequently captious and trivial; and he continually indulged in huge unwieldy digressions. His merits, however, are equally striking. His style, at its best, is marvellously rich and gorgeously rhetorical, and he remains one of our chief masters of romantic impassioned prose. He has great powers of narrative and description, as in his story of *Joan of Arc,* and the wonderful *English Mail Coach* and *Dream Fugue.* He achieved remarkable success in combining grim humour with the horrible in his *Murder considered as one of the Fine Arts*—a piece of sustained irony which would have delighted Swift. But he will always be best remembered by his strangely fascinating autobiographical writings, especially the *Confessions of an English Opium Eater,* which may be classed among the finest things in our literature of personal experience.

JOHN GIBSON LOCKHART (1794–1854), is, like De Quincey, a connecting link between Edinburgh and London, for he was long one of the mainstays of *Blackwood,* while from 1826 to within a few months of his death he was editor of the *Quarterly.* Though closely associated with Wilson, he was a man of very different temper and style of writing, for he was reserved, keen, incisive, and caustic. He produced much miscellaneous work, including four novels (one of which, *Adam Blair,* deserves mention as a powerful study of a good man's sin and remorse); a volume of spirited *Spanish Ballads*; and an admirable *Life of Burns*. His principal title to fame, however, is his magnificent *Life of Scott,* whose daughter, Sophia, he married in 1820. His position as a critic is interesting. Like many other men in that period of transition in literary taste, he was partly of the old order and partly of the new. He was romantic with Scott, and sympathised with Wordsworth, but the work of the younger generation—of Shelley, Keats, and Tennyson at the outset of his career—aroused his hostility. The ascription to him of the authorship of the infamous *Blackwood* attack on Keats rests indeed on insufficient evidence; but it is certain that he wrote the almost equally savage criticism in the *Quarterly* of Tennyson's 1833 volume. His nickname of the 'Scorpion' points to his special gift of sarcasm, which he often used with deadly effect.

100. The London Men. First among these in our affections is CHARLES LAMB (1775–1834), one of the best beloved of English authors, whose memory, as Southey said, 'will retain its fragrance as long as the best spice expended on the Pharaohs'. In nearly all his work, and pre-eminently in the most widely-known portion of it, the ever-delightful *Essays of Elia,* Lamb is as much an egotist as Montaigne, and the substance of what he writes is almost wholly drawn from himself, his experiences, reminiscences, likes, dislikes, whims, and prejudices. But we never complain of this, for in Canon Ainger's language, 'it is the man Charles Lamb that constitutes the charm of his written words.' He was a master of humour and pathos, both of which, and more particularly the peculiar way in which he combined them (blending the finest tenderness with the quaintest fancies) are so entirely personal to him, that we can compare them with nothing else in literature, and have even to coin the epithet 'Lambish' in order to suggest their qualities. On the critical side, his influence was strong in the development of romanticism, and especially of that kind of romanticism which was retrospective in character and largely nourished itself on the literature of the pre-Augustan age. All his sympathies were with this early literature, and the bent of his mind and the direction of his taste are shown in his

Elizabethan tragedy, *John Woodvil*, in his familiar *Tales from Shakespeare* (in collaboration with his sister Mary), and in his *Specimens of English Dramatic Poets who wrote about the Time of Shakespeare*—a work which did much to spread the knowledge of our older English playwrights. His style, though like everything else about him, absolutely his own, is flavoured by constant contact with his favourite writers, Burton, Fuller, and Sir Thomas Browne. He even said, in his whimsical way, that he wrote neither for the present nor for the future, but for antiquity.

In Lamb's contemporary, WILLIAM HAZLITT (1778–1830), we have a capital illustration of the manner in which, as we have seen, the popularity of magazines turned literature into the channels of journalism, though in his case we have to reckon also with the parallel growth of the influence of the lecture-platform. Though irascible, petulant, full of crotchets and intense personal prejudices, Hazlitt was by far the best-equipped and the most satisfactory critic of his day, and his fine catholicity and feeling for what is good, wherever it is found, enabled him to do justice to the romantic school on the one hand, without being unjust to the Augustans on the other. His best criticism is contained in four collections of lectures or essays—*Characters of Shakespeare's Plays, The English Poets, The English Comic Writers,* and *The Dramatic Literature of the Age of Elizabeth.* He has been called 'the critic's critic', and his insight, discrimination, and sureness of taste and touch, go far to justify the title. Nonetheless, we must not forget that, though the best of its kind, his criticism is marked by many of the limitations of his time. It makes no attempt to rise above the critic's personal judgment of his subject, to connect the author in question with the life and spirit of his age, or to interpret literature in that larger historical way of which something was said in the opening chapter of this little book.

LEIGH HUNT, who has already been mentioned as a poet, may also be included here among the periodical prose writers, for, though he was a good deal of a bookmaker as well, he lacked the power of sustained effort, and his books are therefore in the main composed of fragmentary materials. His manner and style bear the unmistakable impress of his own easy-going, irresponsible nature, the butterfly quality of his genius, and his personal charm. He had to live by his pen, and much of his work was done too fast, but his essays, with their quick wit and abundant fancy, are always readable, and his love of literature was honest and deep. As a critic, though he ranks below Hazlitt and Lamb, he holds a distinctive place among the men of his time. His taste was very eclectic, and the breadth of his sympathies is a pleasant feature of his criticism; but, on the whole, his tendency was towards romanticism. The most popular of all his books is his delightfully written *Autobiography*, which Carlyle, who was not easy to satisfy in such a matter, called 'a pious, ingenious, altogether human and worthy book'.

101. Other Prose Writers of the Period. Prominent among these, yet standing entirely apart from every set and group, was WILLIAM COBBETT (1762–1835), political reformer, journalist, pamphleteer, and maker of many books. A coarse, vigorous, independent man, Cobbett was one of the most striking personalities and one of the most widely influential writers of his age, though little of his voluminous work comes under the head of general literature. Perhaps his most characteristic book, and the one which has the most permanent interest, is his *Rural Rides*. His *English Grammar* is probably unique among grammars, because it is thoroughly entertaining. As a prose writer (and Hazlitt regarded him as one of the best in the language) he belonged to the race of Bunyan, Defoe, and Swift. He is vernacular, strong, simple, and clear. He evidently put into practice his own principle that a writer should always take the first word that comes to him, as this is sure to be the word which most fully conveys his meaning. This theory served him extremely well; but one would hesitate to apply it generally.

An antithesis to Cobbett in almost every conceivable particular is presented by LANDOR, whose poetry has already been referred to. As Cobbett is one of our best vernacular and colloquial writers, and as De Quincey is one of our chief masters of romantic prose, so

Landor is unsurpassed in the severe, sententious, sculpturesque style. His principal prose work, the *Imaginary Conversations,* are dialogues between great characters of the past. Their composition extended over many years, and there are some 150 of them in all. They cover a wide range of subjects in life and literature; some are purely dramatic; others are reflective and philosophical. It has been well said of him that he was not a great thinker, but a man of great thoughts. Besides these *Conversations,* Landor produced three other works of a somewhat similar character—*The Citation of William Shakespeare*; *Pericles and Aspasia,* a tale of the golden age of Athens told in letters; and the *Pentameron,* a series of dialogues between Petrarch and Boccaccio, especially noteworthy for their fine criticism of Dante.

SOUTHEY was as industrious as a prose writer as he was as a poet, and as a whole his prose has worn better than his verse. His masterpiece is the admirable *Life of Nelson.* On the other hand, COLERIDGE'S prose is as fragmentary as his verse. His criticism was, however, always suggestive and stimulating, and it exercised a profound influence in the establishment of the romantic principle in literature. His *Biographia Literaria* is rambling and unequal, and its style is in general poor; but it contains many pages of such subtle analytical and interpretative power that they are enough by themselves to give him high standing among English writers on the theory of poetry.

This chapter could be extended considerably by the inclusion of the many writers who, during this period, did excellent work in history and philosophy. But this is not the place to discuss the value of their contributions to the literature of their special subjects, and no useful purpose would be served by a mere catalogue of their names and writings.

21

The Age of Wordsworth:
The Novel

102. Scott. We have seen (§91) that after ten years of great success as a writer of romances in verse, Scott turned from the romance in verse to prose fiction, and that he was led to make this change in part because the original vein which he had opened up was getting exhausted, and in part because the sudden rise of Byron threatened the supremacy which he had long enjoyed. But though with *Waverley* (1814) he struck out definitely into a new line, it is quite clear that in his later narrative poems he had been unconsciously gravitating towards the novel. This is shown by a comparison between *The Lay of the Last Minstrel* and the last important production of the series, *Rokeby*. The *Lay* was simply an elaboration of the old ballad form. *Rokeby* was to all intents and purposes a novel in verse. In this work for the first time, as he himself perceived, the interest was made to centre not in incident but in character, and the chief figures were handled in a way much more suitable to the medium of prose than to that of verse. In *Rokeby*, then, verse was not an aid, but a hindrance, to his powers. The transition from verse to prose was therefore natural. Nor was the idea of writing a prose romance so entirely new to him as is commonly supposed. It had occurred to him, he tells us, before the time of the *Lay*, when he had entertained 'the ambitious desire of composing a tale of chivalry, which was to be in the style of *The Castle of Otranto,* with plenty of Border characters and supernatural incident'—in fact, a sort of *Lay,* but in prose. Accident turned him to the verse romance instead, and success prompted him to devote his energies to it. A little later, however, the reception accorded to *The Lady of the Lake* convinced him that there was a large English reading public interested in the Highlands, and conceiving that he might turn his own first-hand knowledge of the Highlands to good account, he 'threw together' the opening chapters of *Waverley.* He did not, however, persevere with this experiment, and the manuscript was thrown aside and forgotten. Then a fresh stimulus came from the Irish Tales of Maria Edgeworth (see §104). These Scott read with enthusiasm; he was particularly struck by their detailed pictures of the characters and manners of the Irish people; and it now came to his mind that what Miss Edgeworth had done for Ireland, he might do for Scotland. Once more his interest in prose fiction was awakened, but this time his mind ran in the direction of the novel of contemporary life. Just then, by happy accident, while hunting in a drawer for some fishing tackle, he lighted upon the draft of the first chapters of *Waverley.* He read them; found that they fell in with his plan; and sat down to complete the work—a task which, by one of his wonderful feats of improvisation, he accomplished in three weeks.

The history of Scott's gradual approach to the novel is important because it helps us to realise that two different lines of influence ran together in determining the character of his work. On the one hand, there were all those influences which had combined to make him a romantic poet and to send him back for themes and inspiration to the past. On the other hand, there were all those influences which came to him through his direct contact with and intimate knowledge of almost every aspect of actual Scottish life. Before *Waverley* little attempt had been made to blend the interest of romance and realism—the story of chivalry and adventure with the story of character and manners. In *Waverley* the two kinds of interests merged. Scott's work in fiction thus represents the amalgamation of the eighteenth century novel of manners and the eighteenth century historical romance. In other words, he set the story of manners for the first time in an historical framework.

103. Characteristics of Scott's Novels. The *Waverley Novels*, the work of eighteen years of extraordinary creative activity, consist of twenty-seven novels and five tales. Collectively they cover about eight centuries. Arranged in historical order they are as follows: Eleventh century, *Count Robert of Paris*; twelfth century, *The Betrothed, The Talisman, Ivanhoe*; fourteenth century, *Castle Dangerous*; fifteenth century, *The Fair Maid of Perth, Quentin Durward, Anne of Geierstein*; sixteenth century, *The Monastery, The Abbot, Kenilworth, Death of the Laird's Jock*; seventeenth century, *The Fortunes of Nigel, A Legend of Montrose, Woodstock, Peveril of the Peak, Old Mortality, The Bride of Lammermoor, The Pirate*; eighteenth century, *My Aunt Margaret's Mirror, The Black Dwarf, Rob Roy, The Heart of Midlothian, Waverley, Redgauntlet, Guy Mannering, The Highland Widow, The Surgeon's Daughter, The Tapestried Chamber, The Two Drovers, The Antiquary*; nineteenth century (1812), *St. Ronan's Well*. Most of Scott's novels are strictly historical in the sense that they include historical events and characters, though some—like *Guy Mannering, The Antiquary,* and *The Bride of Lammermoor* (all ranking with his very finest work)—are rather private stories with an historical background. In the range of his historical interest Scott stands alone among English writers, but he is always at his best when dealing with the Scotland of the seventeenth and eighteenth centuries. In the regular historical novels his practice is to create some private individual as his nominal hero, to send him out on his adventures and then to contrive that he shall so be caught up in the great public movements of his time that his fortunes shall be involved in and determined by them. Thus in his first novel, Edward Waverley sets out to join his regiment at Dundee in the critical year 1745, gets entangled in the Jacobite rising, meets the Young Pretender, and fights at Prestonpans and Culloden: his personal doings merging in the great currents of history. In this way he was enabled to depict the past, not on its large heroic side only, but also on its domestic and unheroic sides, and to make us feel its substantial reality by linking its interests with individuals situated like ourselves. As Carlyle said of his work: 'These historical novels have taught all men this truth, which looks like a truism, and yet was as good as unknown to writers of history, and others till so taught; that the by-gone ages of the world were actually filled by living men, not by protocols, state papers, controversies, and abstractions of men.'

It must not of course be supposed that Scott's treatment of history is entirely accurate. He often takes great liberties with facts and his anachronisms are numerous. When these are anachronisms of detail only they are relatively unimportant; but sometimes they are fundamental, and then they become serious, as in the case of *Ivanhoe,* which, however brilliant as a romance, is totally untrustworthy as a picture of the life of the middle ages. But in general he was marvellously successful in reproducing at least the externals of the periods which he describes, in giving us a vivid sense of their men and manners, and in breathing life into the dry bones of history.

Scott wrote rapidly and often carelessly, and, as he himself frankly confessed, his novels are for the most part very defective in construction. He is at his best in description and action. As an interpreter of character his method is wholly unlike that of the modern psychological novelist; he does not indulge in elaborate analysis, but paints in broad, bold outlines and with a big brush. When he attempts to deal with complex mental and moral conditions he naturally fails, and he has little power over the stronger passions, except (and the exception is significant) those of patriotism and loyalty. But with simple characters he achieves remarkable success, and especially with his men and women drawn directly from the Scottish life he knew so well—his lawyers, soldiers, farmers, peasants, old-fashioned serving men, and low comedy figures. His humour is racy, full-blooded, and always genial and wholesome. His historical characters are not always quite faithful as portraits, but he possessed, as few other writers have ever done, the secret of making them vital and human; and his James I, Louis XI, Elizabeth, and the

Young Pretender (to mention only a few examples) are fine pieces of imaginative re-creation.

In his general treatment of life we note again his lack of spiritual insight and grasp. As he nowhere takes us much beneath the surface of things he gives us little more than the external panorama of history. Yet whatever shortcomings may be pointed out in it, Scott's work is still very great work. It has emphatically the qualities which ensure permanence in literature; for it is full of creative energy; it keeps us in touch with the large currents of human life; it is manly, robust, and sound.

104. Other Novelists of the Time. Scott's principal contemporaries in prose fiction were three women who worked in a field entirely different from his—that of the modern social and domestic novel. The first in order of time was MARIA EDGEWORTH (1767–1849), whose influence on Scott's own production has already been noted. She was a fairly voluminous writer, but her best work is to be found in some of her short tales and in three Irish novels, *Castle Rackrent*, *The Absentee*, and *Ormond*. Her stories are over-didactic, but they have humour and pathos, and though very unequal, are brightly and simply written. SUSAN EDMONSTONE FERRIER (1782–1854), whose three novels, *Marriage*, *Destiny*, and *The Inheritance*, were also greatly admired by Scott, was a clever painter of Scottish, as Miss Edgeworth was of Irish characters and manners. Midway between these two in date of birth comes JANE AUSTEN (1775–1817) with her *Sense and Sensibility*, *Pride and Prejudice*, *Mansfield Park*, *Emma*, *Persuasion*, and *Northanger Abbey*. Miss Austen's range was narrow, and as she never ventured beyond her own experience and powers, she achieved, as no other English novelist ever has achieved, an even level of perfection. Her books are composed of the most commonplace materials, and are wholly lacking in all the elements of great passion and strong action. They are therefore slight in texture. But her touch was so sure, her humour so subtle, her characterization so life-like, that all competent critics regard her as one of the finest artists that English fiction has ever produced.

With men-writers, meanwhile, fiction exhibited greater variety of matter and method. CHARLES ROBERT MATURIN (1782–1824) carried on the wildest traditions of the romance of fantasy and horror in a number of tales of which *Melmoth the Wanderer* was the most successful, while THEODORE HOOK (1788–1841), one of the fun-makers of his generation, produced a string of loosely written novels which, though they seem very flat today, greatly amused the public of their own time. Far more important than the work of either of these men is that of JOHN GALT (1779–1839), whose *Ayrshire Legatees* and *Annals of the Parish* contain some admirable pictures of contemporary Scottish life. With THOMAS LOVE PEACOCK (1785–1866), a close friend of Shelley, fiction became the vehicle of witty satiric commentary upon the things—and they were many—in society and literature which the author disliked. He continued to write till almost the end of his long life, but we name him here because his really characteristic work—*Headlong Hall, Melincourt, Nightmare Abbey,* and *Crochet Castle*—was all done before 1832. As a matter of convenience, we may here also mention two followers of Scott in the historical romance—GEORGE PAYNE RAINSFORD JAMES (1801–60), and WILLIAM HARRISON AINSWORTH (1805–82), whose best work appeared before the middle of the century. Neither has the slightest claim to literary distinction, but a few of the former's almost countless tales—such as *Henry Masterton* and *Richelieu*—are still readable; while the latter's *Old Saint Paul's* gives a wonderfully vivid description of London in the days of the Plague and the Great Fire.

TABLE OF THE AGE OF WORDSWORTH

Verse	General Prose	The Novel
Lyrical Ballads, 1798		
Landor's *Gebir,* 1798		
Campbell's *Pleasures of Hope,* 1799		
Cowper, d. 1800		

Scott's *Border Minstrelsy*, 1802	*Edinburgh Review*, founded 1802	Edgeworth's *Castle Rackrent*, 1800
Scott's *Lay of the Last Minstrel*, 1805		Edgeworth's *Popular Tales*, 1804
Byron's *Hours of Idleness*, 1807		
Moore's *Irish Melodies*, 1807		
Scott's *Marmion*, 1808; *Lady of the Lake*, 1810		
Tennyson, b. 1809	*Quarterly Review* founded, 1809	
Byron's *Childe Harold* (i, ii), 1809; (iii) 1816; (iv) 1818		
Browning, b. 1812		Jane Austen's *Sense and Sensibility*, 1811
Scott's *Rokeby*, 1813		Thackeray, b. 1811
Shelley's *Queen Mab*, 1813		Dickens, b. 1812
Wordsworth's *Excursion*, 1814		Jane Austen's *Pride and Prejudice*, 1812 *Waverley*, 1814
Coleridge's *Christabel*, 1816		
Shelley's *Alastor*, 1816		
Hunt's *Story of Rimini*, 1816		
Keats' first poems, 1817	*Blackwood's Edinburgh Magazine* founded, 1817	Jane Austen, d. 1817
Byron's *Manfred*, 1817 Byron's *Beppo*, 1818		
Keats' *Endymion*, 1818	*London Magazine* founded, 1817	

	Coleridge's *Biographia Literaria*, 1817	
	Hazlitt's criticisms, 1817–20	*Ivanhoe*, 1819
Byron's *Don Juan*, 1819–23		
Keats' *Hyperion*, 1820		
Shelley's *Prometheus Unbound*, 1820	De Quincey's *Opium Eater*, 1821	George Eliot, b. 1820
Byron's *Cain*, 1821	Lamb, *Elia*, 1821–23	
Keats, d. 1821	Wilson's *Noctes Ambrosiance*, 1822–33	
Shelley's *Adonais*, 1821		
Rogers' *Italy*, 1822		
Shelley, d. 1822		
Byron, d. 1824	Landor's *Imaginary Conversations*, 1824–53	
Tennyson's *Poems*, 1830	Moore's *Life of Byron*, 1830	
Mrs. Hemans' *Songs of the Affections*, 1830		
Browning's *Pauline*, 1831, 1833		
Crabbe, d. 1832		Scott, d. 1832

22

The Age of Tennyson
(1832–1887):
Verse

105. The Age of Tennyson. What, following our method of division, we here call the Age of Tennyson corresponds very closely as a period of literature with the Victorian Age in general history. Victoria ascended the throne in 1837, and it was during the decade between 1830 and 1840 that many of the writers who were to add special distinction to her reign began their work. But, though her own life extended till 1901, we may conveniently take the year of her jubilee—1887—as marking the close of this last epoch in our survey. By that time a fresh race in literature had arisen, while those of the former generation who still survived had nothing of importance to add to their production, and indeed, like Tennyson's Bedivere, found themselves 'among new men, strange faces, other minds'.

Wonderfully rich and varied in personal quality—and its astonishing variety is one of its outstanding characteristics—the literature of the Age of Tennyson at the same time everywhere embodies the spirit of Victorian England, and reflects the influences which combined to make the half century in question an era of surprising change along many lines. It is such a literature as, in the mass, could not conceivably have been produced at any other time in the world's history. The enormous complexity of the period, and the bewildering diversity of the elements which entered into its civilisation, render exhaustive analysis within brief limits impossible. But it is fortunately not difficult to indicate the two great dominant movements, or 'main currents', as Brandes would call them, in the general life of the time. They are, in the political and social spheres, the progress of democracy; in the intellectual sphere, the progress of science.

Reference has been made to the conservative reaction which followed the excitement of the French Revolution. By 1837 that reaction had practically spent its force as well in England as on the Continent. The Reform Bill of 1832 had already destroyed the political supremacy of the landed aristocracy, but, as it left the greater part of the labouring classes still un-enfranchised, it did not satisfy those who had pressed for and been led to expect a far more radical measure. Agitation for electoral reform accordingly continued, and the great popular movement called Chartism kept England for some ten years in a state of political unrest, which was still further stimulated by the industrial depression and widespread misery of the 'hungry forties'. It is with perfect justice, therefore, that the first decade of the new queen's reign has been described as 'an anxious and critical time in modern English history'. But the very dangers and difficulties by which the country was beset stirred the social consciousness and gave immense impetus to philanthropic energy and the spirit of humanitarianism. The repeal of the Corn Laws ushered in an era of much improved industrial conditions, and after 1848 the Chartist movement died out. Then, at long intervals, came the Reform Bills of 1867 and 1884–85, which we may regard as stages in a peaceful revolution which transformed the essentially oligarchic England of William IV's time into the 'crown'd republic' whose praises Tennyson sang. Important as these political changes were, however, they were by no means the most important aspects of the democratic expansion of the Victorian Age. More significant and more vital were the social and intellectual changes by which they were accompanied, as in the breaking down of the old feudal landmarks and distinctions, the more and more general recognition of the claims of the many against those of the long privileged few, the growth of sympathy between man and man and class and class, and the spread of popular education, with all the increased opportunities for personal development which this entailed. Beyond any other period in our history the Victorian Age was an age of social interests and practical ideals, and it was by these that much of its literature was inspired and fed. For proof of this assertion we need only turn to the works of such writers as Carlyle, Ruskin, Dickens, Kingsley, and Mrs. Browning.

Meanwhile the progress of science kept pace with the progress of democracy, and in the fifty years with which we are here concerned men added far more to their positive knowledge of themselves and the universe than their forefathers had done in all the preceding eighteen centuries of our era. Nor is this unparalleled increase of knowledge the only point to be considered. In estimating the influence of science upon life and literature, it is further to be remembered that by reason of the spread of popular education, newspapers, magazines, and cheap books, the facts and speculations of the experts were no longer kept to the experts themselves, but passed rapidly into the possession of the reading public at large. This was, for example, the case with the greatest of all modern generalisations, the doctrine of evolution, which we specially associate with the names of Darwin, Wallace, and Herbert Spencer, and concerning which it is not too much to say that before the Victorian Age had closed it had completely revolutionised all current ideas about nature, man, and society. A vast upheaval in thought was the consequence of this rapid progress and popularisation of knowledge; new theories came into conflict with old faiths; the ancient intellectual order was shaken at its foundations. Hence the Victorian Age was marked throughout by the prominence of the spirit of inquiry and criticism, by scepticism and religious uncertainty, and by spiritual struggle and unrest; and these are among the most persistent and characteristic notes of its higher literature. At the same time, the analytical and critical habit of mind which was fostered by science profoundly affected literature in other ways, and a marked development of realism was one conspicuous result. Finally, we must recognise the far-reaching changes which were brought about by the practical application of science to life in the railway, the steamship, and the telegraph. By breaking down the barriers which had hitherto separated town and country and nation and nation, by facilitating travel and the intercourse of different peoples, and by making the transmission of thought easy and rapid, these mechanical agencies did much to destroy the old provincialism, to help the progress of democracy, and to change fundamentally the spirit of the world. They have therefore to be included among the chief social forces in the literature of Victorian England.

We cannot, however, get even an approximately complete idea of these social forces unless we bear in mind one important principle of historical interpretation—that every strong movement invariably sets up a counter-movement. In our study of the literature of the Age of Tennyson the power of the great counter-movement against the domination of science, for example, can never be left out of account. In fact, science affected literature as much by the opposition it created as by its direct influence; it tended to materialism alike in thought and in life; and a great deal that is noblest in Victorian literature was inspired by the desire to check this tendency, and to proclaim the eternal value of spiritual things. At this point, too, we must recognise the significance of the romantic revival, in connection with which much striking work was now done. Here, as always, romanticism was largely associated with an imaginative return to the past; but its prompting motives were dissatisfaction with the ugliness of modern materialistic civilisation and a determination to escape from the narrow limitations of the realistic theory of art. In the end the romantic spirit combined with the spirit of social reform, and its protest against materialism assumed a practical character.

Owing to the astonishing wealth and variety of the literature of the Age of Tennyson only the barest sketch of it can be attempted here. Many names must be omitted altogether, and even those writers who are selected on account of their personal or historical importance must be treated with the utmost brevity. Dealing first with verse, we will give the greatest space to the two chief poets of the time—Tennyson and Browning.

106. Tennyson. ALFRED TENNYSON was born in 1809, won the Chancellor's medal at Cambridge in 1829 for a poem on *Timbuctoo*, became poet Laureate in 1850 (the year of his marriage) in succession to Wordsworth, was raised to the peerage as Lord Tennyson in 1884, and died in 1892. His activity as a poet extended over more than sixty years. His first important work appeared in 1833, but it was by the two volumes of 1842 that his position was assured as, in Wordsworth's language, 'decidedly the greatest of our living poets.' Then came *The Princess* in 1847; *In Memoriam*, a philosophic elegy inspired by the death of his dear friend, Arthur Henry Hallam, in 1850; *Maud: A Monodrama*, in 1854; and *Enoch Arden and Other Poems* in 1864. In the meantime he had begun work on the story of Arthur and the Round Table, a subject which occupied his attention for many years, for, while the first four *Idylls of the King* were published in 1859, the twelfth and last instalment of the series was not issued till 1885. For upwards of a decade he devoted his energies mainly to the drama, his principal productions in this new field being the three historical plays, *Queen Mary* (1875), *Harold* (1876), and *Becket* (1884). His later writings included, along with many very different things, the remarkable philosophical poems, *The Ancient Sage, Vastness,* and *Akbar's Dream,* and the superb lyric (now always printed, in accordance with his directions, as the last poem in any complete edition of his works) *Crossing the Bar.*

Perhaps after Milton the most conscientious and accomplished poetic artist in our literature, Tennyson is noteworthy for the even perfection of his style, his wonderful mastery of language at once simple and ornate, and the exquisite and varied music of his verse. But from the strictly historical point of view he is specially interesting as the most thoroughly representative poet of his age. He was to

Victorian England what three centuries earlier Spenser, as we have seen (§26) had been to the England of Elizabeth, and much that is most deeply characteristic of its spirit entered into the texture of his writings. As Mr. Stopford Brooke has said: 'For more than sixty years he lived close to the present life of England, as far as he was capable of comprehending and sympathising with its movements; and he inwove what he felt concerning it into his poetry.' The extraordinary diversity of his work is itself typical of the strongly marked eclecticism of his age. He wrote on classical, romantic, and modern subjects; on subjects taken (like Wordsworth's) from humble and rustic life; on English history and Celtic legend; on the deepest problems of philosophy and religion; and the range of his method and style is scarcely less remarkable than that of his matter. But even more typical are the content and quality of his poems. His *Locksley Hall* of 1842 is full of the restless spirit of 'young England' and of its faith in science, commerce, and the progress of mankind; while its sequel, *Locksley Hall Sixty Years After* (1886) shows the revulsion of feeling which had occurred in many minds when the rapid development of science seemed to threaten the very foundations of religion, and commerce was filling the world with the sordid greed of gain. In *The Princess* the poet undertook to grapple with one of the rising questions of the day—that of the higher education of women and their place in the fast-changing conditions of modern society; *Maud* quivers with the patriotic passion of the time of the Crimean War and with the general ferment by which this was accompanied; in the *Idylls of the King,* while the medieval machinery is retained, the old story is turned into a parable the lessons of which are obviously intended to bear directly upon contemporary life. The change which Tennyson's thought underwent in regard to social and political questions itself reveals his curious sensitiveness to the tendencies of his time; for the sanguine temper of his early manhood, the doubts, misgivings, and reactionary utterances of his middle age, and the chastened hopefulness of his last years, are alike reflections of successive moods which were widely characteristic of his generation. But politically and socially he stands out as, on the whole, the poetic exponent of the cautious spirit of Victorian liberalism. He was essentially the poet of law and order as well as of progress; he held tenaciously to the great heritage of English tradition; and while he firmly believed that in the divine scheme of things

> 'The old order changeth, yielding place to new,
> And God fulfils himself in many ways
> Lest one good custom should corrupt the world,'

he was quite as firmly opposed to 'raw haste', rash experiments, and everything that savoured of revolution. Nor must we neglect to note that, apart altogether from any special political principles, Tennyson's poetry is often the vehicle of the spreading democratic sympathies of Victorian England. Recluse and aristocrat as he was, he was profoundly interested in common people and common things; and it is not the least significant feature of his work in the mass that along with *The Princess, Maud*, the *Idylls of the King*, it contains such things as *The May Queen, Enoch Arden*, and *Dora*.

While, however, Tennyson's poetry is thus historically interesting on the social and political sides, it is even more important as a record of the intellectual and spiritual life of the time. A careful student of science and philosophy, he was deeply impressed by the far-reaching meaning of the new discoveries and speculations by which the edifice of the old thought had been undermined, and especially by the wide bearings of the doctrine of evolution; and at once sceptical and mystical in his own temper, he was peculiarly fitted to become the mouth-piece of his century's doubts, difficulties, and craving for the certainties of religious faith. The 'two voices' of that century are perpetually heard in his work; in *In Memoriam*, more than in any other contemporary piece of verse or prose, we may read of its great conflict of doubt and faith; while in many later poems—as notably in *The Ancient Sage*—we may see how the poet challenged the current materialism and asserted the eternal verities of God and immortality. Here, too, the particular quality of

Tennyson's poetry of nature should be emphasised. He studied nature as closely and knew it as well as Wordsworth, and, like Wordsworth, he was always absolutely faithful in his rendering of even the minutest details. But Wordsworth had seen nature with the eye of the poet only, while Tennyson saw it with the eye of the scientist as well. He loved its beauty, but he felt also its indifference and cruelty, and, as a famous passage in *In Memoriam* (54–56) shows us, his keen sense of the cosmic struggle was one of the most disturbing elements in his thought. It must, however, be added that his persistent belief in evolution always steadied and encouraged him, and helped him to look beyond the struggle towards the 'one far-off divine event to which the whole creation moves'.

107. Browning. ROBERT BROWNING was born in 1812, began to write poetry early—his *Pauline* appeared in 1833—and, like his friend Tennyson, devoted his long life entirely to literature. He published *Paracelsus* in 1835; *Strafford* (a tragedy produced by Macready at Covent Garden) in 1837; *Sordello* in 1840; and a collection of dramatic and miscellaneous poems under the general title of *Bells and Pomegranates* at intervals between 1841 and 1846. In the last-named year he married Elizabeth Barrett, whose reputation as a poet then stood higher with the general reading world than his own, for, like Wordsworth, he was a long time in reconciling popular taste to the peculiarities of his method and style. The fifteen happy years of his married life were spent in Italy, and during this period he wrote *Christmas Eve and Easter Day* (1850); and *Men and Women* (1855). After his wife's death in 1861 he settled again in England, and published *Dramatis Personae* in 1864, and his enormous dramatic-narrative poem, *The Ring and the Book*, in four volumes, in 1868–69. By this time he had completely conquered his public, and during the twenty remaining years of his life his popularity was as great as Tennyson's. His fertility continued unabated, but except for occasional lyrics, it cannot be said that his numerous later writings did anything to add to his reputation. His last volume, *Asolando*, was published on the very day—December 12, 1889—that he died in the Palazzo Rezzonico in Venice.

In contrast with Tennyson, Browning was bold, rugged, and altogether unconventional in matter and style, and though never careless in his writing (as is sometimes erroneously supposed), he was too vehement and too impatient to bestow time and effort upon the polishing of his verse. Much of his work—and especially of his later work—is in consequence prolix and ill-digested; it is often also marred by harshness and crudities of expression and by faults in taste; while despite the heroic attempts of some of his more extravagant admirers to rebut the charge, the obscurity of not a little of his production cannot be denied. But notwithstanding many obvious defects, his greatness as a poet is quite beyond dispute; and though it is necessary to qualify the claims put forth by adherents of the 'Browning cult', critics of all schools now combine in recognising the supreme strength and beauty, and the enduring poetic value, of what is best—and of this there is much—in his work.

His genius was essentially dramatic; but as his interest was centred throughout in the moral and spiritual forces and conflicts of individual men and women rather than in the world of action, it was not through the machinery of the regular stage-play that he found his most natural outlet. His characteristic art-form (a form which has been used by other poets, but by none so effectively), was the detached speech, or dramatic monologue, in which he takes some striking individual—generally at a critical moment—and instead of dissecting him from the outside, as the ordinary novelist would do, penetrates to the depth of his nature and through his own utterances compels him to reveal the innermost secrets of his life. Psychological insight, analytical subtlety, and power of dramatic interpretation are among the main features of Browning's poetry; splendid examples of his method are to be found in many of the poems in *Men and Women* and *Dramatis Personae*; while, except for the introduction and conclusion, this is the method adopted in the largest (if not the greatest) of his works, *The Ring and the Book*.

As a moralist and religious teacher Browning held a very distinct place among the writers of the Victorian Age. An uncompromising foe of scientific materialism, he preached God and immortality as the central truths of his philosophy of life, and he preached them as one absolutely assured of their reality. Nor was it only the negations of the current philosophy that he challenged. His poetry was throughout a protest also against the pessimistic mood engendered by them. The melancholy, hesitating spirit so often expressed by Tennyson finds no place in his verse, and he looked boldly at the evil of existence without for a moment losing his robustly optimistic faith. 'Hope hard in the subtle thing that's spirit,' was the note of his message to his generation; and to the many about him who were asking doubtfully whether after all life was really worth the living, he gave answer in the words of his Pippa—'God's in His heaven—all's right with the world.'

108. Other Poets of the Period. After Tennyson and Browning, who stand head and shoulders above all their fellows, it is not easy to settle the order of precedence among the many poets of the Victorian Age; but the third place may perhaps be assigned to MATTHEW ARNOLD (1822–88). A thorough classicist by sympathy and training, and with an admiration of the Greeks so strong that it sometimes led him astray, Arnold believed that all really great poetry is impersonal or objective poetry (like the drama and the epic), in which the poet escapes from himself and from the conditions of his own world, while subjective poetry, or the poetry of self-expression, necessarily and as such belongs to a lower artistic plane. It was in accordance with this theory that his most ambitious poems—*Sohrab and Rustum, Tristram and Iseult, Balder Dead,* and *Empedocles on Etna*—were written; but carefully wrought as these productions are, they impress us as rather academic, imitative, and unreal. All critical principles notwithstanding, the bias of his genius was towards the poetry of self-expression, and his best work was done when, ignoring theory, he gave his mind free play. Most of his personal poetry is steeped in the melancholy spirit of an era of transition. Its keynote is struck in the *Stanzas from the Grande Chartreuse*:

> Wandering between two worlds, one dead,
> The other powerless to be born;

and it carries with it a heavy burden of doubt. Yet Arnold's ethical temper was so noble, and his hold upon the great ideals of conduct and duty so steady, that his sadness, though at times depressing, is never enervating. In style he was cold and clear; his ear was imperfect, and there is little verbal felicity or natural magic in his verse; but its fine restraint and sculpturesque purity are worthy of high praise. Arnold has never been a popular poet, but he has always had his audience 'fit, though few'.

With Arnold it is natural to associate ARTHUR HUGH CLOUGH (1819–61), both because the two men were friends (Arnold's *Thyrsis* is a noble monody on Clough's death), and because they were in many ways spiritual kinsmen. Clough's personal poetry was regarded by Mr. Lowell as 'the truest expression in verse of the moral and intellectual tendencies, the doubt and struggle towards settled convictions, of the period in which he lived'; it resembles Arnold's in its sceptical quality, its transparent sincerity, and its moral earnestness and courage. Among his longer poems there is one—the delightful *Bothie of Tober-na-Vuolich*—which deserves to be better known than it is. But though, for the reason assigned, he is mentioned here, Clough's place is only among the minor poets.

The case is different with ELIZABETH BARRETT BROWNING (1806–61), who holds her position as the most considerable and vigorous, if not the greatest, of all our women-writers of verse. She wrote far too much and too fast; she was singularly deficient in the faculty of self-criticism; and her faults were many and glaring. Her poetry is frequently marked by over-wrought emotionalism, which often becomes hysterical and sometimes degenerates into downright gush; she is often spasmodic and even vulgar; and prolixity, diffuseness, straining after effect, and gross abuses in diction and rime, have to be reckoned among her characteristics. But at her best she exhibits the redeeming qualities of noble sincerity, genuine passion, and undeniable power over language. Her romantic poems show the continued influence of the spirit of the outgoing age; poems like *Casa Guidi Windows,* her love of liberty and Italy; poems like the *Cry of the Children,* the same humanitarian enthusiasm as we have in the novels of Dickens and Kingsley and in Hood's *Song of the Shirt.* Such social purpose is also the inspiration of her most ambitious effort, *Aurora Leigh,* a long poem in blank verse which, save for its form, might really be classed as a novel. Arnold, we have noted, held that, the poet should go out of his age as well as out of himself in his search for subject-matter. Mrs. Browning, on the contrary, maintained by theory and practice that it should be one chief aim of the poet to meet the age face to face. Hence the realism and the reform spirit which were so prominent in contemporary prose fiction are here found invading poetry as well. But, though *Aurora Leigh* was probably Mrs. Browning's most popular achievement, her finest work is to be sought in the series of sonnets entitled *Sonnets from the Portuguese,* in which she enshrined her love. These have their place among the masterpieces of the love-poetry of our literature, and as an expression of a woman's passion are practically unique.

I have spoken of the romantic revival as one of the principal counter-movements against the dominant scientific and commercial spirit of the Victorian Age, and have noted that its protest took the characteristic form of a return to the past. The medievalism, the influences of which have already been traced from the middle of the eighteenth century onward, after waning for a time, now again became a potent force in literature and art. It is represented in both by the painter-poet, DANTE GABRIEL ROSSETTI (1828-82), the leading figure in the artistic movement called Pre-Raphaelitism, the very name of which is indicative of its inspiration and purpose. Singularly unmodern in all his sympathies and ways of thinking, and with practically no interest in the life of his time, Rossetti was, in Mr. Hall Caine's language, 'an anachronism in these days.' The real home of his imagination was, in fact, not the London of the nineteenth century in which his lot was cast, but the Florence of Dante's era, and his identification with medieval ideas and feelings was so complete that in such poems as *The Blessed Damozel, World's Worth*, and *Ave*, we seem to breathe the very atmosphere of the *Vita Nuova, Paradiso*, and the works of the great Catholic painters. This is the more remarkable because, so far as his intellectual convictions were concerned, Rossetti was not a Catholic but an agnostic. As a ballad-writer he was very successful, especially in dealing with situations of tragic intensity, as in *The White Ship, Sister Helen*, and *Eden Bower*; as a sonnet-writer, as in the fine series, *The House of Life*, he ranks with our greatest. His technique was very remarkable, and he had a curious felicity in diction and riming. But his poetry as a whole is not very wholesome in tone, and its rare and exotic beauty is at times more than a little suggestive of decadence.

Rossetti's sister, CHRISTINA GEORGINA ROSSETTI (1830–94) is the only other woman-poet in our literature who can fairly be placed beside Mrs. Browning. Her work is characterised by deep religious feeling, a pronounced strain of mysticism, and much metrical charm. It is not through Christina, however, but rather through WILLIAM MORRIS (1834–96), that the main line of Rossetti's influence, and more broadly, of the romanticism represented by him, is to be traced. Morris's early works—*The Defence of Guenevere and Other Poems* (1858), *The Life and Death of Jason* (1867), and *The Earthly Paradise* (1868–70)—are purely romantic in method and style, though their undertone of sadness served to remind the critical reader that, while the poet deliberately turned his back upon his time, he could not altogether escape its troubled spirit. Later, under the influence of Ruskin and of his own growing revulsion from the ugliness of modern commercialism, Morris became a socialist. His medievalism thus changed from vague sentimental regret over the past into a positive programme for the future. This transformation of the 'idle singer of an empty day' (Morris's early description of himself) into an ardent and active reformer, is very interesting as showing the powerful sway of social interests during the Victorian period. It was with him, in particular, that the protest of romanticism against materialism assumed, as I have said, a practical form.

The last to die of the great race of Victorian poets, ALGERNON CHARLES SWINBURNE (1837–1909), also belonged to the romantic stock, though many other influences in the complex culture of his time entered into his work. Extremely prolific and versatile, he wrote Greek tragedies (*Atalanta in Calydon* and *Erechtheus* rank among our very finest attempts to revive the pure classic form); an English dramatic trilogy on Mary Stuart; experiments in medieval mystery plays; long narrative poems of great passion and beauty, of which *Tristram of Lyonesse* is perhaps the best; a large body of political poems, the revolutionary fervour of which is strongly suggestive of one of the writer's chief masters, Victor Hugo; odes of many kinds; monologues, and gorgeous lyrics without number. It is, however, primarily as a lyrist that he will hold his place in our literature. He showed almost unparalleled mastery over the resources of language and metre, and his daring in the use of both was unbounded. But his facility was often fatal and his fondness for mere verbal effects was a frequent snare. His power of saying things was astonishing, but on the whole he had very little to say, and despite the genuine inspiration of much of his writing, it suffers from its relatively unsubstantial character. Swinburne was capable of producing miracles of word-music, but something more than word-music is necessary to ensure the permanence of a poem.

Such remaining poets of the Age of Tennyson as have here to be mentioned must be put into a paragraph. For convenience they may be arranged in the chronological order of their births.

SIR HENRY TAYLOR (1800–86) did most of his work in verse in the dramatic form. He wrote tragedies in the severer Elizabethan manner, of which the best is *Philip van Artevelde,* and one romantic comedy, *The Virgin Widow, or A Sicilian Summer.* ROBERT STEPHEN HAWKER (1803–75), the extremely eccentric vicar of Morwenstow in Cornwall, was a man of curiously medieval cast of mind, and even shared many of the crudest superstitions of the simple village folk among whom he lived. His finest poem, *The Quest of the Sangraal,* is full of the genuine spirit of the great medieval adventure, and therefore presents an interesting contrast with Tennyson's thoroughly modernized narrative in the *Idylls of the King*. EDWARD FITZGERALD (1809–83) one of Tennyson's closest friends, produced little verse, but that little included one of the best-known and most fascinating of all modern English poems—his free translation, or paraphrase, of the *Rubaiyat* (or Quatrains) of the Persian astronomer-poet of the eleventh century, Omar Khayyám. This translation had little success at first, but it gradually won its way, and it has now long been recognised as one of the poetic masterpieces of the time. Its history is therefore strikingly different from that of the *Proverbial Philosophy* of MARTIN FARQUHAR TUPPER (1810–89), a collection of highly didactic pieces in loosely rhythmical prose, which for many years sold by the hundred thousand, but are now relegated to the dust-heap of unread things. Another poet who enjoyed great fame in his day, and is now hardly more than a name, was PHILIP JAMES BAILEY (1816–1902), whose enormous *Festus*, upon which his reputation rests, created a sensation upon its first publication and was treated by serious reviewers as belonging to the same class as *Paradise Lost* and *Faust*. Tennyson passed sound judgment upon it when he described it, in effect, as a dull poem containing many grand things. The obvious straining after originality of expression, which we have noted in the case of Mrs. Browning, is conspicuous again in it, and its overwrought sentiment, its forced and unnatural phraseology, its pomposity and inflation, are worthy of remark, because it is this poem which is commonly regarded as the principal agency in creating, or at least fostering, what was known as the 'spasmodic school' of poetry. Other writers of this school of some note in their time were SYDNEY DOBELL (1824–74), the author of *The Roman* and *Balder*, and ALEXANDER SMITH (1830–67), whose *Life Drama* (published when the writer was only twenty-one) gave promises which were never redeemed. Dobell and Smith are examples of exploded reputations. On the other hand, the work of JAMES THOMSON (1834–82) is likely to gain rather than lose in critical appreciation as time goes on. His *City of Dreadful Night* is a poem of pessimism and blank despair; but whatever one may think of the views of life embodied in it, one can hardly praise too highly its gloomy power, its imaginative strength, and the sonorous and stately music of its verse. To the foregoing list, by no means complete, of Victorian poets, we may just add the names of a few writers, who did noteworthy work in verse, though they gained their principal laurels in other fields. LORD MACAULAY won fame with his stirring *Lays of Ancient Rome,* and the versatile LORD LYTTON with a romantic epic, *King Arthur,* and the more important *Lost Tales of Miletus.* THACKERAY had a real talent for serious as well as for humorous poetry, and some of his lyrics are very tender and true. George Eliot's poetry is considerable in quantity, and her *Spanish Gypsy, Agatha, The Legend of Jubal,* and *How Lisa loved the King,* have many of the great intellectual and moral qualities of her prose fiction, but they are wanting in real poetic inspiration. KINGSLEY'S verse, on the contrary, leaves every reader with a sense of regret that there is so little of it. His *Saint's Tragedy* and *Andromeda* are both things of note, and his songs and ballads are admirable.

23

The Age of Tennyson:
General Prose

109. Carlyle. Incomparably the greatest figure in the general prose literature of his age, and one of the greatest moral forces of the modern world, THOMAS CARLYLE was born in 1795 at Ecclefechan, Dumfriesshire, where his father was a stonemason. He sprang straight from the rugged Scottish peasantry, and the stern doctrines of the old Calvinism in which he was bred left, in spite of all his intellectual growth, a lasting impression upon his mind. From the Academy at Annan, where he received the rudiments of his education, he proceeded to Edinburgh University, where he matriculated in 1809. Leaving without taking a degree, he then taught for a time at Annan and Kirkcaldy. His parents' design had been that he should enter the Scottish Church, but radical changes in his religious views made this impossible. Endowed with a passionately earnest nature, he suffered agonies from the doubts which assailed him during the many dark years in which he wandered in the 'howling wilderness of infidelity', striving vainly to recover his lost belief in God, in life, and in himself; and then suddenly there came a moment of mystical illumination, or 'spiritual new birth', which restored him, not indeed to his former religious convictions, but at least to the mood of courage and faith. The history both of the protracted spiritual conflict and of the strange experience by which it was ended, is written with immense power in the second book of *Sartor Resartus*. Unfortunately, though mental relief was now obtained, he was already the victim of the acute dyspepsia which was henceforth to make his life miserable and to colour much of his thought. Private teaching and hack-writing (which included a translation of Goethe's *Wilhelm Meister*) provided him with a scanty and precarious livelihood, and in 1825 he published in book-form his first important piece of independent work, his admirable *Life of Schiller*. In 1826 he married Jane Welsh, a woman of brilliant intellectual parts, and for some years contributed much to the magazines, especially on subjects connected with German literature—a literature in which he had found 'a new heaven and a new earth'. On her father's death, Mrs. Carlyle inherited a small farmhouse amid the dreary moorlands of Craigenputtoch, in Dumfriesshire; and it was while living there that he produced his most characteristic book, which is also one of the most remarkable and vital books in modern English literature, *Sartor Resartus*. In the summer of 1834 he moved to London. His *French Revolution* appeared in 1837; his lectures on *Heroes and Hero-Worship* (delivered in 1839–40) in 1841; *Past and Present* (the most penetrating and influential of all the many books which were inspired by the critical social and industrial conditions of the time; see §105) in 1843; the *Letters and Speeches of Oliver Cromwell* in 1845; *Latter-day Pamphlets* (a piece of ferocious social criticism) in 1850; the *Life of John Sterling* (a valued friend who had died several years before) in 1851; the *History of Frederick the Great,* his last important work, in instalments of two volumes a time, in 1858, 1862 and 1865. The death of his wife in 1866 was a blow from which he never recovered, and as he was now hopelessly pessimistic in regard to the movements and tendencies of the world about him, his remaining years were filled with sorrow and bitterness of soul. He died in 1881, and was buried, not in Westminster Abbey, as was suggested, but in accordance with his own wish, at Ecclefechan.

Carlyle's style, with its enormous wealth of vocabulary, its strangely constructed sentences, its breaks, abrupt turns, apostrophes and exclamations, is unique in our prose literature, and if at times it may seem uncouth and even chaotic, we must still regard even its most conspicuous mannerisms as the expression of the writer's peculiar personality. He spoke contemptuously of art as art, and had no patience with the merely bookish side of literature; yet he was in his own way one of our greatest literary artists. In his mastery of vivid and telling phraseology he is unrivalled. As we may realise by going no further than his wonderful prose-epic, *The French Revolution*, his descriptive power and power of characterisation were alike remarkable. He employed sarcasm, irony, and invective with tremendous effect; and while his intense spirituality and fine imagination give him a place among the prophets and poets, rich and abundant humour was a no less salient feature of his genius. In all the essentials of his philosophy he was fundamentally a puritan of the puritans. In him indeed the strenuous and uncompromising ethical spirit of seventeenth century puritanism found its last great exponent. Unyielding in temper and fiercely in earnest, he was intolerant of moral weakness no less than of downright wrongdoing, and held that apathy and indifference were among the most deadly evils of the time. The keynote of his teaching was sincerity; he hated conventions and unrealities with a consuming hatred; the burden of his message was that there is no salvation in shams, even in the shams that have grown sacred through age, and that in society, politics, and religion, we must seek reality at all costs. History for him was 'the larger Bible'—the revelation of God's righteous dealings with men; and the lessons which he read in the past he carried over and applied to the present. His position in the modern world may perhaps be sufficiently defined in the statement that he was in absolute antagonism to all its most characteristic ideals and tendencies. He had no faith in democracy, which was for him the last word of political unwisdom, and was never weary of insisting that the great masses of the people need the guidance and leadership of the 'hero' or 'able man'. He poured the vials of his wrath upon the easy-going optimism which had been bred by rapidly developing commercial prosperity, and with all the impassioned zeal of a Hebrew prophet, proclaimed a spiritual standard of life to a generation which had fallen into idolatrous worship of the 'mud-gods of modern civilisation'. He denounced scientific materialism and the utilitarianism (or 'pig-philosophy') which went along with it, and with a power far beyond that of any of his contemporaries, preached God and spiritual freedom as the only life-giving truths. Carlyle could not indeed turn back the currents of his age; but it would not be easy to exaggerate his influence upon it.

110. Ruskin. By virtue of the extent and variety of his work, his vigour and originality, his influence on art, letters, and life, and the range and beauty of his style, John Ruskin is entitled to rank next after Carlyle in the general prose of his time. He was born in 1819, and though the place of his birth was London, he came of a Scottish stock. His father was a rich wine merchant, and as boy and youth he enjoyed all the advantages which wealth can afford; yet his early training was as rigidly puritan as Carlyle's had been, and everything in his home surroundings helped to deepen the ingrained earnestness of his nature. At Oxford he won the Newdigate prize with a poem entitled *Salsette and Elephanta* (1839), and four years later published the first volume of *Modern Painters,* the primary purpose of which was to vindicate the genius of Turner, and, with a view to this, to expound the true principles of landscape-painting in general. Successive volumes appeared at intervals—the fifth and last in 1860; but by this time the work had outgrown its original design, and had expanded into a comprehensive, though extremely rambling treatise on aesthetics. In the meantime he became as much occupied with architecture as with painting, and produced the companion volumes *The Seven Lamps of Architecture* (1849) and *The Stones of Venice* (1851–53). As we may learn particularly from the last-named work and from *The Two Paths* (1859), however, his study of the history of art had led out into the study of social conditions; his interest was thus aroused in the practical problems of his own day; and the inspiration of Carlyle, whom in this respect he proclaimed his master, completed the transformation of the art critic into the philan-thropist and reformer. In later life, especially a Slade Professor at Oxford, he continued his work in the history and theory of art; but most of his time and energy was now devoted to social propaganda, and even his academic utterances were deeply coloured by his new enthusiasms. With splendid unselfishness he now gave his genius, his strength, and his wealth to the great social causes which he had taken to heart, and while he directed his efforts to all sorts of practical ends, he continued to expound his social and economic theories in lectures, essays, and books. *Unto this Last* (1861), *Munera Pulveris* (1862), *Time and Tide by Wear and Tyne* (1867), and the series of 'letters to the working men of England', entitled *Fors Clavigera* (1871–84); set forth his political economy, and his educational and institutional ideals; his more general ethical teachings may be found, for example, in *Sesame and Lilies* (1865) and *The Crown of Wild Olive* (1866). He spent the closing years of his life in failing health at his home on Coniston Water, in the Lake District, and there he died in 1900.

It will be seen that Ruskin's work, which is very great in bulk and miscellaneous in character, falls roughly into two divisions; his writings on art, mainly before 1860; and his writings after 1860, on social, economic, and ethical questions. The connection between these two sides of his activity, however, is far closer than might at first sight be supposed. His later practical teachings were, indeed, the logical outcome and development of his teachings on art. His aesthetics rested ultimately on moral foundations. True art, he insisted, can be produced only by a nation which is inspired by noble national aims, and lives a pure, righteous, and happy life; and it was therefore, he deemed, all but useless to preach art to nineteenth century England, sunk as it was, as regarded the wealthier classes, in sordid materialism, and, as regarded the great submerged masses of the people, in poverty and misery. A complete purification of the entire social system—an 'entire change of heart', as he put it—was necessary before any revival of art was possible in England; and it was by this line of reasoning that he was forced to the conclusion that even as a lover of art his best work could for the moment be done in the field of social service.

Apart from the significance of its basic moral principle—that all great art is 'the expression of an art-gift by a pure soul'—Ruskin's aesthetic doctrine has special importance for its emphasis upon the need of a constant, direct, first-hand study of nature. Here, as we see, he was following in art the lead of Wordsworth in poetry, and like Wordsworth, he helped to break down the tyranny of convention and tradition, and to put men once more into living touch with living reality. The artist, he insisted, must abandon altogether the stereotyped formalism of the schools, and instead of trying to paint like some famous master—say, Raphael—must go straight to nature for himself, and strive to reproduce faithfully what he finds there, 'rejecting nothing, selecting nothing, and scorning nothing.' It was this part of Ruskin's philosophy which specially inspired the Pre-Raphaelites (see §108). He was also an eloquent advocate of the claims of Gothic (or Christian) as against classic (or pagan) art, and exercised immense influence in developing in his generation a love for the painting and architecture of the middle ages. At this point we should remember that while the strongly accentuated puritanism of his character allied him to such men as Knox and Carlyle, his equally strong romantic bias connected him with Scott, of whom, in contrast with Carlyle, he was all his life long an ardent admirer.

In regard to his social and economic teaching, which when first enunciated was ridiculed as hopelessly quixotic and absurd, it is enough here to say that it must be interpreted as, at bottom, an attempt to apply the principles of Christianity directly to the practical business of life, national as well as individual. Hence his violent attack upon the accepted political economy of the time. In his denunciations of the sordid spirit of modern commercial England and its idolatrous worship of wealth and material success, he followed up the teachings of Carlyle, and in turn became the chief leader of William Morris (see §108).

Many faults may be found with Ruskin as a writer. He is

whimsical and capricious; his discursiveness is irritating; his temper dogmatic; his manner often so petulant and aggressive as to stir the reader to revolt; in thought and phrase he is often fantastic; and his inconsistencies are so numerous and glaring as to shake our faith in the substantial value of his doctrine. But his spirit was always pure, noble, and chivalrous, and as a preacher of righteousness—and this was essentially his rôle—his influence told immensely for good. His style calls for the highest praise; and alike in the rich ornate prose of his early, and in the easy colloquialism of his later writing, he is in the front rank of our greatest masters. A special feature of his style is his marvellous power of word-painting.

111. Macaulay. In treating Carlyle and Ruskin as the greatest general prose writers of their age, we are adopting the revised judgment of history. Contemporary opinion would have given the first place to Macaulay, who in popularity far exceeded both of them. THOMAS BABINGTON MACAULAY was born in 1800, and after a brilliant academic record at Cambridge, opened a career of extraordinary and varied success with an essay on Milton in the *Edinburgh Review* for August, 1825. He went to the bar, entered the House of Commons, and made a reputation as an orator and statesman; but all the time he was writing steadily for the *Edinburgh*. He was in India as legal adviser to the Supreme Council from 1834 to 1838, and on his return to England re-entered public life, and after many years of strenuous political activity was raised to the peerage as Baron Macaulay of Rothley. His chief literary work was now his *History of England from the Accession of James II*, the first two volumes of which were published in 1848, instantly scoring a success such as no purely historical production had ever before enjoyed. Despite a collapse in health which left him a permanent invalid, he persevered with his great undertaking, and his third and fourth volumes appeared in 1855. The fifth was issued after his sudden death in 1859.

Macaulay's amazing vogue with the great public (and it is rightly said that even his purely literary essays have been widely read by persons who as a rule never think of reading criticism) may be explained by reference to a combination of qualities in his genius, of which some must be reckoned as excellences of the highest order, while others have rather to be set down on the adverse side of the account. He had a marvellous faculty for making everything he touched interesting; whatever might be the subject of his discourse, his animation was unbounded and he rarely wrote a dull page. As a mere story-teller he could risk comparison with his greatest contemporaries in fiction, and he was as clear as he was energetic, vivacious, and picturesque. At the same time, we have to remember that save for his exceptional endowment of genius, he was an almost typical Englishman of his generation, and therefore delighted the average man because he expressed so eloquently the average man's point of view about things instead of transcending or attacking it. Practical and positive in temper, untroubled by doubts and wholly indifferent to 'the burden of the mystery' of life, he was the very embodiment of sturdy commonsense; he hated the vague and the mystical, and he had a firm faith in the 'happy materialism' of his age. Readers who were simply bewildered by Carlyle and Ruskin, and resented, or were perhaps disturbed by, the persistency with which these great moral teachers challenged their comfortable optimism, found in Macaulay, with his downrightness and sanity, a man after their own hearts. His shallowness, too—and in his interpretation of history and character he was undeniably shallow—made it all the easier for them to understand him; while his brilliant style—which in its lucidity, vivacity, hardness, and epigrammatic force is an exact index of his personality—gave a wonderful charm to everything he said. Macaulay was not a great thinker; he was not a great literary critic; and as biographer and historian, though always painstaking, he was often led into inaccuracy by his love of sweeping statements and striking contrasts. But his achievements were still remarkable. More than any other writer he may be said by his essays to have popularised a taste for literature, and his *History* remains the most generally attractive piece of historical narrative in the language.

112. Arnold. The last prose writer to whom it is necessary here to give a separate section is MATTHEW ARNOLD. The son of Thomas Arnold, the famous headmaster of Rugby, he was born in 1822, distinguished himself at Oxford, was for a time private secretary to Lord Lansdowne, and from 1855 to within two years of his death worked hard as a lay inspector of schools. He also held the chair of poetry at Oxford from 1857 to 1867, and in 1883 and 1886 made lecturing tours in America. He died in 1888. Of his poetry, in the main the work of his earlier manhood, we have already spoken (§108). His prose falls naturally into two divisions; in the one he deals with literature, in the other, with life. His writings on literature are to be found chiefly in his two volumes of *Essays in Criticism* (1865 and 1888), *Mixed Essays* (1879), and Oxford *Lectures on Translating Homer* (1861, 1862), all of which are marked by the same qualities of insight, acumen, delicacy of perception, and fineness of taste. Regarding literature as essentially a 'criticism of life', he was mainly concerned with the moral values of the writers discussed, and in practice he went far to realise his own conception of criticism as 'a dis-interested endeavour to learn and propagate the best that is known and thought in the world'. Yet he had lived too much with the Greeks to overlook the claims of art as art. He was not a great scholar; he was neither profound nor systematic, and his judgment was sometimes disturbed by caprice. But his literary criticism as a whole is wonderfully full, suggestive, and illuminating. As a critic of life, Arnold addressed himself to the task of breaking down the 'hard unintelligence' and enlarging the mental and moral horizon of the great English public, in his *Culture and Anarchy* (1869) and *Friendship's Garland* (1871); while in *Literature and Dogma* (1873) and *God and the Bible* (1875), he entered the theological field, and undertook to reconstruct essential Christianity on a basis of pure naturalism. His prose is admirable for its lucidity, grace, and charm, though he occasionally irritates by mannerisms and a trick of repetition. Always polished and urbane despite his colloquialism, he could nonetheless employ raillery and sarcasm with deadly effect. He had also an extraordinary gift of crystallising his ideas in telling and memorable phrases. He was one of the most stimulating writers of his time, and though his temper was very different from Carlyle's or Ruskin's, he did much useful work by carrying on, in his own way, their attack upon the materialism of modern life.

113. Other Prose Writers of the Time. Out of the remaining innumerable company of Victorian prose writers who gained distinction in various fields, I here select for mention those few, and those few only, of whom even the briefest review of the period is bound to take some account.

In history, HENRY THOMAS BUCKLE (1821–62) showed the profound influence of physical science by his *History of Civilisation in England,* in which he made an attempt to eliminate the personal factor from human affairs, and to explain progress entirely by reference to natural causes and general laws. In part at least as a result of the example of Macaulay, though in part also as a result of the analytical tendencies of the age, many Victorian historians adopted the practice of writing at great length and in immense detail upon relatively short periods. Conspicuous illustrations may be found in *The History of the Norman Conquest,* a solid piece of work, by EDWARD AUGUSTUS FREEMAN (1823–92); the brilliant but inaccurate *History of England from the Fall of Wolsey to the Defeat of the Spanish Armada,* by JAMES ANTHONY FROUDE (1818–94); the laborious series of volumes on the period of the Stuarts and the Civil War, by SAMUEL RAWDON GARDINER (1829–1902), and the equally painstaking and substantial *History of England in the Eighteenth Century,* by WILLIAM EDWARD HARTPOLE LECKY (1838–1903). The method of concentration, on the other hand, is admirably exemplified in the *Short History of the English People,* by JOHN RICHARD GREEN (1837–83), the best book of the kind that we have. In this, the strong democratic influence of the time is apparent; it is a history, not of kings and wars only, but, as the title states, of the people.

The seven volumes of JOHN ADDINGTON SYMONDS (1840–93) on

The Renaissance in Italy (a work of great merit, though sadly marred by prolixity and extreme floridness of diction), may be taken as a connecting link between history and aesthetic criticism. In this latter field the most important writer after Ruskin was WALTER HORATIO PATER (1839–94), who produced slowly and with infinite labour, and wrote in a highly elaborated, singularly beautiful, but rather too artificial style. His volume, *The Renaissance,* and his *Greek Studies,* contain the best of his criticism; but he also did some fine and practically unique work in philosophical romance, as in his *Imaginary Portraits* and *Marius the Epicurean.*

Literary criticism and the art of the general essay were meanwhile cultivated with much success by many writers; among them, by Froude in his *Short Studies on Great Subjects,* and by SIR LESLIE STEPHEN (1832–1904), in his *Hours in a Library,* a collection of biographical studies of great value by reason of their learning, catholicity, and sureness of taste. Swinburne also wrote a great deal of literary criticism, but his enthusiasms and his prejudices alike were so violent that little confidence can be placed in his judgment. The essays, critical and general, of Stevenson the novelist (*Familiar Studies of Men and Books, Memories and Portraits, Virginibus Puerisque*) may, on the contrary, be reckoned among the most important things of the class in recent literature.

The popularisation of knowledge, of which I have spoken, naturally led to the production of a large body of literature in which scientific subjects were so handled as to be made interesting to the intelligent general reader. Two famous scientists, JOHN TYNDALL (1820–93) and THOMAS HENRY HUXLEY (1825–95) proved themselves masters in the art of luminous exposition, and Grant Allen (1848–99) made a distinct mark in the same line. Similarly, theology passed into general literature, as notably in the lectures and essays of JOHN HENRY NEWMAN (1801–90), whose influence was so wide and deep that he has been regarded as, after Carlyle, the most dominating personality in the literature of his age. One other writer, who stands apart from all the foregoing groups, has also to be mentioned, JOHN

RICHARD JEFFERIES (1848–87). In his *Gamekeeper at Home, The Amateur Poacher,* and other books of the same kind, he wrote of nature with rare powers of observation and description, but perhaps the most fascinating of his works is *The Story of my Heart,* an account of his inner experiences and development.

24

The Age of Tennyson:
The Novel

114. General Characteristics. The literary and social significance of the rise and establishment of prose fiction during the eighteenth century has already been pointed out (§73), and in the light of what was then said, its prominence in the literature of the Age of Tennyson will be readily understood. Yet the special place which it has now come to fill must still be emphasised. The mere fact that it was soon recognised as incomparably the most popular form of literature with the great and ever-increasing general reading public will itself go far to explain, on the well-known principle of supply and demand, its attractiveness to innumerable writers of the most varied powers and aims; but its breadth and elasticity, and the freedom it gave to each new practitioner to do his own work in his own way, must also be taken into account. Absorbing into itself a very large part of the creative energy of the time, the novel thus became a vehicle of ideas as well as a means of amusement. Writers of different schools of thought employed it to embody their general criticism of life, while it was found to lend itself equally well to the purposes of those who, having some special thesis to expound, desired to reach the largest possible body of readers. It was inevitable that it should thus come to reflect all the forces which were shaping the complex modern world. The spread of science made it realistic and analytical; the spread of democracy made it social and humanitarian; the spirit of religious and moral unrest, of inquiry and criticism, was often uppermost in it; often, too, it revealed the powerful influences of the romantic revival. In its very variety of matter and treatment, therefore, the Victorian novel is the index of the many-sided interests and conflicting elements of the Victorian age. At this point the well-marked tendency towards specialisation in fiction should also be noted. Here and there, it is true, novelists aimed (as Fielding had done in *Tom Jones*) to give a fairly comprehensive picture of contemporary)' society. But as a rule aspects of life were picked out for separate treatment, and subdivision of labour and interests was the result. Thus, for example, we have novels of the sea and of military life, of high life, middle-class life, low life, criminal life, of industrial life, political life, artistic life, clerical life, and so on; while frequently the subdivision follows geographical lines, as in the fiction which is concerned with Irish life, or Scottish life, or even, it may be, the life of different English counties. It is largely through the free development of these subdividing tendencies that prose fiction has expanded on all sides until it has become practically coextensive with all the aspects and activities of the modern world.

It would be impossible, even if it were necessary, to undertake here a detailed consideration of the Victorian novel. Only so much needs to be said about it as will serve to complete our brief survey of Victorian literature in general. I shall, therefore, first touch upon the broad characteristics of the three chief novelists of the time—Dickens, Thackeray, and George Eliot—after which I shall try just to indicate the significance of the work done by their more important contemporaries in fiction.

115. Dickens. CHARLES DICKENS (1812–70) sprang suddenly into fame with the *Pickwick Papers* (1837), and at twenty-five found himself the most popular of English novelists—a position which he still holds today. Technically considered, his work falls into two chronological divisions. He began as a follower of the traditions of Smollett (see

§76), whom as a child he had read with great enthusiasm, and who, despite the immeasurable difference between them in spirit and tone, may be regarded as his master; and his early novels—*Pickwick*, for instance, and *Nicholas Nickleby*—are, like Smollett's, bundles of adventures, connected, so far as they are connected at all, only by the characters who figure in them. In *Martin Chuzzlewit* (1843), *Dombey and Son* (1846–48), and *David Copperfield* (1849–50), some effort is made towards greater unification, but even these books belong substantially to the loose, chronicle type. *Bleak House* (1852–53) may be said to open his second period, because here for the first time we find a systematic attempt to gather up all the diverse threads of the story into a coherent plot. It cannot be held that Dickens was very successful with his plot-building, and even in his latest books there is still a great deal of merely episodical material. But it was in accordance with this changed structural method that the novels after *Bleak House*—*Little Dorrit* (1855–57), *A Tale of Two Cities* (1859), *Great Expectations* (1861), *Our Mutual Friend* (1864–65), and the unfinished *Edwin Drood*—were planned.

Dickens's qualities are obvious to all who read, and in particular, his overflowing irresistible humour, his unsurpassed descriptive power, and the astonishing vitality of his characterisation. Criticism has, of course, to point out, in regard to his characterisation, that the range of his success was, after all, very limited; and it is, moreover, questioned whether even his humorous creations (and it was in the field of the odd and the grotesque that his great achievements lay) belong in any sense to the world of realities. It must be admitted that with him character was generally heightened into caricature. Yet the fact remains that no other writer in our literature, save only Shakespeare, ever called into being so many men and women who have become permanent elements of that humorous tradition into which we of the English-speaking race are privileged to be born. Dickens's principal fault was the over-wrought quality of much of his emotion. It is here that he has suffered most from changes of taste. In his craving after effect he continually had recourse to heavily-loaded emphasis, and, as a result, his work became crude. He loved melodrama, and his melodrama was too frequently theatrical; in his many passages of studied sentiment and pathos he was often extravagant and mawkish.

His novels belong entirely to the humanitarian movement of the Victorian era, of which they are indeed, in the domain of fiction, by far the most important product and expression. He was from first to last a novelist with a purpose. In nearly all his books he set out to attack some specific abuse or abuses in the existing system of things, and throughout he constituted himself the champion of the weak, the outcast, and the oppressed. Humanitarianism was indeed the keynote of his work, and as his enormous popularity carried his influence far and wide, he may justly be reckoned one of the greatest social reformers of his age. At the same time, he shared to the full its sanguine spirit. Despite its many evils—the hardness of heart and the selfishness of those in high places—the greed and hypocrisy which were so prevalent—the wicked class prejudices which divided man from man—the world was still for Dickens a very good world to live in. A man of buoyant temper and unflagging energy, he put his unwavering optimism into everything he wrote, and his contagious high spirits were undoubtedly a factor in his success.

116. Thackeray. Dickens's world was that of the lower and lower middle classes, and when he left this, he nearly always failed. The world of his great rival, WILLIAM MAKEPEACE THACKERAY (1811–63), on the other hand, was that of 'society'—of the clubs, the drawing rooms, and the well-to-do. This world he called, in his first really successful and most thoroughly characteristic book, *Vanity Fair* (1847–48), and his use of this phrase out of the *Pilgrim's Progress* indicates both the nature of his subject-matter and his own attitude towards it. The sub-title of the same work—*A Novel without a Hero*—still further points to the spirit of his writing and the foundation principles of his art. Thackeray was essentially a social satirist and a realist. He knew nothing of Dickens's humanitarianism and tremendous zeal for reform. But his persistent and telling attacks upon snobbery, affectation, and humbug may after all be regarded as the parallel, though on a different plane, of Carlyle's terrific denunciations of quackery, shams, and insincerity. His conscious rupture with romanticism in fiction was inspired rather by moral than by purely artistic considerations. The romantic novel, with its high-flown sentiment and distorted views of motive and character, gave, he believed, a totally false impression of life, and thus did immense harm; and he held with his great master, Fielding, that 'truth is best, from whatever pulpit'. He made it his business, therefore, to portray the world as he himself had found it; and as he had not found it in the least romantic, he would not paint it in romantic colours. In fact, in his reaction against the long popular romantic tradition he practically changed the centre of gravity of interest in fiction, making vice rather than virtue the pith and substance of his stories. We must indeed recognise the increasing geniality of his books. He began by dealing almost exclusively with the sordid and ugly aspects of life, as in *Barry Lyndon*; the more comprehensive picture in *Vanity Fair* allowed a much larger place for purity and unselfishness; and after *Vanity Fair*—in *Pendennis, Esmond, The Newcomes, The Virginians* and *Philip*—the good element gained in prominence and importance. Yet to the end, though the satire became less ferocious and sweeping and the tone more tender and sympathetic, the evil of life still bulked large in Thackeray's thought. He was not, as has often been alleged, a cynic, for though his caustic criticism occasionally gives plausibility to the charge, he, felt, as the cynic does not, the pity and pathos of human things, as well as their absurdities. But his general view of existence, in contrast with that of Dickens, was profoundly melancholy. The text of his many moralisings may be stated in his favourite phrase—*Vanitas vanitatum*.

Thackeray's interest was always centred in character; he paid little or no attention to questions of construction, and his novels belong to the sprawling, inorganic kind. His characterisation, however, redeems all faults of technique, for it is marvellously penetrative and truthful. As a writer of colloquial prose, he holds a place well to the fore in our literature, and merely as a writer, though not always correct, he is always charming. Despite the immediate purpose of his social satire, he did some of his best work with materials furnished by the past. His *Henry Esmond* (1852), with its wonderful re-creation of the life and atmosphere, and even of the tone and style of the early eighteenth century, is one of the very finest historical novels in the language.

117. George Eliot. The novel, then, was humananitarian in the hands of Dickens and satiric in the hands of Thackeray. In the hands of MARY ANN, or MARIAN EVANS, always known by her pen-name of GEORGE ELIOT (1819–80), it became moral and philosophical. As Dickens's world was that of the London streets and Thackeray's that of the clubs and drawing-rooms, so hers was for the most part that of the old-fashioned provincial life with which she had been familiar in her girlhood. In one novel, indeed, *Romola*—a tale of the Renaissance in Florence—she made an excursion into the past; but she was always at her best when, as in *Adam Bede* (1859), *The Mill on the Floss* (1860), *Silas Marner* (1861), and *Middlemarch* (1871), she kept close to the scenes and the types of character she had early known and loved. Superficially considered, her work thus somewhat resembles that of Jane Austen (§104), and due note must be taken of its excellence as a representation of men and manners in Midland village and country town. But where Jane Austen had written only of the externals of the social comedy, George Eliot was concerned with great moral struggles beneath the surface of an existence which to the casual observer would seem dull and commonplace. With her power of weaving tragedy, and tragedy as poignant and deeply moral as anything to be found in Aeschylus or Shakespeare, out of home-spun materials (as in Hetty Sorrel's pitiful story in *Adam Bede*) she is thus, like Wordsworth in *Michael,* an exponent of the democratic movement in our modern literature. Humour of a rich and delicate kind, and pathos which was never forced, are to be reckoned among her principal gifts; and though the foundation of her art was avowedly uncompromising truth to life, her realism was everywhere tempered with the widest and tenderest sympathy. But the distinctive features of her work are to be sought in the philosophic element which fills so large a place in it, and which, like her realism, connects her with the scientific tendencies of her age. George Eliot was a great thinker; beginning her career as a novelist late in life, she brought to it scholarship such as no other English writer of fiction has ever possessed; she was in intimate touch with all contemporary discoveries and speculations; and while she early abandoned the evangelical Christianity in which she had been bred, her earnest religious nature gave her a wonderful insight into all phases of spiritual experience. Her work thus takes its place, not with light literature, but with the most serious literature of the century; her novels are great essays on life, though their teachings are embodied in the concrete forms of art. Her central theme was habitually the conflict between the higher and the lower life—duty and inclination; and as this theme was almost always worked out by her tragically—as the movement of the story was commonly from weakness to sin and from sin to nemesis—her books are profoundly sad. But as with all really great tragedy, hers is a purifying sadness. She had, however, the faults of her qualities, and these faults have proved extremely detrimental to her posthumous fame. Her tendency from the first was towards the excessive use of analysis and commentary; this tendency grew upon her as her creative faculty waned, and her later writings—like *Daniel Deronda,* for example—are almost choked by science and psychology.

118. Other Novelists of the Period. As in a brief catalogue of these it is difficult to find any other basis of classification, I will arrange them here mainly in order of birth, only departing from this as convenience may suggest.

With no claim to rank as a literary artist, CAPTAIN FREDERICK MARRYAT (1792–1848) deserves mention as our raciest and most amusing novelist of the sea (*e.g., Peter Simple, Mr. Midshipman Easy*). Though born, as will be seen, before the eighteenth century was out, his first novel, *Frank Mildmay,* was not published till 1829. A year before this EDWARD BULWER LYTTON, afterwards LORD LYTTON

(1803–73) had caused a sensation with *Pelham*. Lytton was a man of infinite cleverness and versatility, and in his work in fiction he scored success in many styles; in melodramatic tales of society and crime (*e.g., Paul Clifford, Ernest Maltravers, Eugene Aram*); historical romance (*e.g., The Last Days of Pompeii, Harold, The Last of the Barons*); tales of the supernatural (*e.g., Zanoni*); stories of social purpose (*e.g., The Coming Race*), and novels of domestic life (*e.g., The Caxtons, My Novel*). The brilliancy of his achievement in all these fields will not be denied; but this brilliancy often degenerates into meretricious glitter, and much of his writing is marred by extravagance and unreality. The same defects are conspicuous in the novels (*e.g., Henrietta Temple, Coningsby, Tancred*) of BENJAMIN DISRAELI, EARL OF BEAGONSFIELD (1804–81). One of these, however, *Sybil* (1845), calls for mention apart because, as a powerful exposure of abuses connected with the relations of capital and labour, it belongs to the humanitarian movement in contemporary fiction. Very different in quality was the work of GEORGE BORROW (1803–81), an eccentric man of many crotchets, who travelled much (see, *e.g., The Bible in Spain*), studied the gypsies (see, *e.g., The Gypsies in Spain*), and produced two rambling autobiographical novels, *Lavengro* and its sequel, *The Romany Rye*. Three years younger, CHARLES LEVER (1806–72) wrote many volumes, but is chiefly remembered today for two books of rollicking Irish fun and military adventure, *Harry Lorrequer* and *Charles O'Malley*. With CHARLES READE (1814–84) social purpose is generally dominant (*e.g., Foul Play, Put Yourself in His Place, Hard Cash*), but the best of his books is his vigorous and exciting historical romance, *The Cloister and the Hearth*. MRS. GASKELL (1810–65) may also be included here among the humanitarian novelists (*e.g.,* her pathetic story of factory life, *Mary Barton*), but for most readers now she lives as the author of the quaint and charming village idyll, *Cranford*. ANTHONY TROLLOPE (1815–82), a far too voluminous writer, was a realist of the realists, and his photographic pictures of early Victorian provincial life (*e.g., Barchester Towers, Dr. Thorne*) already begin to possess an historical value. He was at his best as a novelist of clerical life (*e.g. The Warden, Framley Parsonage*).

In her first and most successful book, *Jane Eyre* (1847) CHARLOTTE BRONTË (1816–55) put an intensity of passion and a frankness of description into the novel which were quite new to the women's fiction of the time, and shocked not a few old-fashioned people. Her sister EMILY (1818–48) also ranks highly; her chief work, *Wuthering Heights,* is considered a masterpiece. The third sister ANNE (1820–49) is less important; her chief novels are *Agnes Grey* and *The Tenant of Wildfell Hall.* In CHARLES KINGSLEY (1819–75), an enthusiastic disciple of Carlyle and an ardent social reformer, we reach one of the most vigorous of the humanitarian novelists of the mid-Victorian age. His *Alton Locke, Yeast,* and *Two Years Ago,* are full of the unrest of their time and of the writer's passionate earnestness in the cause of the masses; but his finest work as literature was done in his two historical novels, *Westward Ho* and *Hypatia.* His brother, HENRY (1830–76), though far less known, is sometimes accounted the better novelist. His *Geoffrey Hamlyn* has been pronounced by competent judges our best novel of Australian life. WILLIAM WILKIE COLLINS (1824–89) has his standing secure in English fiction as our greatest master of sensation and plot (*e.g., The Woman in White, The Moonstone*). It was in part at least under his influence that his friend Dickens changed, as we have seen, from the inorganic to the organic type of story. RICHARD DODDRIDGE BLACKMORE (1825–1900) wrote at least one book which will live—his spirited Exmoor romance, *Lorna Doone.* SIR WALTER BESANT (1836–1901) may roughly be said to belong to the school of Dickens in virtue in particular of the strong humanitarianism and direct social purpose of much of his work (*e.g., All Sorts and Conditions of Men, Children of Gibeon*); but he often worked with much success on somewhat different lines, as in his capital eighteenth century story, *The Chaplain of the Fleet.* Two of the most important names in the long list of our Victorian novelists come at the last, and with these (as still living writers cannot be mentioned *here**) our survey may fitly close. One of

---

* See Chapters XXV and XXVI.

these is GEORGE MEREDITH (1828–1909), the other ROBERT LOUIS STEVENSON (1850–94). Though never widely popular, Meredith is now acknowledged as one of our very greatest English writers of fiction, and two of his works, *The Ordeal of Richard Feverel* and *The Egoist*, seem already to have taken rank among the classics. One of the most delightful of personalities and of stylists, with a spirit and a touch all his own, Stevenson perhaps more than any other man of his generation led the way from realism to romance, and there can be no doubt in the mind of any judicious reader that his *Treasure Island, Dr. Jekyll and Mr. Hyde, Kidnapped*, and *The Master of Ballantrae*, are hall-marked for immortality. He and Meredith together carried on the finest traditions of fiction till well on towards the end of a long period of extraordinary and many-sided activity.

TABLE OF THE AGE OF TENNYSON

Verse	General Prose	The Novel
Tennyson's *Poems*, 1833	Carlyle's *Sartor Resartus*, 1833, 1834	Lytton's *Pelham*, 1827 Dickens's *Boz*, 1834–36
Browning's *Pauline*, 1833	Carlyle's *French Revolution*, 1837	Dickens's *Pickwick*, 1837
	Lockhart's *Life of Scott*, 1836–38	Thackeray's *Yellowplush Papers*, 1837
	Macaulay's *Essays*, 1843	
	Ruskin's *Modern Painters*, 1843–60	Disraeli's *Sybil*, 1845 Thackeray's *Vanity Fair* 1847–48 Bronte's *Jane Eyre*, 1847
Arnold's *Strayed Reveller*, 1848	Macaulay's *History*, 1848–60	Kingsley's *Alton Locke*, 1850
Arnold's *Poems*, 1855	Froude's *History*, 1856–69	Trollope's *Warden*, 1855

Mrs. Browning's *Aurora Leigh*, 1856	Buckle's *Civilisation*, 1857–61	
		George Eliot's *Clerical Life*, 1858
Tennyson's *Idylls of the King*, 1859–86		George Eliot's *Adam Bede*, 1859
Clare, d. 1864		Meredith's *Richard Feverel*, 1859
		Thackeray, d. 1863
	Arnold's *Essays in Criticism*, 1865 1888	
Swinburne's *Poems and Ballads*, 1866		Dickens, d. 1870
Browning's *The Ring and the Book*, 1868, 1869		
Morris's *Earthly Paradise*, 1868–70		
Rossetti's *Poems*, 1870–72		
	Pater's *Renaissance*, 1873	Lytton, d. 1873
	Symonds' *Renaissance in Italy*, 1875–86	
	Stevenson's *Virginibus Puerisque*, 1881	George Eliot, d. 1880
	Carlyle, d. 1881	
Rossetti, d. 1882		Trollope, d. 1882
Arnold, d. 1888		
Browning, d. 1889		
	Ruskin, d. 1900	
Tennyson, d. 1892		
		Stevenson, d. 1894

25

The Age of Hardy
(1887–1928)

119. Epilogue to the Victorian Age. If the first jubilee of Queen Victoria in 1887 is taken as a convenient landmark to denote the virtual end of the Age of Tennyson, the remaining fourteen years of the queen's reign may be regarded as a sinuous corridor leading to the new century. At the death of Tennyson in 1892 no dominant personality remained to interpret the sentiments of the British nation or to represent its general voice in melodious aphorisms. Soon, indeed, there was no general voice to represent, for Browning's idea of human diversity and complexity attracted the younger generation more than Tennyson's desire to suggest a grand simplicity and unity of purpose throughout Creation. The old hope in the ultimate discovery of One Universal Truth gave place to the disturbing contemplation of an endless series of competing truths. Dogma was dead. With this change of outlook the apparently, solid foundations which had sustained the Victorian Age began to crumble, and the cause lay as much in certain defects in nineteenth-century popular idealism as in the impatience of the new generation. The splendour of the Victorian achievement was such that it is heightened, not dimmed, by stripping away whatever served only to add a meretricious glitter. Through the scientists and inventors the bounds of thought and speculation and of man's control over Nature were vastly extended in the Victorian Age; but this enlargement (allied with industrial progress, colonial expansion, and multiplication of material wealth) bred in a large and influential section of Victorian people a dangerous sense of self-sovereignty and illimitable attainment. Queen Victoria's Diamond Jubilee in 1897 was as proud a display of pageantry and magniloquence as any that modern man has permitted himself to give, and in some later reading of history the jubilee rites of that summer may seem to be the point at which the prosperity and assurance of the Victorian Age began to pale toward their decline. While the period was at high noon it was second only to the Elizabethan Age—yet to lament unduly the passing of Victorian greatness would be to ignore the first lesson of history. Greatness is periodic. It makes exhausting demands upon human energy and must be followed by periods of relaxation, in which the general stature of genius is diminished. In such periods any main current of tendency in literature and ideas can rarely be distinguished. The little geniuses have, commonly, no intelligent regard for the uses of tradition: they either imitate slavishly or revolt arrogantly. Nor have they themselves the power to create a new tradition.

Such a period and such a group of little geniuses followed the Age of Tennyson, and though for the purposes of the present chapter the forty years between 1887 and 1928 are called the Age of Hardy, this is not intended to suggest that Hardy was in any special sense a spiritual or intellectual director during that time. He was much admired by his juniors as a man of outstanding and exceptional genius, but he was no modernist.

120. The Eighteen-Nineties. From beginning to end the great Victorian writers devoted themselves to a literature of purpose. In the last decade of the century a new group of authors and artists set out to demonstrate that 'all art is useless' in the sense of being free from allegiance to ideas of morality and standards of conduct. OSCAR WILDE (1856–1900), the foremost of this group, was attracted by the theories of Walter Pater, who with surprise and reluctance found himself adopted as the mentor of the Aesthetic Movement. Pater's final essay in *The Renaissance* had suggested a tentative philosophy of life arising from the cultivation of moments of 'exquisite passion': 'The service of philosophy, and of religion and culture as well, to the human spirit, is to startle it into a sharp and eager observation. Every moment some form grows perfect in hand or face; some tone on the hills or sea is choicer than the rest; some mood of passion or insight or intellectual excitement is irresistibly real and attractive for us,—for that moment only. Not the fruit of experience, but experience itself is the end.... The theory or idea or system, which requires of us the sacrifice of any part of this experience, in consideration of some interest into which we cannot enter, or some abstract morality we have not identified with ourselves, or what is only conventional, has no real claim upon us.' To Pater himself, cloistered in scholarly calm, this amounted to little more than an interesting intellectual conception; but when put into living practice by the young 'decadents' of the nineties it developed into the pursuit of pure sensation divorced from moral control. Sinister rumours gathering around Wilde led to the arrest and trial of this brilliant poseur, who was sent in 1895 to Reading Gaol for two years. Thereafter he was variously represented as a satyr and as a martyr, and the controversy prevented a balanced appreciation of his work. It is now possible to see him in a clear light, and to recognize that his flashing wit, his penetrating paradoxes and his gay audacity remain as stimulating, as illuminating and as entertaining in our own time as they were at first. His elaborately decorated style has for the most part worn well; if there is perceptible tarnish it is in patches only. There is still pleasure to be had from the polished and jewelled prose of *Intentions,* a series of dialogues on literature and the arts—with dissertations on lying, poison, and masks, subjects with which the decadents absurdly considered it almost an obligation to be familiar. Wilde's wit was more than a display of verbal gymnastics: it often crystallized into a memorable phrase some truth or some serviceable critical judgment which a pedestrian or a pedantic style would obscure in a mist of words. Even when his wit was exercised playfully it left a lasting mark, as in *The Importance of Being Earnest*, a comedy of manners on a level with Sheridan's best. The fairy tales (*The Happy Prince* and others) are blemished by the sophistication and heavy-lidded world-weariness apparent below, their surface simplicity; and among the poems few are free from a suggestion of musty tinselled bedragglement. That something of Byron which lived in Wilde prevents the most intimate display of his bleeding heart from carrying the conviction of sincerity rightly demanded from a testament of suffering. *De Profundis* (Wilde's *apologia*) and *The Ballad of Reading Gaol* are affecting, but nothing more: neither touches the depths. Always a deliberate and calculating artificer, Oscar Wilde was incapable of absolute sincerity and simplicity; he was always posturing, even in his agony.

The best qualities of the decadents, and the worst, were personified in Wilde and illustrated by his work. It would be superfluous in this brief survey to speak in detail of other members of the group, though several (more or less closely associated) need to be mentioned: AUBREY BEARDSLEY (1872–98) and CHARLES CONDER (1868–1909)—without whose drawings and paintings the eighteen-nineties would lose a striking part of its typical character; ARTHUR SYMONS (1865–1945), whose early poems employed 'the *décor* of the town' and celebrated the hectic passions of the streets, using a symbolistic style based on modern French poetry. ERNEST DOWSON (1867–1900), equally hectic; and LIONEL JOHNSON (1867–1902), a true poet on the fringe of the decadent movement but free from its hotter extravagances.

JOHN DAVIDSON (1857–1909) vented a defiantly introspective nature in a sequence of four long poems ending with *The Testament of John Davidson*, which seemed in the opening years of the twentieth century to give him rank as a poet of some philosophic importance. Seen from a distance in time, however, his *Testaments* display less deep thought than feverish personal preoccupation—

> ... on the adamantine bastion hung
> A figure crucified, which was myself;

and Davidson is now little remembered except for a few lyrics in the anthologies.

Two periodicals, *The Yellow Book* (1894–97) and *The Savoy* (1896) were founded for the publication of writings and pictures in the mode of the nineties. These magazines should be referred to by those who wish to understand the foibles of the period and to capture some breath of its spirit. In later numbers *The Yellow Book* became less and less the organ of a coterie, and drew into its list of contributors many writers who achieved wider distinction in the next decade.

121. Thomas Hardy. Some exploration of the literary hothouse of the nineties was necessary before turning to Hardy, since it is in the works of the decadents that the chief signs of an organized anti-Victorian movement are seen. But no revolt comes without some preceding sounds of discontent. As early as the sixties certain cherished Victorian ideals were being challenged here and there, and in Hardy's work there was from the beginning an implied disagreement with current conventions—as there was also in Samuel Butler's *Erewhon* (1872) and more especially in his *The Way of All Flesh*. For the next twenty years, however, these were to be lonely voices Except for a period in London during young manhood, THOMAS HARDY passed his life near Dorchester, close to which he was born in 1840 and died in 1928. Early training as an architect gave him an intimate knowledge of local churches, utilized to advantage in his writings; and in other ways, also, his personal experience was bound up with the people and customs, the monuments and institutions, of Dorset and the contiguous counties of south-western England, which he placed permanently on the literary map by the ancient name Wessex. As a writer Hardy was a living paradox. A natural poet, much of his poetry is nevertheless in prose. He had the poet's largeness, minuteness and intensity of vision—a threefold faculty displayed throughout his novels; yet among his hundreds of typical lyrical poems hardly a score are free from grating harshness and pinchbeck angularity. The explanation of the paradox is that Hardy's genius was entirely sculpturesque. Given a granitic block of stubborn prose he could chisel as a master and carve not only tremendously impressive figure-groups but also vast sculptured landscapes with all the varied detail of nature, even to a filigree of bare branches against the sunset. But lyrics cannot be induced from granite chips; or if they are, only by some miracle such as happened twice or thrice to Hardy and produced *Tess's Lament, Weathers,* and *In Time of 'the Breaking of Nations'*. His emphasis upon the human tragedy is held in right proportion and perspective in most of his novels, where it is balanced by the massivity of the scene and the unquenchable courage of the men and women. Scarcely more than twice did Hardy's skill in the novelist's craft desert him. The last chapter of *Tess of the D'Urbervilles* outraged the religious conscience of 1891; today it offends the aesthetic conscience by its violation of our critical sense of order and imaginative sufficiency. There is a failure in artistry when an artist says more than exactly enough. Hardy had said enough in *Tess* before the beginning of the last chapter. As it stands, the novel is a masterpiece, but it is scarred by an unhappy final stroke. *Jude the Obscure,* the last novel, is more fatally injured by ruthlessness. At no time are Sue and Jude permitted to escape the shadowing hand of malignant destiny. They are defeated and broken. Their lack of spiritual resilience, their crippling inability to do what many of Hardy's people do magnificently—stand erect and hit destiny full in the face—prevent *Jude the Obscure* from being the greatest of Hardy's novels. Its power is overwhelming, yet the power is so misdirected and dissipated that potential tragedy is distorted into dark madness.

It was perhaps unfortunate that the manuscript of Hardy's first novel (never published) went to George Meredith, at that time a publishers' reader. Meredith advised the young author to give more attention to plot, advice Hardy appears to have taken too literally. The manner in which thereafter he *constructed* his books led more than once to a disregard of probability and to overmuch trust in coincidence. This apparent mechanical contrivance would have debased Hardy's novels to the level of third-rate journeywork if his ability in other branches of the craft had been less extraordinary man it was. Many of his characters, both major and minor, are created with the fullness, vigour and assurance of a Shakespeare or a Dickens; while his power to suggest immensity of place was unique. Whether it is the dour vastness of Egdon Heath in *The Return of the Native,* the luscious ripeness of Blackmoor Vale in *Tess,* or the tree-girt solitude of *The Woodlanders,* Hardy's places are fully as memorable as his people. On Egdon, indeed, the men and women are pigmies—the Heath is itself the demon, moulding and conditioning the lives of those who dwell upon it and who are part of its own life. In the use of tragedy Hardy bears comparison with the great figures in world literature, and he falls short of their stature chiefly because he inclined to pursue his afflicted characters past the limits at which both art and nature are customarily satisfied to halt. In the use of pathos, however, he is unsurpassed. Is there anywhere in literature a finer delicacy, a more exquisite handling of sorrow, than in the description of Tess's christening of her child by candlelight in the bedroom? Among other instances are Marty South's lament over Giles at the close of *The Woodlanders,* and the tragedy of the dog whose well-meaning zeal drives Gabriel Oak's flock to destruction (*Far from the Madding Crowd*).

Hardy's novels and poems are, throughout, the work of a man painfully dissatisfied with the age in which he lived. He was homesick for the past—the past of England before the strong roots of English manhood and womanhood had been overlaid by what seemed to Hardy a thin soil of finicking niceness miscalled education and culture. He distrusted modern civilization because he suspected that its effect was frequently to *decivilize* and weaken those to whom Nature and old custom had given stout hearts, clear heads and an enduring spirit. Ancient and modern are constantly at war in his books, where none is happy who has felt the alienating touch of school-bred refinement. Though Hardy's mind was shaped to some extent by the theories of later German philosophers, he thought gratefully of the simple paganism lingering on in Wessex beneath the Christian veneer. Wessex was still the old England. Its woods, its heaths, it barrows, its barns and byres—all these stood in memory of a noble antiquity making mute protest against invading aggressive modernity. What Wessex meant to Hardy, and its significance as a symbol in relation to his whole work, is indicated at the opening of *The Return of the Native,* in a chapter which is among the supreme achievements in English prose.

Resenting the animosity stirred by *Tess* and *Jude,* Hardy abandoned novel-writing in 1896, and at the age of nearly sixty resumed the practice of verse, interrupted thirty years before. *Wessex Poems* (1898) included a few pieces dated earlier than 1870, and, among these, *Hap* is a compressed preliminary statement of (as it proved) Hardy's unchanging idea of the ordering of the universe. That idea, expressed repeatedly in his poems, reached its final expression in *The Dynasts,* an epic-drama of the Napoleonic wars. Hardy held that there is no active intelligence, no just and loving God, behind human destiny, but that Creation is swayed by an unconscious mechanical force, sightless, dumb, mindless, and equally indifferent to either the sufferings or the joys of mankind. Not until the last page of *The Dynasts* is any hope offered of possible release from the fell clutch of circumstance; and then only a faint suggestion that, at some unguessable future moment, consciousness may begin to stir in the blind and senseless 'Immanent Will' and inspire it to 'fashion all things fair.'

The Dynasts (completed in 1908) is Hardy's most extensive work, and one of the greatest creations in literature. For this vast epic-drama two traditional forms were adapted and combined, and from their union Hardy produced a new and original form. The epic is foreign to the modern genius, and what would have been extended passages of narrative verse in a traditional epic are here abbreviated into vivid 'stage-directions' to fill the spaces between the scenes of the spoken drama. *The Dynasts* is a masterly example of Hardy's genius in the organization and control of literary material. It was an astonishing feat to secure balance, order, proportion and perspective in handling hundreds of characters, a time-period of fifteen years, and a scenic range covering practically the whole of Europe. All the historical personages are introduced, and, as well, the common people who bore the chief part of the suffering caused by the clash of dynasts. Hardy's pity for all suffering creatures was terribly acute. He himself agonized in the agony of others, and he was never able to cultivate that protective skin of semi-apologetic callousness by which the majority insulate themselves against a torturing participation in the world's sum of misery.

122. Poets of the Transition (1892–1913). Four years after Tennyson's death the laureateship declined upon ALFRED AUSTIN (1835–1913), a political journalist who aspired to be a philosophical poet but was capable of little more than sentimental balderdash in verse. There were poets in the land, however, between 1892 and 1913, though it was not until the later date that new poetry began again to be read by large numbers of people. These twenty years may therefore be treated as a transition period.

There were, first, the poets who took patriotism and imperialism as their keywords. W.E. HENLEY (1849–1903) had higher gifts as an editor and critic, perhaps, than as a poet: under his direction the *Scots Observer* and the *National Observer* fostered the talent of numerous young writers. Henley's services in verse to the patriotic ideal in its cruder form are represented chiefly by the anthology, *Lyra Heroica*, and by a volume of his own poems, *For England's Sake*. He is at his best in the free-verse stanzas, *A late lark twitters from the quiet skies*, though more widely admired for *Invictus*, a piece of spectacular fist-shaking against heaven which satisfies the raw sentiments of immature heterodoxy. (Sir) WILLIAM WATSON (1858–1935) would have justified with dignity the popular notion of the poet laureate's function had he been appointed to succeed Tennyson. He is a little too good to be included with the ruck of lesser poets, yet not nearly good enough to go with the great. His best poetry echoes the stately accents of the past—as in the elegies, *Wordsworth's Grave* and *Lachrymae Musarum* (on the death of Tennyson)—without any fire of distinctive personal genius. Nevertheless, his patriotic lyrics as well as his ceremonial and other occasional poems show a sense of order and proportion—except when (as in *The Purple East*) indignation betrayed him into verbal hysteria. Opinions of RUDYARD KIPLING'S verse (his prose is considered in § 128) are still in a fluid state. Many intelligent critics, including T.S. Eliot, agree in accounting him an impressive writer; others, not less intelligent, who admire his prose without reserve, are exasperated by what they regard as Kipling's cock-of-the-walk mentality and by his big-drum and mouth-organ ditties. But his soldier tales and poems succeed in giving precisely the modestly heroic impression of the British soldier that a large section of the nation loved; and whatever may be thought of his verses in Kiplingese, those other poems which express a quiet love of England and its byways have the evident marks of good poetry—restraint, first-hand imagery, varied music. Though in these qualities ALFRED NOYES (*b.* 1880) is less well equipped, his poetry has the tunefulness and pictorial emphasis that give immediate pleasure. Critics who question his stature as a poet are influenced by the conviction that, in music, imagery and thought, NOYES fails to provide the *permanent* satisfaction which is a principal function of poetry.

Three poets of this transition period stand apart from the rest: Francis Thompson, A.E. Housman, and Robert Bridges. The life of FRANCIS THOMPSON (1859–1907) was a tangled comi-tragedy of invertebrate will, drugs, penury, intellectual fastidiousness and imaginative splendour. Through a total incapacity to adjust himself to even the simplest practical demands of daily living, he passed by stages from a cultured home-life to match-selling in the London gutters, from which Wilfrid and Alice Meynell (herself a poet and essayist of rare quality, reticent yet deeply thoughtful) were compelled to wrench him before he would settle amid the family circle they freely opened to him in their own household. Cured temporarily of drug-taking, he published between 1893 and 1897 three collections of verse—including *The Hound of Heaven,* an *Ode to the Setting Sun,* and a group of *Poems on Children*—which ensure for Thompson a place among the English poets. *The Hound of Heaven* is unique both for its metaphysical import and its magnificently opulent diction. This revelation of the implacable pursuing love of God came incandescently from one who had passed through spiritual agony and known divine compassion. Personal experience was fused in the crucible of poetic vision until it became as a clear flame in a rushing wind. Thompson's medievalism caused him to use words in a manner that gives them the effect of gorgeous vestments at a solemn ritual, and in this direction poetry could go little farther than he carried it. In other moods he could be delicately simple (as in some of the poems on children) without relaxing the emotional intensity which charges his work with power.

A.E. HOUSMAN (1859–1936) published only two small books of verse, *A Shropshire Lad* and *Last Poems*. The perfection of his technique, his achievement of beauty without ornament and without exhortation, and the adamantine fortitude of his philosophic pessimism, made him much admired by younger poets who could praise where they could not follow. Very few, indeed, will be able (and fewer will desire) to follow Housman either technically or philosophically. His art consisted in that most difficult of literary exercises—ruthless pruning without denuding; his philosophy encouraged the utter abandonment of hope and self-pity, substituting nothing but endurance. Housman's hopeless world, as seen through his poems, is a marvellously clean and invigorating place, and his is the distinction of being the first English poet of importance to shed religious belief without being either sorry for himself or proud of himself.

ROBERT BRIDGES (1844–1930) practised as a surgeon until he was nearly forty, when he retired and cultivated in seclusion his love for poetry and learning. Between 1885 and 1905 he wrote a series of verse-dramas and masques (entirely neglected by the theatres), and slowly became known to a widening circle by many beautiful lyrics and several equally beautiful longer poems, including *The Growth of Love* and *Eros and Psyche*. But by 1913, when he was appointed Poet Laureate, Bridges' work was still known only to a minority of readers; and not until the last months of his life did he become widely recognized as one of the few major poets by whom the laureateship has been held. *The Testament of Beauty,* a lengthy philosophical poem published at the end of 1929, was received with general admiration, though it is much more difficult than the earlier neglected poems. This is not the place, nor is it yet the time, to attempt a tabloid exposition of a poem into which had gone the matured wisdom of a lifetime marked by an unusual alertness and activity of mind and spirit. Though *The Testament of Beauty* has difficulties, it also has passages of clear and simple beauty attractive to poetry-lovers who are not philosophically minded. A legend grew up, earlier, that Bridges' poetry (not excepting the lyrics) is passionless. Certainly it does not throb with any undisciplined emotion, but passionless it is not. English love poetry was enriched by Bridges, who voiced deep feeling in poetic forms that approach perfection. He was always an experimenter, especially in seeking to naturalize classical metres in English. Most of these experiments failed, though the 'loose alexandrines' he invented and used in *The Testament of Beauty* provide a flexible medium for argument and reflection. Bridges would undoubtedly have been more popular if he had had an obvious message for his generation. That, in truth, he *had* a message is manifest in his last poem, but its delivery was long delayed, and when it came it could not be briefly paraphrased for the enlightenment of unready minds.

123. The 'Revival' of Poetry. Bridges' succession to the laureateship in 1913 coincided with an effort by several young poets to popularize contemporary poetry. Largely through the enterprise of RUPERT BROOKE (1887–1915), though under the editorship of (Sir) Edward Marsh, an anthology of new verse was issued in the autumn of 1913 with the title *Georgian Poetry.* Immensely successful, this volume started a boom in poetry which was still developing when the first World War gave it a further impetus. Men in unusually stressful circumstances then found in poetry an outlet for unusually insistent emotions and thoughts. A flood of war poetry began, and lasted until the peace. Much of it was interesting and exciting enough while it was being written and first read, but little has survived the winnowing of time. Rupert Brooke himself was a real poet, though not a great one. And it is reasonable to suggest that he would not have developed into a great poet even if the war had not flung him into a premature grave on the island of Skyros. His collected poems include some remarkable and memorable pieces: the *1914* sonnets, *The Great Lover, The Old Vicarage, Grantchester*; but the glamour of his personal charm and the moving sacrifice of his eager youth and physical beauty inflated his poetic reputation. From the multitude of war poets, JULIAN GRENFELL and SIEGFRIED SASSOON may be singled out: the first as giving (in *Into Battle*) the most sincere expression to courageous idealism; the other as beginning (in *Counter Attack*) that war of the fountain pen against the machine gun which continued, at first spasmodically and later in mass formation (through novels, plays and poems), for years after the war ended.

The sole alternative to cataloguing the Georgian poets is to name only some of those who stand above the general level. RALPH HODGSON'S *The Bull, The Song of Honour, Eve,* and *The Gipsy Girl* are remarkable for strength, imaginative force, subtle music, and masterly concentration. Bridges' successor as Poet Laureate, JOHN MASEFIELD (b. 1874), passed from sea songs and ballads to narrative poems combining a rough vigour of diction with religious fervour and an insufficiently austere conception of the nature of beauty. Though Masefield at his best is impressive, he is not in general a fastidious craftsman. Parts of *Dauber* and most of *Reynard the Fox* are, certainly, very good indeed. In the latter, the accurate adjustment of the metrical movement to the beat of the horses' hoofs, and to the increasing exhaustion of the fox, is admirably managed, and accentuates by comparison the hasty technique of *The Everlasting Mercy, The Widow in the Bye Street,* and *The Daffodil Fields.* Masefield's most satisfying poems are the *Saltwater Ballads* (which include several notable additions to our sea poetry),some sonnets in the *Lollingdon*

Downs series, *Reynard the Fox, Biography,* and *August 1914,* where the moving sense of still loveliness over the English countryside preludes the tremendous tragedy of the War.

124. Dramatists of the Transition. T. W. Robertson's work in stage naturalism in the eighteen-sixties prepared the way for (Sir) A. W. PINERO (1855–1934) and HENRY ARTHUR JONES (1851–1928), who in the eighties and nineties popularized the 'problem play'—though the 'problems' seldom escape being the offspring of the divorce court and the theatrical imagination. These two playwrights were, however, unusually accomplished dramatic craftsmen, and if their material had been worth the efficiency they brought to its handling, the English stage would have recovered earlier the prestige it lost a century before. Henry Arthur Jones was less popular than Pinero, but he was sometimes a better dramatist. Even when his situations are wholly 'of the theatre' he could make them seem momentarily and excitingly credible. The interrogation of Felicia Hindmarsh by Sir Daniel Carteret in *Mrs. Dane's Defence* may be in substance wholly artificial, yet there is genius in the management of the scene. Each sentence heightens suspense and moves the action nearer to its preposterously thrilling climax.

125. George Bernard Shaw. The 'efficient' dramatists, the creators of 'the well-made play', had no permanent contribution to make to English drama, for they neglected to take Life into the theatre. BERNARD SHAW (1856–1950) brought about a revolution in the drama by hauling Life unceremoniously into the theatre, undeterred by the knowledge that at first he had little idea of what more to do with Life when he had flung it in a heap on the stage. Yet if his earliest plays are a mass of raw humanity, the mass is at least strugglingly *alive,* not ossified by theatrical convention. Shaw came in the traditional almost-penniless condition from Dublin to London in 1876, and through local politics and journalism imposed himself upon public notice. He then set out to impose himself upon the theatre—less out of special liking for the theatre than out of a moral passion for the establishment of righteousness in social relationships. Therefore when he dragged Life into the theatre, it began at once to talk about housing conditions, religion, finance, prostitution—about everything that Shaw thought to be muddled and mismanaged and pernicious. The public had to be compelled against its will to listen, and no one without Bernard Shaw's impudent wit and humour, pugnaciousness, pertinacity and puritan passion could have compelled it to listen. The stage by Shaw's contrivance became the ventilating shaft of modern civilisation; and what splendid exhilarating fun the ventilating process became! Shaw quickly learned how to organize for stage use the living material he had collected. The interval between *Widowers' Houses* on the one hand and *Candida* and *You Never Can Tell* on the other, was a matter of only two or three years, but in the interval Shaw developed from a propagandist to a playwright dealing with real problems and nearly-real people. In *Man and Superman* he presented his philosophic idea of the Life Force—an animating spirit instilled into man with the purpose of energizing him to produce a higher type of creature, the Superman, as God's coadjutor on earth. Faced by man's inertia and unreadiness to co-operate in the divine plan, the Life Force is made in *Man and Superman* to select woman as the more willing instrument in the devisal of means for evolving the Superman. Shaw's conception of a Life Force ran through most of the later plays, coming to fuller development in *Back to Methuselah,* where it merged into his larger theory of Creative Evolution, signifying the idea of man-made-perfect through the conscious development of the will-to-be-made-perfect. Bernard Shaw is an inexhaustible subject. Notwithstanding the denials of antagonistic critics, it is certain that he powerfully influenced the thought of a large and increasing body of people in Britain and abroad for fully sixty years, passing buoyantly through a period of embittered opposition not unlike that encountered by Kipling from a different political direction. Later generations must be left to determine the truth or untruth of the repeated charges that Bernard Shaw was a shallow thinker and a merely destructive critic: there is a good case for the defence in reply to both charges.

As a dramatist, Shaw's unmatched abilities lay in his combination of effervescing wit and strong commonsense; his probing spirit of inquiry by which he pierced the stoutest hide of humbug—even that of his own admirers; and his dialectical brilliance. *Saint Joan* comes nearest among Shaw's works to the general idea of what a good play should be, though it has not the prophetic vision which makes *Heartbreak House* so memorable.

126. Irish Drama and Poetry. For roughly ten years, up to 1899, WILLIAM BUTLER YEATS (1865–1939), the son of an Irish painter, strove to bring into existence an Irish National Theatre. When at length he succeeded, there began a brilliant period of Irish drama, to which Yeats himself contributed several notable poetic plays, including *The Land of Heart's Desire* and *The Countess Cathleen*. His genius, however, was more poetic than dramatic, and his early lyrics, then admired equally by the people and by other poets, set him in the forefront of contemporary poetry. His later work is mentioned in the next chapter. GEORGE WILLIAM RUSSELL (1867–1935) was also an outstanding personality in modern Irish literature. Writing under the pseudonym 'A.E.', Russell became an honoured figure as poet, dramatist (*Deirdre*, 1902), essayist and editor. In addition, he performed valuable services in agricultural reform, and exercised a powerful influence upon contemporary Ireland. The Irish National Theatre, housed at the Abbey Theatre in Dublin (through the munificence of Miss A.E.F. Horniman, C.H., a devoted patron of the theatre in England and Ireland), attracted a capable body of new dramatists, the chief of whom in the first period was J.M. SYNGE (1871–1909), author of *The Playboy of the Western World, Riders to the Sea,* and other plays; and in the second period SEAN O'CASEY (*b.* 1884) was rightly acclaimed for two plays of contemporary town life in Ireland, *Juno and the Paycock* (1925) and *The Plough and the Stars* (1926), but when he afterwards turned to less comprehensible experimental pieces—e.g. *The Silver Tassie* (1928) and *Within the Gates* (1933)—he was not so successful. LADY GREGORY (1852–1932) was drawn to the theatre by Yeats, and besides helping in organization and management, herself contributed a succession of uncommonly well-observed little plays of modern Irish life and character—*Seven Short Plays* (1909) and others. She also wrote the history of the modern Irish drama in *Our Irish Theatre*.

127. Other Playwrights. Bernard Shaw's claim on the attention of his generation derived from the importance of his plays as commentaries upon contemporary affairs, though as time passes they will almost certainly be seen to have more permanent features than this. The claim of (Sir) J.M. BARRIE (1860–1937) upon the attention of posterity may, on the other hand, arise from the fact that he eschewed specifically modern problems and dealt in terms of fantasy with men and women in situations as familiar or as unfamiliar (according to the reader's point of view) in one generation as in another. Shaw's unquenchable optimism never permitted him to abandon hope in man's ability and ultimate preparedness to set about the task of producing the Superman. Barrie, in settled pessimism, took refuge from the ugliness of modern life in a world of delicate sentiment and make-believe, which in his plays is entirely consistent with itself and only untenable when criticized (as it should not be) in terms of twentieth-century dailiness. He did skirt about the edges of a modern problem in *The Admirable Crichton*, only to fly from its full implications in the last act. Barrie's equipment as a craftsman of the theatre was as full as that of any other dramatist working in his period; as a humorist he was by turns sunnily human and wryly disillusioned; while as the author of *Peter Pan* he completely satisfied the critic in the nursery, the one kind of critic whose judgment is not warped by arbitrary prejudices or mental dyspepsia. Lewis Carroll's creation of *Alice* in 1865 was one of those strokes of sublime genius that do not occur more than once or twice; and few imaginative exercises can be more refreshing than to consider a meeting of Peter and Alice as companions in Wonderland.

Beside those already mentioned, other early twentieth-century dramatists are less important. JOHN GALSWORTHY (1867–1933) wrote three excellent plays, *Strife, The Silver Box,* and *The Skin Game,* compared with which his remaining dramatic works seem hardly more than humanitarian tracts; HARLEY GRANVILLE-BARKER (1877–1946), the author of one superlatively good social comedy, *The Voysey Inheritance* (probably the best naturalistic play of the period), was also a force in the theatre both as actor and producer; *Milestones* by ARNOLD BENNETT and EDWARD KNOBLOCK is a fascinating study in the dynamics of progress and the statics of human stubbornness; while *Pompey the Great*, *The Tragedy of Nan* and *Good Friday* are among John Masefield's contributions to modern tragic drama.

128. Novelists of the Transition. The English novel during most part of the nineteenth century was predominantly romantic in tone, even when drab or 'realistic' in subject matter. From about 1885 onward, alongside a diminishing romanticism represented by Stevenson and others, there came into prominence certain novelists whose aim was to treat realistic themes *realistically*—that is, in a dispassionate, non-sentimental, and non-condemnatory manner. Much might be written about the errors and illusions of the new realists, and of the extent to which they mistook mere ugliness for frankness and 'seeing life steadily and seeing it whole'. It must here suffice to record that *Esther Waters* by GEORGE MOORE (1857–1933) was a landmark in this movement toward aesthetic realism. GEORGE GISSING (1857–1903), working independently in the same direction, though not a literary theorist, wrote a number of grim novels close to such 'facts of life' as Gissing had observed; and sometimes (as, for example, in *Born in Exile*) introducing much slightly-veiled autobiography. The world dealt so harshly with Gissing (for which the world was not alone to blame) that his consequent disgruntlement is not surprising. The pity is that his novels are disgruntled also. Not even the literary integrity by which his fiction is usually graced atones for the note of whining resentment. But for this weak self-pity Gissing would have counted among the major nineteenth-century novelists, and even with all his faults he was a writer of real quality. In later years, having escaped from miserable circumstances, he wrote *The Private Papers of Henry Ryecroft*, a book of reflections in fine prose.

George Moore passed by stages from modern realism to a series of novels more or less historical—*The Brook Kerith* (a masterpiece dealing with the legend that Jesus lived on among the Essene monastic community, and introducing Saint Paul); *Abelard and Heloise*; *Ulick and Soracha*. These books were experiments in a prose style of remarkable clarity, precision and strength—achieving a beauty entirely inherent in the texture of the prose and independent of verbal ornamentation, which George Moore austerely rejected in his final period.

RUDYARD KIPLING (1865–1936) had no equal among English short-story writers of the traditional type. In that form he was the master of many moods, passing with ease and assurance from brutality to fantasy, from folklore to farce—performing brilliantly in each. He widened the range of fiction with his stories of machinery and of animals, his gift of efficiency and conviction going far toward persuading readers that machines as well as animals must surely have minds and souls, of which Kipling appeared to know from A to Z the nature and intimate workings. *Kim* is the only novel comparable in merit with his short stories. It does magnificently for the Tibetan borderland what *Pickwick* did for England, though *Kim* is less boisterously comic.

Two writers of historical fiction produced work of some note at the end of this transition period: STANLEY WEYMAN (1855–1928) (*A Gentleman of France, The House of the Wolf, Chippinge*) and MAURICE HEWLETT (1861–1923) (*Richard Yea-and-Nay, The Queen's Quair*). Hewlett was also in other ways a novelist of more than ordinary merit. His *Open Country* deserves to be remembered, and *The Forest Lovers* stands with ANTHONY HOPE'S *The Prisoner of Zenda* as a pleasing product of the romantic imagination. CONAN DOYLE'S Sherlock Holmes has become an 'immortal', though the later cultivation of detective fiction has made his methods and observations seem primitive.

129. Twentieth Century Novelists. For a quarter of a century after Dickens' death the custody of tradition in the English novel was vested in Meredith and Hardy. None of the writers mentioned in § 128 was within the direct tradition, and not until the nineteen-hundreds did younger writers begin to produce novels sufficiently important to justify hope that the passing of the great Victorians would not prove irreparable. In a backward view the early fantastic romances of H.G. WELLS (1866–1946) can be seen in right relation to his entire work. Though at first *The Time Machine* and its successors in that particular kind seemed scarcely more than amazingly clever frivolities, it is possible to trace in them the early stages of Wells' growth as a critic of institutions and constitutions. *Love and Mr. Lewisham, Kipps,* and *The History of Mr. Polly* established him as a novelist of substantial quality with a special genius for comedy and humanitarian zeal, in the direct line of descent from Dickens. While aware of the real merits of the earlier books, many people ranked *Tono-Bungay* as Wells' best novel. Characterization, narration, description, adventure—the management of these in *Tono-Bungay* earned admiration, and the book is, moreover, a serious and illuminating study in English social history between (say) 1880 and 1910. The national change of balance from aristocracy to an incongruous combination of democracy and charlatanism is displayed as it appears to the mind of George Ponderevo, who, though possessing the then 'new' outlook, nevertheless expressed doubts shared by the author himself as to whether even a convinced democrat could view the changed order with equanimity. From 1912 onward H.G. Wells put into practice more and more his stated theory that the novel should no longer seek merely to entertain, but should serve as a platform for the propagation of ideas and the discussion of any and every topic of contemporary social and political interest. As a consequence, Wells' later novels became an interesting series of elaborated pamphlets masquerading only half-heartedly as fiction, though, for all his sociological and political fervour, the creative literary artist and the master of comic narrative occasionally broke through again, as in *Mr. Britling Sees It Through* and in the earlier part of *Christina Alberta's Father*.

JOSEPH CONRAD (Josef Konrad Korzeniowski) (1857–1924) came as a youth from Poland to serve on French and afterwards on British merchant ships, learned the English tongue, was driven from sea-life by illness, and settled in England to write in English the best sea stories in our language (see *The Nigger of the 'Narcissus', Typhoon,* and others). He disliked being regarded as mainly a writer about the sea, setting a higher value upon his penetrating psychological novels (*Chance,* for example). He was the first novelist who attempted with success in English to make the novel a work of art in the full and exact sense, following the example of the Anglicized-American Henry James, whose manner was, however, less robust and vigorous. In cultivating the literary art Conrad did not abate the tremendous living intensity and spiritual depth which make his novels unique. As a means of conveying intimate aspects of character and revealing subtle shades of truth, Conrad used a peculiarly involved and sometimes per-plexing narrative method. But any initial difficulty presented by his complexity of form is more than compensated by the rewards of intellectual excitement, quickened perception and deepened understanding of motives. *Lord Jim* is as near to the absolute greatness of poetic tragedy as any novel could be, and if *Victory* has to be placed lower when tested by the same standard, it is because it lacks the austerity of *Lord Jim* and plunges into exotic romanticism. Conrad's success as an impressionist in words was due to the high value he set upon exactitude of observation and reproduction. His impressionism is never woolly or diffused but is always the calculated outcome of a precise style. A unifying idea, as well as a theory of art, runs through Conrad's novels and tales: *the imperative need for loyalty to a human principle.* On the sea, men are united by the ever-lurking threat of a contingent common peril—the anger and treachery of the ocean. Against this enemy, human solidarity must be maintained. There must be no breaking or betrayal of that solidarity; or if there is (as there was by Lord Jim) atonement must be made after travail. The idea of human solidarity (the phrase has now a political significance rarely applicable to Conrad) is insistent in all his work, and is accompanied by the complementary ideal of fidelity in all human relationships.

Mention of *The Old Wives' Tale, Clayhanger,* and *Riceyman Steps* by

ARNOLD BENNETT (1867–1931) and *The Forsyte Saga* by Galsworthy rounds off the list of major traditional novels in this period. These two writers gave, in the books named, large-scale pictures of different social strata in modern England: Arnold Bennett of the typical middle-class in trade and industry; Galsworthy of the professional and aristocratic classes. Their respective literary styles corresponded with their subject matter. Bennett's was efficient workmanlike middle-class prose; Galsworthy's, graceful and suave. Arnold Bennett also wrote, among much else of less merit, at least one first-rate humorous novel, *Buried Alive,* afterwards dramatized with success as *The Great Adventure.*

WILLIAM DE MORGAN (1839–1917), after spending the main part of his life in designing and manufacturing ceramics (decorated tiles and pottery), turned to novel-writing while recovering from an illness. Thereafter, during his last eleven years, he produced nine long novels. The first three—*Joseph Vance* (1906), *Alice-for-Short* (1907), *Somehow Good* (1908)—are the best, and though he wrote in the tradition of the great Victorian novelists he had read in the years before pottery became his chief concern, De Morgan was far more original than derivative and excelled in both humour and controlled pathos.

130. Miscellaneous Prose. The revolutionary changes in journalism which came in the closing years of the nineteenth century through the varied influences of Alfred Harmsworth, T. P. O'Connor and Bernard Shaw, led the newspapers by degrees to assume some of the functions of magazines and thereby to provide a new medium for the periodical essay. Not all the essayists of the period were contributors to the newspapers and weekly reviews, but two at least—ROBERT LYND and A.G. GARDINER (Alpha of the Plough)—did admirable work under the conditions of limited length imposed by the press. In a rather wider field E.V. LUCAS made a definite mark, particularly with a type of book combining qualities of a familiar essay and of the novel: *Over Bemerton's* is a characteristic example of these 'entertainments' and probably the best. (Sir) MAX BEERBOHM (1872–1956), a prodigy of the nineties with a small book of essays called *The Works of Max Beerbohm,* survived long beyond that decade to become not only the most brilliant caricaturist of his generation but also a parodist of genius (*A Christmas Garland*), while his gifts as an essayist increased (*And Even Now*). KENNETH GRAHAME'S *The Golden Age*, *Dream Days*, and *The Wind in the Willows* have become classics for both children and grown-ups; and with *When We Were Very Young* A.A. MILNE added to the brief list of good books of verse for children.

C.M. DOUGHTY (1843–1926) stands at the head of the travel writers of the period, though it is doubtful whether his massive *Arabia Deserta* will in the future be found digestible by more than a small class of hardy and assiduous readers. W. H. HUDSON (1841–1922) succeeded Richard Jefferies as a popular writer of nature books. Hudson had little of Jefferies' lyrical ecstasy in style, his prose being more notable for its cool clarity (*A Shepherd's Life* and *Far Away and Long Ago*).

A genuine advance was made in biography by LYTTON STRACHEY (1880–1932), whose epoch-making books, *Eminent Victorians* and *Queen Victoria*, altered the outlook of a whole generation of English biographers. Strachey found biography a depressed industry and transformed it into a fine art.

TABLE OF THE AGE OF HARDY

Fiction	Verse	Drama
Hardy's *Return of the Native*, 1878	Bridges's *Shorter Poems*, 1873–80	
Hardy's *Mayor of Casterbridge*, 1885		
Kipling's *Plain Tales from the Hills*, 1887	G.M. Hopkins d. 1889	
Gissing's *New Grub Street*, 1891		
Hardy's *Tess of the D'Urbervilles*, 1891		

Gissing's *Born in Exile*, 1892	Kipling's *Barrack Room Ballads*, 1892	
	Thompson's *Hound of Heaven*, 1893	Pinero's *Second Mrs. Tanquerqy*, 1893
Moore's *Esther Waters*, 1894		
Hardy's *Jude the Obscure*, 1895	Yeats' *Poems*, 1895	Wilde's *Importance of Being Earnest*, 1895
Wells' *Time Machine*, 1895		
	Housman's *Shropshire Lad*, 1896	
Conrad's *Nigger of the 'Narcissus'*, 1897		H.A. Jones' *The Liars*, 1897
		Pinero's *Trelawny of the 'Wells'*, 1897
	Wilde's *Ballad of Reading Gaol*, 1898	Bernard Shaw's *Plays: Pleasant and Unpleasant*, 1898
	Hardy's *Wessex Poems*, 1898	
Conrad's *Lord Jim*, 1900		H.A., Jones' *Mrs. Dane's Defence*, 1900
Kipling's *Kim*, 1901		Shaw's *Man and Superman*, 1903
Butler's *Way of All Flesh*, 1903		Barrie's *The Admirable Cruchton*, 1903
Conrad's *Nostromo*, 1904	Hardy's *Dynasts*, 1904–06–08	Barrie's *Peter Pan* 1904
Wells' *Kipps*, 1905		Synge's *Playboy of the Western World*, 1907
De Morgan's *Joseph Vance*, 1906		Barrie's *What Every Woman Knows*, 1908
Arnold Bennett's *Old Wives' Tale*, 1908		
Wells' *Tono-Bungay*, 1909		Galsworthy's *Strife*, 1909

	Meredith d. 1909	Synge d. 1909
	Swinburne d. 1909	Granville-Barker's *Voysey Inheritance*, 1909
	Rupert Brooke's *Poems*, 1911	
	Masefield's *Everlasting Mercy*, 1911	Bennett & Knoblock's *Milestones*, 1912
	Walter de la Mare's *Listeners*, 1912	
	De la Mare's *Peacock Pie*, 1913	
	Georgian Poetry 1911–1912, 1913	
Lawrence's *Sons and Lovers*, 1913		
Mackenzie's *Sinister Street*, 1913–14		
Conrad's *Victory*, 1915		
George Moore's *Brook Kerith*, 1916		
Wells' *Mr. Britling Sees It Through*, 1916		
Douglas' *South Wind*, 1917		
De Morgan d. 1917	Ralph Hodgson's *Poems*, 1917	
	Siegfried Sassoon's *Counter Attack*, 1918	Drinkwater's *Abraham Lincoln*, 1918
	Hopkins' *Poems*, 1918	
		Shaw's *Heartbreak House*, 1919
		Galsworthy's *Skin Game*, 1920

		Shaw's *Back to Methuselah*, 1921
Galsworthy's *Forsyte Saga*, 1922	Eliot's *The Waste Land*, 1922	
Joyce's *Ulysses*, 1922		
Bennett's *Riceyman Steps*, 1923		
Forster's *A Passage to India*, 1924		
Conrad d. 1924		
		O'Casey's *Juno and the Paycock*, 1925
		Coward's *Hay Fever*, 1925
Hardy d.	1928	
	Bridges' *Testament of Beauty*, 1929	
	Bridges d. 1930	

26
The Present Age
(1930–1955)

131. Old Legacies and New Tendencies. The division of literature into periods convenient for study may create an impression that the writers in each 'age' can be treated independently of their predecessors and successors. That view should be discouraged. We are the heirs of all our ancestors; our descendants will be the heirs of our forerunners and of ourselves. Whatever seems new in literature is found on examination to have roots stretching back into a more or less remote past. However fresh the shoots or strange the blossoms, their nourishment has come from the soil and the air which gave life to things that may now seem finished and done with. What, it may be asked, have we of the Atomic Age to do with the Classical Age in Greece of nearly 2500 years ago? Or even with the Victorian Age in England of only a hundred years ago? Answers can be found in the literature of our own time, for the apparently most 'advanced' writers in the present age have been deeply indebted to both those periods, as well as to periods in between. James Joyce's *Ulysses*, in form the most 'revolutionary' novel of the twentieth century, is designed upon the plan of Homer's *Odyssey*; T.S. Eliot's poetry (as his notes to *The Waste Land* show) draws from many past sources, English and foreign, while no influence is stronger in the work of Eliot's younger contemporaries than that of the Victorian poet Gerard Manley Hopkins. Indeed, without Hopkins, who was almost entirely unknown during his own lifetime, present-day poetry would be very different from what it is. But, of course, no good writer depends wholly or even mainly on the past. Present experience in his personal life and in the wider social and political life of the world he lives in is no less important, and it influences his work deeply if the times are troubled.

When Thomas Hardy died in 1928 the world appeared to be recovering from the consequences of the first World War, though the recovery had been slow and painful, and longsighted people were still uneasy about the outlook. The League of Nations had failed to bring about the state of international harmony hoped for by its founders, and poverty and social unrest persisted in many places. Then, as the nineteen-thirties approached, a worldwide financial crisis struck both rich and poor, threatening ruin to whole nations as well as bringing misery and want to unnumbered families and individual persons. In Britain (and elsewhere) millions of unemployed created a grave social problem, and hitherto flourishing industrial regions became 'distressed areas'. An account of the state of the country at that time can be found in J.B. Priestley's *An English Journey* (1934). In Germany the burden of unemployment created the conditions that Hitler exploited as a stepping-stone to autocratic power, which he used to re-arm the nation and thus re-employ the multitudes of workless in feverish preparations for military supremacy. The god of war, overthrown in 1918, was mounting his throne again, not only in Germany but also in Japan, whose militarists made war in China; in Italy, where Mussolini dreamt of a modern Roman Empire and prepared for conquest in Abyssinia and Libya; and in Spain where a civil war raged with terrifying savagery.

In these circumstances many writers became convinced that literature was useless if it did not serve a definite social and political purpose, and those who failed to share this conviction were thought to be skulking in the ivory tower of mere literary art. The poetry and prose of the nineteen-thirties returned therefore to the serious mood which had dominated the mid-Victorian period; but with a difference. The Victorians had been mainly preoccupied with the 'condition of England' question (i.e. the problem of how to uplift the poor), and their literature was permeated by a spirit of non-violent humanitarianism. The writings of the nineteen-thirties, however, were as much preoccupied with the condition of the whole world, for air-travel had made the world appear as small a place as Britain a century before, and humanitarian hopefulness had been displaced by partisan propaganda which, by implication if not explicitly, offered some particular political doctrine as a means to world salvation.

The case for literature with a purpose is obvious, the case against it is less so. Literature is more than pamphleteering, otherwise many thousands of pamphlets now forgotten would still be read as much as novels and poetry are read. Literature is not the mere statement of a problem, however important, nor simply the pleading of a cause, however worthy. Literature is a creative art, written by creative literary artists. The motive power of artists is imagination, which endows them with vision and the perception of truth in its full aspect. A vision of truth is the peculiar and special contribution which a great poet or a great novelist is qualified to give to mankind: it is a vision of the beauty and perfection that is humanity's ideal aim, the end toward which all things move. But they move with agonizing slowness, painful step by painful step; and it is with this almost imperceptible progress that politicians and sociologists are concerned. Politics, it has been said, is *the art of the possible.* In contrast it can be said that poetry is *the art of the desirable.* When a poet attempts to harness his talent to current practical problems he is more likely to cripple his own imagination than to serve mankind, for a poet very rarely allows importance to significant facts while he commands a vision of ultimate truth. If he loses that vision through a misapplied concern with facts he sacrifices his birthright and betrays his mission: he becomes (modifying lines' used by George Meredith in another connection in *Modern Love*) a rapid falcon condemned to do the flitting of a bat. Such is the end to which poets have come when they have been unwisely possessed by a conviction that literature is unworthy if it does not develop a social conscience in relation to immediate affairs. Much literature in the nineteen-thirties was conscience-ridden in that way, and the writers and works of the period when sifted by posterity will in all probability be valued in proportion to the degree in which they looked beyond the disturbances of their own period. From his ivory tower the poet or novelist may see more and speak more saving wisdom than if he descends to bustle about in the political cockpit.

132. Gerard Manley Hopkins. There is no parallel in literary history to the case of GERARD MANLEY HOPKINS (1844–89), who published nothing in his own lifetime, yet after his collected poems were first issued in 1918 had so deep and wide an influence upon the younger generation that the aspect of modern poetry was changed right up to the present time, and his influence is still unexhausted. Hopkins went from Highgate School to Balliol College, Oxford, where he became a follower of the Anglican High Church party until in 1866 he turned Roman Catholic and two years later joined the Society of Jesus. As a devout Jesuit he considered it a religious duty to discontinue writing poetry, but when a ship-wreck in December 1875 caused the drowning of five Franciscan nuns he was inspired to compose his outstanding poem *The Wreck of the Deutschland*. Besides being deeply religious, Hopkins was a profound scholar (he served as Professor of Greek at Dublin University from 1884) with an exceptionally austere, subtle and complex mind. Though he loved the beauties of Nature ('Glory be to God for dappled things—For skies of couple-colour...finches' wings; Landscape plotted and pieced—' he wrote in *Pied Beauty*), Hopkins turned away from the romantic style of poetry which had been practised throughout the nineteenth century and continued in vogue until the closing stages of the first World War. He adopted metrical forms and a verse technique which owed something to John Donne and other metaphysical poets of the seventeenth century, but he was far more an innovator than a borrower. To describe his own system of prosody he used the term 'sprung rhythm', and the word 'inscape' to denote his aim in the treatment of subject material. Neither of these expressions can be defined apart from a close study of the poems and of the letters in which he wrote about them to his friends, one of the chief of whom, Robert Bridges, edited the 1918 volume, though he was not in particular sympathy with Hopkins' methods and convictions. *A Hopkins Reader,* compiled by John Pick in 1953, contains a liberal selection of the poems and letters and provides the most useful and illuminating introduction to a difficult writer who is regarded by his admirers and disciples as one of the greatest English poets.

Since it is strange that a poet who died in 1889 should be included in a chapter dealing with a much later period, attention must be given briefly to the reasons why Hopkins has appeared to our contemporaries, both religious and non-religious, as closely akin to themselves. It is impossible to know what effect his work would have had if he had published it while he was alive, but it is at least probable that it would have made little impression, for the spirit of Victorian times was mostly at variance with his own, and the 'climate of opinion' was not favourable to intellectual complexity and such spiritual probing. Although there had been 'little wars', although there was still much poverty, the educated classes had enjoyed long periods of peace and prosperity. For them life was simple and comfortable. All that was changed by the coming of war in 1914. The firm safe bottom of the world dropped out; life suddenly ceased to be either simple or comfortable. While the older generation still clung hopefully to their memories of a stable world, younger people were more conscious of a troubled present and a perplexing future. In literature the smooth romantic writings which had satisfied their parents and had until 1914 pleased themselves, now appeared superficial and empty. The polished surface of life was shattered and they looked down into a dark abyss which, however frightening, it was their stern task to explore. Religion had been a main source of comfort to their elders, but a religion requiring hardly more than a quiet round of Christian observances had ceased to satisfy. Life had become broken and craggy, no longer like a pastoral landscape, but, rather, a prospect of granite mountains and chasms.

It was into this prospect that Gerard Manley Hopkins' poems were thrown, and before long they were recognized as the work of a spiritual explorer whose vision had penetrated below life's surfaces and whose poetic craft was appropriate to the needs of the new generation. Here was a kind of poetry which did not act as a smoothing-plane gliding over a surface of appearances but as a rock-drill driving down into realities; and realities were the aim of religious and irreligious alike. Hopkins, it seemed, had found and passed to them a poetic instrument which they could employ for their own purposes, whether or not their particular purposes were like his own.

But while it is simple to take an instrument in hand it is less simple to use it effectively. Because they were tired of easy poetry and had responded to Hopkins' poetry because it was not easy, a good many of his followers neglected to observe that there is no virtue in difficulty as an end in itself. However difficult Hopkins may at times be, he is always saying something worth saying, something which it is worth the reader's while to labour to comprehend. The far-reaching influence of Hopkins after 1918 was not altogether fortunate for English poetry, since it encouraged lesser minds than his to foster the illusion that clarity is inferior to obscurity, and that obscurity and profundity go hand in hand. The truth is, of course, that a good poet, however difficult, is never obscure, if by obscurity we mean that what he is saying cannot be comprehended by those who learn his language. Milton is obscure until we master the Miltonic language; Browning is obscure until we master the Browning language. On the other hand, many of Hopkins' imitators are obscure because they have no language of their own, no personal poetic technique, and nothing to say that could not be said in plain prose, when its lack of true content would be immediately evident.

For the very reason that his influence has been so great, it is highly important to distinguish between those poets whose work is genuinely illuminated by his example and those others who have merely embraced the Hopkins cult and been led by it into a blind alley.

133. T.S. Eliot and Others. Any literary cult is deplorable, in as much as it may lead other writers into unintelligent imitation and a mass of readers into unintelligent adulation: it destroys the faculty of independent creation and the faculty of independent critical judgment. It is difficult to separate the Hopkins cult from the T.S. ELIOT (*b.* 1888) cult. They have run concurrently and there are close resemblances in the writings of these two poets. Eliot must not be regarded, however, simply as a disciple of Hopkins. Though he has no more escaped the Hopkins influence than any other writer in the present age, he published his first poems (*Prufrock and Other Observations,* 1917) before Hopkins' appeared, and all his work is strongly individual and creatively personal. He was born in the United States in 1888 and was educated there and in France before settling down in England and at length adopting British citizenship. With *The Waste Land* (1922) he established the reputation which made him the leading living poet of the English-speaking world, though his output for some years was extremely small, consisting of little more in verse than two short pieces, *The Journey of the Magi* and *Ash Wednesday.* But during those years he wrote a number of critical works in prose which created as marked an impression in the study of Dante, Milton, and other writers of the past as his poetry was making in its own field. *The Waste Land* presented a disturbing vision of the state of the contemporary world, in free verse interspersed with a variety of literary allusions and quotations and rising to a prophetic tone in which there appeared to be no sound of Christian hope. It was a Jeremiah-like vision of human society as Eliot saw it after the war: confused, dirty, barren in spirit, and altogether horrible. The imagery was deliberately unromantic, in places deliberately ugly and drawn from the shabby side of city life, for this poem was designed to be shocking in a serious way: its purpose was to shock its readers into seeing their 'waste land' as it was—a spiritually dry and materially littered place. For some years the poem was very little understood, and it was much disliked by those who had been brought up on romantic poetry. Not only did it shock through its subject matter, it shocked also by its manner and style, for Eliot devised a kind of verse technique which, far from decorating and softening the picture, actually reinforced its troubling purpose. Yet just as a bare tree, or even a whitened fossil shape, can possess its own special stripped beauty, so Eliot's bare and hardened lines have their ascetic beauty. He had already begun to put into practice the theory of verse-making which he was afterwards to develop and extend into poetic drama, namely that poetry should conform to the rhythms of natural speech and avoid the artifices of literary language. The validity of this can be examined by turning to Eliot's plays—*The Cocktail Party* and *The Confidential Clerk* conform to the theory more closely than the earlier *Murder in the Cathedral* and *The Family Reunion*—and considering whether the lines, when spoken, are distinguishable from prose by hearers who have not already seen them set out as verse on the printed pages. Eliot's development into a religious poet can be traced in most of his work after *The Waste Land*, both in his plays and in his non-dramatic poetry, which culminated in the sequence of poems collected as *Four Quartets* (1944).

Under the sway of T.S. Eliot's authority poets grew timid of poetry marked by verbal richness and buoyancy of spirit, and actors in poetic drama followed the mode so thoroughly that it became the fashion to speak Shakespeare in a manner which made it seem that poetry on the stage was intended to be kept as a guilty secret from the audiences. Audiences were believed not to 'like' poetry, an illusion happily dispelled when Christopher Fry's *The Lady's Not For Burning* had a long and successful London run in 1949 and was taken up afterwards by many repertory theatres and amateur companies. The success of this play is due not to the fact that it is the strange love story of a vagabond and a reputed witch, but to its torrential beauty of language and its verbal wit. Christopher

Fry (*b.* 1907) had much practical experience in the theatre before becoming a successful playwright. His first published play *The Boy With a Cart* (1939) showed the influence of Eliot, an influence which he largely surmounted in *The Lady's Not For Burning*, giving his own abundant gift of words free play and thereby delighting all sorts and conditions of people on differing intellectual and social levels. A few critics scolded Fry for his departure from the current fashion, and as his language withdrew into austerity in later plays (e.g. *A Sleep of Prisoners* and *The Dark is Light Enough*) his appeal became correspondingly restricted.

In the nineteen-thirties several attempts were made, with only limited success or with none at all, by W.H. Auden and Christopher Isherwood collaboratively in *The Dog Beneath the Skin, The Ascent of F. 6,* and *On the Frontier,* and by Stephen Spender in *Trial of a Judge*. These were all concerned in some measure, explicitly or symbolically, with the political troubles of the period, and their interest has dwindled as those particular troubles have receded into the past. Of the promising younger poets of that decade W.H. AUDEN (*b.* 1907) and C. DAY LEWIS (*b.* 1904) continued after the war to maintain the reputation they built up before, though both modified the political views they had then held; Auden, after some time in the United States, succeeded Day Lewis in the Professorship of Poetry at OXFORD. LOUIS MACNEICE (*b.* 1907) and STEPHEN SPENDER (*b.* 1909) were more prominent in the thirties than after, though MacNeice wrote a number of interesting plays for broadcasting in later years.

The outburst of poetry which was so remarkable a literary feature in the first World War was not repeated during the second. That war was entered upon in 1939 with no popular fervour or heroic idealism, and in its darker stages it bred no more uplifting sensation than dogged determination. In that atmosphere poetry could find little sustenance; and, moreover, what poetry was then written, in a chastened mood of endurance, was for the most part beyond the understanding of the common reader. In the years before the war, much was heard of the necessity of poetry for the masses, but those who proclaimed and thought themselves to be meeting the need were out of mental and emotional contact with their desired audience, and modern poetry lost touch with all but studiously persevering readers. Since the second World War ended, although there have been tentative signs of a possible return to a simpler and more generally intelligible style and treatment, no widely acceptable poet has appeared and none whose talent appears to raise him above a modest level of competence. Mainly through his success as a radio broadcaster, a poet who began in the thirties, DYLAN THOMAS (1914–53), reached a larger audience than most of his generation, and received much posthumous acclaim for *Under Milk Wood,* a poetical radio fantasy completed just before his death. Whether his other poetry will take a permanent place in English literature, or whether its more remarkable qualities will be swallowed up by its metaphysical mannerisms cannot yet be decided.

Standing aside from any sweeping current of tendency in the period, the Sitwell family established themselves in a uniquely assured position. They were at first derided as impudent and frivolous, for in their youth they mocked everything conventional, and the early poetry of (Dame) EDITH SITWELL (*b.* 1887) seemed often artificial and toy-like, though it was the outcome of the author's desire to experiment and enlarge the technical range of verse. With the coming of war in 1939, however, the more serious tendencies which had been surely developing in her middle period received a strong impetus and in the light of her work as a whole—so far and independently of what may be still to come—she must be considered as on the level of the greatest English women poets. Though Emily Brontë and Alice Meynell wrote a few perfect short poems they produced nothing that can be compared with Edith Sitwell's more substantial works; and Mrs. Browning was, technically and otherwise, her inferior in all but the *Sonnets from the Portuguese.* (Sir) OSBERT SITWELL (*b.* 1892) was already well known as a poet, novelist, short-story and travel-book writer before he surpassed these varied works with a remarkable autobiography (*Left Hand, Right Hand,* in five volumes with individual titles, 1945–50), which is also a portrait of the age in which he has lived, with many excellent biographical studies and an exceptionally fine study of his own father. SACHEVERELL SITWELL (*b.* 1900) wrote some poetry, but has devoted himself mainly to writings on art.

The earlier work of W.B. Yeats has been mentioned in the preceding chapter of this book. He must be referred to again here, for while he began as a late-Victorian romantic poet he ended as a twentieth-century metaphysical poet fully abreast of the newer generation. His progress can be assessed by comparing the beautiful but simple *Lake Isle of Innisfree* with the beautiful and profound *Byzantium*. His life was both a triumph and a tragedy. He spanned with a double measure of success that few have experienced two contrasting ages, enjoying wide popularity with his early poetry and a deep intellectual respect with his later. This was his triumph. His tragedy was that in an ageing body he retained energies of spirit and urgencies of impulse which declining physical ability could neither employ to the fullness of his desire nor reduce to the measure of his residual strength.

WALTER DE LA MARE (1873–1956) was comparatively little affected by the new trends, keeping steadily along his own path and being for that reason a poet who may rank higher in the judgment of posterity than most of the younger 'experimental' poets who attracted more attention during the later years of his career. He wrote many delightful poems for children in *Peacock Pie* and other volumes, yet, like all first-class writings intended for young people, these have more than a childish substance, and older people find wisdom in them. De la Mare always makes his poems suggest depths of meaning beyond what the words actually say; all good poets do this, but he wrote with an appearance of such simplicity and ease that hasty readers may miss what lies beneath the surface. He hints at mystery and magic and the breathless uncanniness of silence with great skill and impressiveness, and is in every way a rare poet, gay-hearted as well as grave in mind and temper when gravity is appropriate. His poems for mature readers are, of course, more numerous than those for children and they constitute the more important part of his work. He also wrote novels (e.g. *Memoirs of a Midget*) and many short stories, all with an atmosphere of strangeness.

134. The Changing Novel. In an essay entitled *Mr. Bennett and Mrs. Brown* VIRGINIA WOOLF (1882–1941) took Arnold Bennett as a typical example of the older kind of novelists who were, she thought, incapable of creating characters that were more than crude external sketches of men and women. She herself aimed at something finer that would convey the essences of human life. What she achieved in her novels was something so fine and rare that her imaginary fellow passenger Mrs. Brown would hardly have recognized it as real and human. Mrs. Woolf (Virginia Stephen) had been born into a literary household where her father, Sir Leslie Stephen, created a library atmosphere in which learning and fine thinking encouraged those acute sensibilities and sensitive perceptions which were to make the novels she wrote in womanhood unlike any novels written before. When she married Leonard Woolf, another author, she passed into another literary environment where she became a principal figure among the group (which included Lytton Strachey) known in the nineteen-twenties and thirties as the Bloomsbury Set. These intellectuals discussed among themselves political and literary affairs, and their interests ranged far and wide. Yet they lived in what was very largely a secular monastic circle, from which the rougher and coarser textures of common life were excluded. Human life in the main is, however, rough and coarse; to ignore that it is so deludes us into a falsely delicate view of the world and its people. Virginia Woolf's novels are a beautiful monument to excessive delicacy of that kind. She created a fictional world which was not a reflection of the actual world, but only a world made in the image of her own exquisite sensibilities; a better world, maybe, but a bodiless world. Whereas Arnold Bennett and novelists of his sort create characters outside themselves, all Virginia Woolf's characters are aspects of herself. She was a great writer, but not a great novelist. She could put her self-characters into interesting situations but she could not tell a story. Modern novelists have come to believe that a story is unnecessary, but this belief is the outcome of a general decline in inventive power. A novelist who *can* tell a story *does* tell it; he delights in his inventive ability.

It was Virginia Woolf's misfortune to be born into an age when novels were the common form of literature, the only form through which a writer of books could expect to gain a large audience. If Mrs. Woolf had lived in, say, the sixteenth century she would have written poetry, for poetry was then the common form. As she found herself in a prose age she used prose for what was, in truth, poetic material. Her prose is excellent, but it is rather like a beautiful dress on a spiritual form which has existence but no substance. For most readers her easiest book is *Orlando*, which is frankly a fantasy released from the bonds of time and place; in it, therefore, the strangest things can happen without seeming unnatural, and we can linger with pleasure over such passages as that describing the Thames during the great frost, without feeling that we ought to be reading straight on. *The Voyage Out* and *To the Lighthouse* have a firmer structure, but many of her admirers select *The Waves* and *The Years* as Virginia Woolf's masterpieces. Her critical essays (collected in *The Common Reader* and several other volumes) are enjoyed and justly praised by numerous readers who find her novels unsatisfactory and tiresome.

Like Virginia Woolf, E.M. FORSTER (b. 1879) has written literary criticism of exceptional quality, in *Abinger Harvest* and *Two Cheers for Democracy*. As the title of the latter book indicates, he is also a critic of social and political affairs, a fair-minded one with no party bias. Born well before the Victorian Age had received any major shock, he carried into the twentieth century the liberal humanitarian ideals of that period; but his sombre cast of mind did not admit an equivalent measure of Victorian optimism, while the sparse prose style of his novels, and his sense of the spiritual and mental isolation of individual men and women, precluded him from becoming a comforting popular novelist. He found a select and faithful audience among reflective people, and, more perhaps than any other writer of his time, can be called 'a novelist's novelist' whose influence on other writers has been pervasive, though in twenty years he produced only five novels. *Howard's End* was the most widely read until *A Passage to India*, which coincided in the time of its appearance with a mood of readiness upon the part of many people in Britain to believe that imperial rule in India had set up social and psychological strains which were near to breaking point. *A Passage to India* is a troubling novel with a subtly studied character in the unjustly accused Dr. Aziz, and the whole book is permeated by an atmosphere of tragic incompatibility between the two races which admits of no mutual understanding. The basis of personal experience which gave rise to the general idea of this novel can be found in a much later book by Forster, *The Hill of Devi*. He has also written short stories (e.g. *The Celestial Omnibus*, included in his *Collected Short Stories*) which show another side of his creative talent. While the main part of Forster's work falls within the dates of the preceding chapter, the effect of that work on thought and literature has been felt more especially in the present age.

The works of JAMES JOYCE (1882–1941) have already attracted a small army of expositors and explainers. It must be sufficient here to record that *Ulysses,* a long prose epic dealing with twenty-four hours in the lives of a group of drab people in Dublin, has been singled out as the greatest novel of this century and one of the greatest novels of all time. Joyce was an experimenter with language; his originality lay partly in that, partly in his exceptional erudition, and partly in his endeavour to put the whole of life, including its obscenities, into his novels. His most experimental novel, *Finnegans Wake*, resembles a vast musical composition in which words are used as a composer uses notes; sense gives way to sound, words are broken up, verbal puns abound, and the whole work belongs to a dream world. It is, indeed, a night in the dream world of a certain H.C. Earwaker. An earlier book by Joyce, *Portrait of the Artist as a Young Man,* is relatively straightforward.

Nothing has been said in earlier chapters concerning SOMERSET MAUGHAM (b. 1874), though he began to write in the eighteen-nineties. He was for a long time underestimated by critics, who were misled by his popularity among ordinary readers into supposing that no important writer could make so immediate an appeal. By the nineteen-thirties, however, critical opinion had caught up with popular taste, and although some continued to deny literary merit to Maugham, by his eightieth birthday he was generally commended as the writer of many excellent and immensely readable (if sometimes cynical and often sardonic) short stories, and of at least two first-rate novels, *Of Human Bondage* and *Cakes and Ale,* as well as of a number of plays, notably *The Circle* and *Our Betters.*

D.H. LAWRENCE (1885–1930) was a controversial figure who might have been accepted without question as a great novelist if he had not believed it to be his mission to seek to release English people from the pressure of moral restraints which generations have regarded as essential to the cohesion of civilized society.

In the nineteen-twenties ALDOUS HUXLEY (b. 1894) appeared like a modern Jonathan Swift, savagely satirizing his contemporaries in energetic prose. His short stories and novels (such as *Mortal Coils* and *Antic Hay*) delighted even those against whom his barbed arrows of wit and disgust were aimed, until smiles grew rarer as Huxley's wit dwindled and his disgust increased. *Point Counter Point* contained bitter satirical portraits of writers and others at whose identity their intimates might guess, but in its wider implications the book was an attack upon the whole of intellectual society at that time. *Brave New World* envisaged in 1932 a future in which the entire populace would be mentally conditioned by totalitarian despots, a theme developed in still darker tones nearly twenty years later by GEORGE ORWELL (1903–50) in *Nineteen Eighty-Four.* Orwell, after writing several books with limited success, had suddenly become widely known in 1945 for his short political satire on a totalitarian state, *Animal Farm,* in which 'all animals are equal but some are more equal than others'.

(Sir) HUGH WALPOLE (1884–1941) was one of the most applauded novelists of his generation, but as his output increased his power grew less, and in all but a very few novels he was hardly more than a competent and facile writer. An early novel of school life from the masters' angle, *Mr. Perrin and Mr. Traill*, has lasting qualities; *Rogue Herries* is the first and best of a series that went on too long. *Sinister Street*, a fine novel of childhood, and of young manhood at Oxford, made (Sir) COMPTON MACKENZIE (*b.* 1883) famous, but it was not equalled by any of the numerous popular novels he wrote afterwards. When *The Good Companions* by J.B. PRIESTLEY (*b.* 1894) appeared, it seemed possible that he might develop into a present-day Dickens and restore to general favour the full-blooded novel of crowded life, character and adventure, but the novels which followed it were less interesting than the plays he wrote (see § 135).

Among the younger novelists GRAHAM GREENE (*b.* 1904) has taken a leading place since the second World War, when the surfeit of horror and violence prepared a host of readers to look upon such experiences with a combination of outraged fascination, stoical equanimity, and soul-probing. Sin and suffering play an important part in Graham Greene's novels, and he plunges his characters into depths of degradation (*e.g., Brighton Rock* and *The Heart of the Matter*) from which they can be redeemed only by the way of divine compassion and salvation. EVELYN WAUGH (*b.* 1903), like Greene, is a Roman Catholic, and his novels, too, have religious implications. He began as a farcical humorist in such stories as *Decline and Fall* and *Vile Bodies*; more recently he wrote a bitter farcical satire on American funeral customs, *The Loved One*; but his best novel is the soberer *Brideshead Revisited*.

CHARLES MORGAN (*b.* 1894) has written several well-received novels marked rather by a carefully groomed style than by deep thinking and feeling. *The Fountain* and *The Judge's Story*, among others, have been found impressive and enjoyable, and the qualities which characterize the novels appear also in his plays *The Flashing Stream, The River Line,* and *The Burning Glass.*

Outstanding among recent novelists, JOYCE CARY (1888–1957)

was also the most varied in his selection and treatment of subjects. He passed from studies of African life and mentality (*The African Witch* and *Mister Johnson*) to a moving account of wartime evacuee children (*Charley is My Darling*); from a reminiscent novel of life in Ireland (*The House of Children*) to the shameless doings of a rascally artist (*The Horse's Mouth*). Even if the last-named novel is not Cary's best, it is unique in so far as it succeeds in carrying conviction that the hero, the scurrilous down-at-heel Jimson, really is a man of genius.

The rapid growth of university education for women has led increasing numbers of them to take up a literary career. ROSE MACAULAY—who was, in time, somewhat ahead of the larger company of recent women novelists—wrote several amusing and witty satirical novels (*Told by an Idiot,* and others) in the earlier part of her career, following those with an excellent historical novel of the seventeenth century, *They Were Defeated,* and a moving study of the effects of the war upon young people, *The World My Wilderness.* IVY COMPTON-BURNETT, a more difficult but more original and penetrating writer, has been much commended for her dozen or so novels, of which *Parents and Children* is representative; ELIZABETH BOWEN'S novels and short stories have something of the literary distinction of Virginia Woolf's writings, but are firmer in outline and display a more satisfying grasp of human character (*e.g., Death of the Heart*); DOROTHY SAYERS gave the detective novel an intellectual and religious significance, before turning definitely to Christian writings, as in the broadcast cycle of plays *The Man Born to be King.*

The English short story ventured into different paths in the nineteen-twenties, largely under the influence of the Russian writer Tchekov, who concentrated on atmosphere rather than on plot and firm characterisation. KATHERINE MANSFIELD (1888–1923) was perhaps less of a Chekhov disciple than was generally supposed at the time, though her methods were nearer to his than to those of any English writer. Born in New Zealand, she came to Europe as a young woman and spent the remainder of her short life in England and France, with an interval in Germany. Her carefully composed yet sensitive style was allied with a remarkable power of understanding children, and also unhappy and thwarted people, of whom she wrote with cleansing compassion (*Collected Stories of Katherine Mansfield*).

135. Prose Drama. Bernard Shaw continued to write almost up to the time of his death in 1950 at the age of ninety-four, and no younger writer displaced him as the leading play-wright of the first half of the twentieth century. It is the general opinion that he wrote nothing important after *Saint Joan* (1923), but it is obtuse to deny high merit to *The Apple Cart* (1929) and the one-act play *Village Wooing* (1933). These show a deeper understanding of men and women than the less perceptive among his critics will allow that Shaw possessed, while the former of these two plays is, despite weaknesses in technical construction, a model of how a political drama can be written without being narrowly tendentious and dreary. In the other plays belonging to Shaw's last twenty years there are many flashes of wit, wisdom, uproarious fun, and penetrating social and political criticism, though, considered as pieces for stage performance, they are untidy and shapeless. His great virtue as a writer on current topics was that he saw beyond immediate problems and refused to be swayed by popular prejudices, however much that refusal might outrage the less far-sighted. By 1950 the 'shocking' plays he wrote half-a-century before had come to seem plain common sense illuminated by humour as fresh as the morning sunlight.

The only other prose dramatist in the second quarter of this century whose plays are as good to read in print as to see in a theatre is JAMES BRIDIE (1880–1951). He was born in Scotland and practised as a doctor before turning to authorship. He must be regarded as to some extent a disciple of Bernard Shaw, though only in his wit and humour and power of entertaining by dramatic discussion and argument. He chose his themes from a more varied field than Bernard Shaw ranged over, and was more restlessly experimental. Once Shaw had found his own method and style in playwriting he brought his subject material within the compass of his own proved capabilities. Bridie was never content to go on doing well what he had already done well. A success in one direction exhausted its interest for him and he turned to something different, often with disappointing results. Consequently Bridie wrote only three plays (*The Anatomist, Tobias and the Angel* and *Mr. Bolfry*) which are good throughout, and the last-named of these may puzzle anyone who cannot digest the dose of Scottish metaphysics which it administers with dazzling effect. From the rest of his work only fragments of genius can be extracted (as from, e.g., *A Sleeping Clergyman* and *Daphne Laureola*). The darkening political scene in 1928 led him to write *King of Nowhere*; and in 1944, in wild contrast, he kicked up his heels with bewildering abandon in *The Forrigan Reel*.

Plays are written for performance on the stage; whatever literary merit their writers can give them is subsidiary to the main purpose. It often happens, therefore, that a play which is entertaining, or even impressive, in stage performance seems thin when read. But that is preferable to a play which fails on the stage yet is good to read, for in that case the author has chosen the wrong medium and should have written a novel or a pamphlet or some other form of 'reading matter'. A play depends largely upon the power to compress much matter into a little time, and the author has to remember that while listening to spoken words we cannot pause to turn over in our minds what the actors are saying; we have to listen continuously for what is about to be said next. The author must provide the players with dialogue that makes its intended impression moment by moment, and the words must sound like natural spoken language, not like pages from a written essay or a printed book. Theatres are temples of illusion; their business is make-believe. If a writer can create for the audience an illusion of reality he will succeed in the theatre, even though he may not produce anything that is important as literature.

Most playwrights are of that kind, and two of the outstanding recent non-literary ones call for mention here, since they have played a large part in contemporary theatre history. Noel Coward (b. 1899) had early theatrical training and made his mark just after the first World War with a tense and emotionally strained play, *The Vortex*.

He went on to brittle comedies about trivial leisured people, but they are written with such verve and create so cleverly the illusion of people talking in the clipped style then fashionable and behaving in the conventionally unconventional manner then in vogue that he became immensely popular with *Hay Fever* he moved up a step in the literary scale by writing a comedy comparable with Oscar Wilde's, though not equalling Wilde's best. As he grew older Coward grew more serious without growing duller, as in *This Happy Breed*; but light and verbally audacious comedy is his natural medium. Though *Quadrille*, one of his latest pieces, was not favoured by the critics, it provided two great players with excellent parts, and even great players cannot succeed without good acting material. Moreover, the extremely witty and amusing scene between the two women in Act III of *Quadrille* would almost certainly be praised even on literary grounds if it were part of a Restoration comedy instead of a passage in a play of 1952. TERENCE RATTIGAN (*b.* 1911) appeared at first to tread in the footsteps of Noel Coward, but his work as a whole, to date, has been more adventurous in subject and treatment. *The Winslow Boy* is based on an actual case of a naval cadet falsely accused and punished for theft, and Rattigan made a gripping and moving play of the events through which the boy's good name was eventually cleared.

 J.B. Priestley turned to playwriting after his great success as a novelist, with *The Good Companions,* and both as a dramatist and as a novelist his work has been unequal and incalculable. He made his most original contributions to the theatre with plays dealing with the new theories of time evolved by certain philosophers—chiefly the theory that clock-time associated with the notion of past, present, and future is an illusion and that time consists in reality of a continuous present (but, as it is stated here, this is a crude over-simplification of a bafflingly complex theory). Priestley's *Time and the Conways* and *I Have Been Here Before* touch upon such matters. In *Johnson Over Jordan* and other plays he attempted to explore deeper themes, and the relative failure of those attempts led him to scold the public for its inattentiveness, though what fault there was lay mainly in his own omission to recognize that in the theatre good intentions do not counterbalance lapses from sound and persuasive stage craftsmanship.

A number of excellent short plays by LAURENCE HOUSMAN (b. 1865) should be mentioned: *Little Plays of St. Francis*; and *Happy and Glorious*, a series of episodes in the life of Queen Victoria.

136. Miscellaneous Prose. English statesmen have occasionally been distinguished authors also, as Macaulay was, and as three or four Prime Ministers have been. BENJAMIN DISRAELI, EARL OF BEACONSFIELD (1804–81), wrote a good many novels in the nineteenth century, some fantastic and flippantly witty, others serious political studies. ARTHUR JAMES (EARL OF) BALFOUR (1848–1930) was the author of philosophical works (*A Defence of Philosophic Doubt*, etc.). STANLEY (EARL) BALDWIN (1867–1947) published several volumes of inspiriting addresses (*On England*, etc.). None of these, however, seems likely to take as high a place in English literature as (Sir) WINSTON CHURCHILL (b. 1874), whose lifetime of experience as soldier, statesman, and author' has coincided with the most troubled period of modern world history. In *My Early Life* he told an exciting story, including that of his capture and escape during the South African war of 1899–1902, the *Life of Lord Randolph Churchill* (his father and also a statesman) and the *Life of Marlborough* (his great soldier ancestor) brought Sir Winston renown as a biographer; but it was with his histories of the two World Wars in which he played so vital a part that he obtained chief eminence as a writer (*The World Crisis*, dealing with the events of 1914–18, and *The Second World War*, a vast panorama in six volumes). His literary style, vigorous and glowing, may be somewhat distasteful to austere minds with a preference for cold objective prose, but its stirring quality well befits his subjects and the sweep of his practical vision has a swift searchlight quality which none but a great historian who is also a great man of action could command. He has, indeed, been worthily compared in both capacities with Caesar.

There have been very few other British historians whose work is also memorable as literature. There are Gibbon and Macaulay in the past, and in the present G.M. TREVELYAN (a descendant of Macaulay) and C.V. WEDGWOOD. The three-part work on Garibaldi's campaign for making Italy an independent nation established Trevelyan's reputation, and he proceeded to write stimulating volumes on the England of Queen Anne, before his *English Social History: A Survey of Six Centuries* made the wartime generation of the nineteen-forties more eager to read history than fiction. Miss Wedgwood's excellent *William the Silent* was being followed at the time this chapter was written by a larger undertaking, a history of the English Civil War, of which the first volume (1955) was *The King's Peace, 1637–1641*.

When English biography had recovered from the fever set up by unworthy imitators of Lytton Strachey, the way was open for clearer-headed books which were both sound in substance and of commendable literary quality: Lord DAVID CECIL's life of the poet William Cowper, *The Stricken Deer*, and his two volumes on a leading Victorian statesman, *The Young Melbourne* and *Lord M*; *Talleyrand*, by DUFF COOPER (VISCOUNT NORWICH); and (Sir) HAROLD NICOLSON's *King George V, His Life and Reign*.

Philosophy is no easy subject to present for general reading, though when treated by a skilful man of letters it can be inexhaustibly fascinating, as BERTRAND RUSSELL (*b.* 1872) made it in a number of volumes which were on a more easily comprehensible plane than the erudite works he addressed to specialists in mathematical philosophy. His *History of Western Philosophy* covers an extensive subject in a pleasurable and enlightening style that is within the range of common understanding.

In the present age few parts of the world have remained unexplored, and attention is turning speculatively to the prospects of adventure and discovery in outer space. Nevertheless, numerous travel books continue to be written and the popularity of this kind of literature is undiminished. Few such books have lasting quality, however, but among recent travellers who have produced notable accounts of their journeyings PETER FLEMING (*Brazilian Adventure* and *One's Company*) and FREYA STARK (*The Southern Gates of Arabia*, etc.) are outstanding. Somewhat earlier GERTRUDE BELL (1868–1926) wrote *The Desert and the Sown* and *Amurath to Amurath*; and Norman Douglas (1868–1952) *Siren Land* and *Old Calabria*, though his most original work was the unique satirical novel, *South Wind*, set in the island of Capri.

As a person T.E. LAWRENCE (1888–1935) has been the most controversial figure among twentieth-century writers. An Oxford scholar and archaeologist, he surprisingly developed remarkable gifts of military leadership when, in the first World War, he headed the desert Arabs in their struggle for independence against Turkey. When the war ended he was disillusioned by his conviction that the Allies had failed in their promises to the Arabs, and he joined the Air Force as an ordinary recruit, refusing to take commissioned or non-commissioned rank, and assuming the name T.E. Shaw. Since he sought to escape from the flood of publicity which had engulfed him as 'Lawrence of Arabia', he might have done better to retire to the quiet of a scholarly life at Oxford, for his (as it was regarded) eccentric behaviour attracted further unwelcomed attention. He was killed accidentally while riding a fast motor-cycle. In 1926 Lawrence published an expensive privately-circulated account of the successful desert campaign, *Seven Pillars of Wisdom,* which at once gave him the rank of a great writer. Perhaps his greatness in this respect was too readily declared by his admirers, who were prepared to accept him without qualification as a hero-genius. He learned the craft of writing through close consultation with Bernard Shaw and others, and this eclecticism of literary style, combined with the desire to treat objectively his own part in the Arab struggle for freedom, makes his book impersonal and remote in tone. But as a feat of conscious writing and for its word-portraits of the personalities Lawrence encountered, *Seven Pillars of Wisdom* stands on a lonely eminence to which in the future it is possible that no larger company will feel invited than is now attracted to DOUGHTY's *Arabia Deserta* which Lawrence virtually rediscovered after its long neglect. *Revolt in the Desert,* a condensed version of the original book, was issued in 1927; *Seven Pillars* became available to all after Lawrence's death.

HILAIRE BELLOC (1870–1953) and G.K. CHESTERTON (1872–1936) may fittingly close this section, for their works included a considerable outpouring of miscellaneous prose, and in character and temperament they belonged so much to a passing age of idealism that Belloc may be regarded as the last of the Romantics. He was born a Catholic, Chesterton became one, and they often worked in double harness in antagonism towards what Belloc in one of his book titles called *The Servile State, i.e.,* the state in which the individual weighs little against bureaucracy and despotism. What the ultimate rank of these two writers may be cannot now be guessed. Some of the poems of each will probably endure, and Belloc's travel book *The Path to Rome*. Chesterton wrote too much and often too carelessly: in total he was more a casual journalist than an author of genius, though his *Father Brown* detective stories may be sufficiently out of the common run to survive for some time. Belloc was a convinced propagandist whose fervour for the causes he cherished was prone to obscure his sense of historical accuracy.

TABLE OF THE PRESENT AGE

Fiction	Verse	Drama
	Osbert Sitwell's *England Reclaimed,* 1927	
V. Woolf's *Orlando,* 1928		
Priestley's *The Good Companions,* 1929		
Maugham's *Cakes and Ale,* 1930	Edith Sitwell's *Collected Poems,* 1930	Shaw's *The Apple Cart,* 1930
Bennett d. 1931		Bridie's *Tobias and the Angel,* 1931

V. Woolf's *The Waves*, 1931

A. Huxley's *Brave New World*, 1932

Geo. Moore d. 1933

Galsworthy d. 1933

Eliot's *Murder in the Cathedral*, 1935

Day Lewis's *Collected Poems 1929–36*

Kipling d. 1936

A.E. Housman d. 1936

G.K. Chesterton d. 1936

V. Woolf's *The Years*, 1937

Priestley's *Time and the Conways*, 1937

Barrie d. 1937

Joyce's *Finnegans Wake*, 1939

Yeats d. 1939

Auden's *Selected Poems*, 1940

Yeats' *Last Poems and Plays*, 1940

James Joyce d. 1941

Virginia Woolf d. 1941

De la Mare's *Collected Poems*, 1942

Bridie's *Mr. Bolfry* 1943

Cary's *The Horse's Mouth*, 1944

Eliot's *Four Quartets*, 1944

De la Mare's *Collected Rhymes and Verses*, 1944

Orwell's *Animal Farm*, 1945

E. Sitwell's *A Song of the Cold*, 1945

H.G. Wells d. 1946

Rattigan's *The Winslow Boy*, 1946

		Granville-Barker, d. 1946
	Robert Graves' *Collected Poems*, 1948	
Orwell's *Nineteen Eightyfour*, 1949	E. Sitwell's *The Canticle of the Rose*, 1949	Bridie's *Daphne Laureola*, 1949 Fry's *The lady's Not For Burning*, 1949 Eliot's *The Cocktail Party*, 1950 Bernard Shaw d. 1950 Bridie d. 1951
	Osbert Sitwell's *Wrack at Tidesend*, 1952	
	Dylan Thomas' *Collected Poems*, 1952	
Belloc d. 1953		
	Dylan Thomas d. 1953	
Boerbohm d. 1956		
	De la Mare d. 1956	
Cary d. 1957		